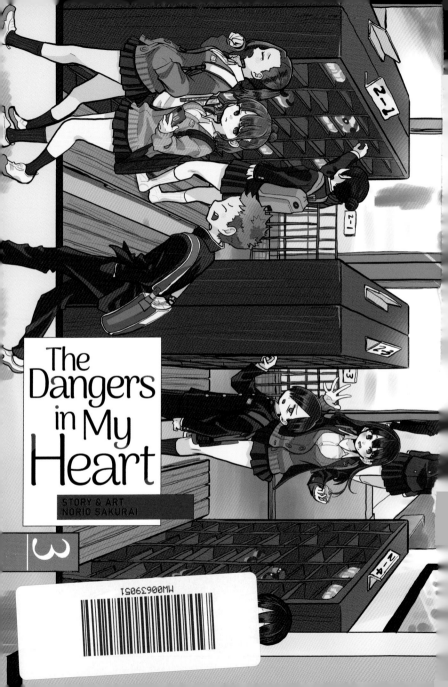

The
Dangers
in My
Heart

STORY & ART
NORIO SAKURAI

3

Class Newsletter, Vol. 03

CONTENTS

	I Use LINE	003
Karte.31	I Can't Keep My Distance	019
Karte.32	We Swapped Places	027
Karte.33	I Tuned In	039
Karte.34	I Did Some Tutoring	049
Karte.35	I Am Not Like My Mother	057
Karte.36	I Attempted to Make Contact	071
Karte.37	I Was Really Drenched	079
Karte.38	I Had a Dream	087
Karte.39	I Became Her Practice Partner	105
Karte.40	I Can't See	115
Karte.41	I Was Used	125
Karte.42	I Hate Yamada	139
Karte.43	We Use LINE	149
Karte.44		
	Dark Mage	015
Extra.1	I Had My Height Measured	065
Extra.2	Strawberries and Bavarois	099
Extra.3		

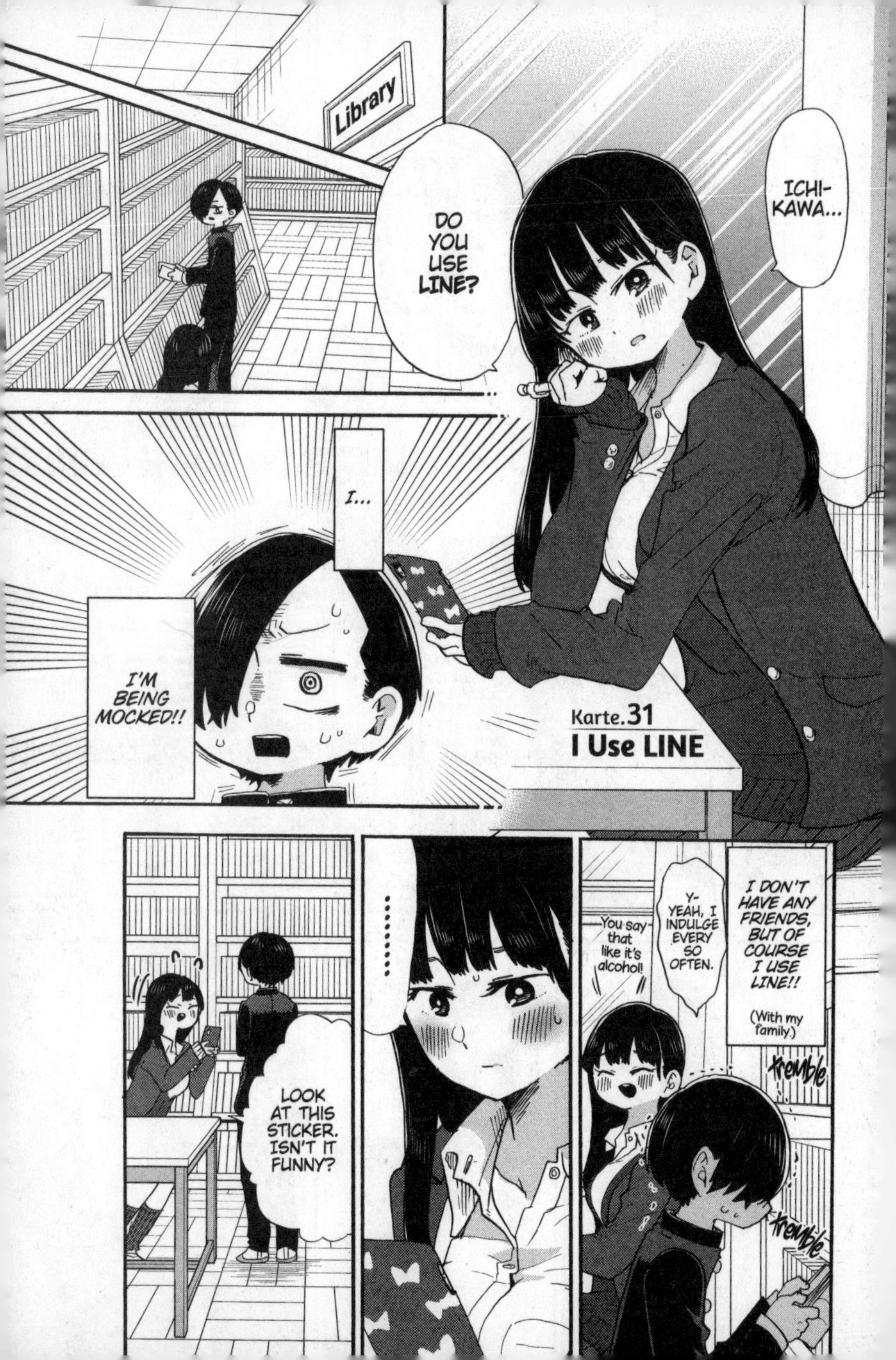

ICHI-KAWA...
DO YOU USE LINE?
Karte.31
I Use LINE
Library
I...
I'M BEING MOCKED!!
I DON'T HAVE ANY FRIENDS, BUT OF COURSE I USE LINE!!
(With my family.)
Y-YEAH, I INDULGE EVERY SO OFTEN.
You say that like it's alcohol!
tremble
tremble
....
LOOK AT THIS STICKER. ISN'T IT FUNNY?

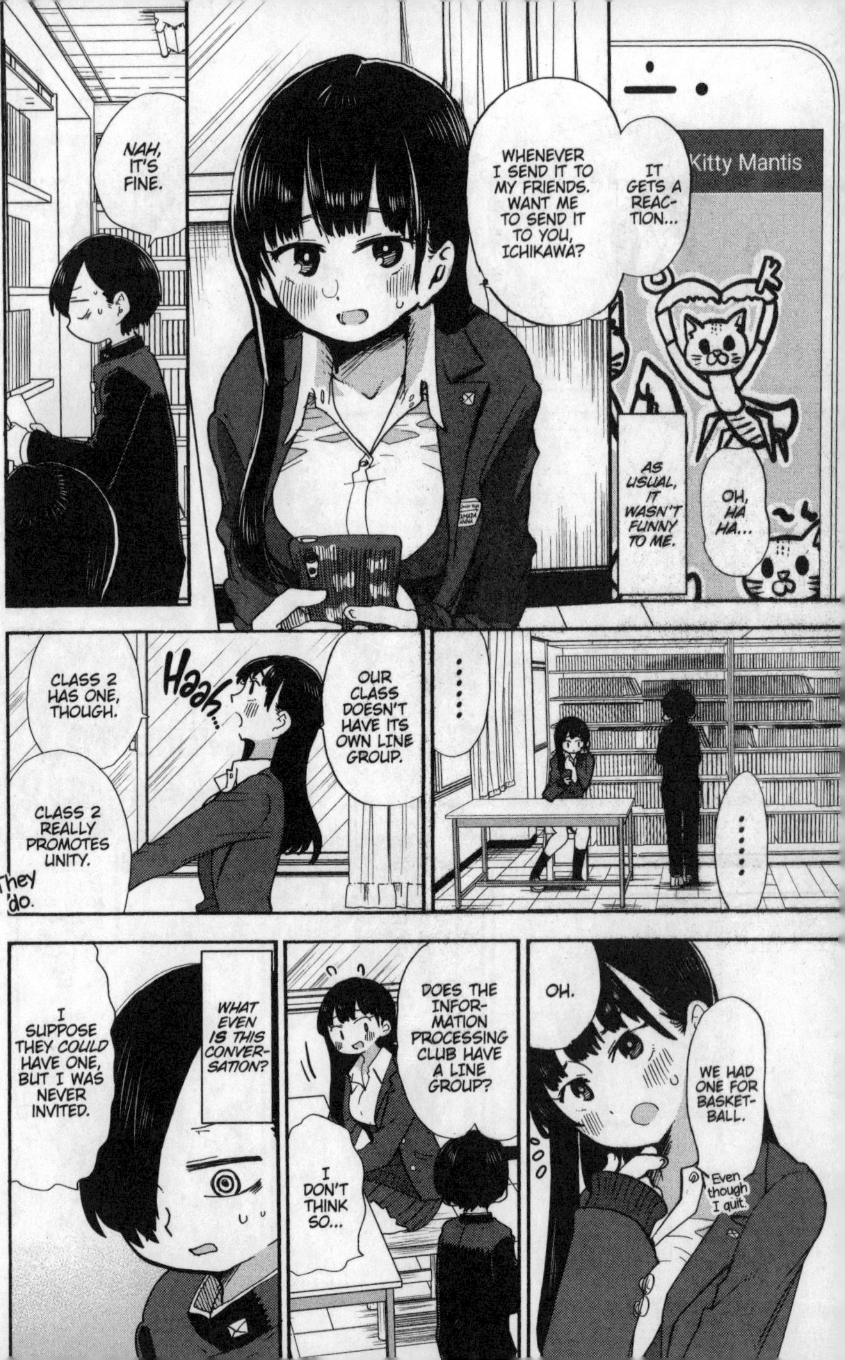
Kitty Mantis
IT GETS A REACTION...
WHENEVER I SEND IT TO MY FRIENDS. WANT ME TO SEND IT TO YOU, ICHIKAWA?
OH, HA HA...
AS USUAL, IT WASN'T FUNNY TO ME.
NAH, IT'S FINE.
......
......
OUR CLASS DOESN'T HAVE ITS OWN LINE GROUP.
Haah...
CLASS 2 HAS ONE, THOUGH.
CLASS 2 REALLY PROMOTES UNITY.
They do.
OH.
WE HAD ONE FOR BASKETBALL.
Even though I quit.
DOES THE INFORMATION PROCESSING CLUB HAVE A LINE GROUP?
I DON'T THINK SO...
WHAT EVEN IS THIS CONVERSATION?
I SUPPOSE THEY COULD HAVE ONE, BUT I WAS NEVER INVITED.

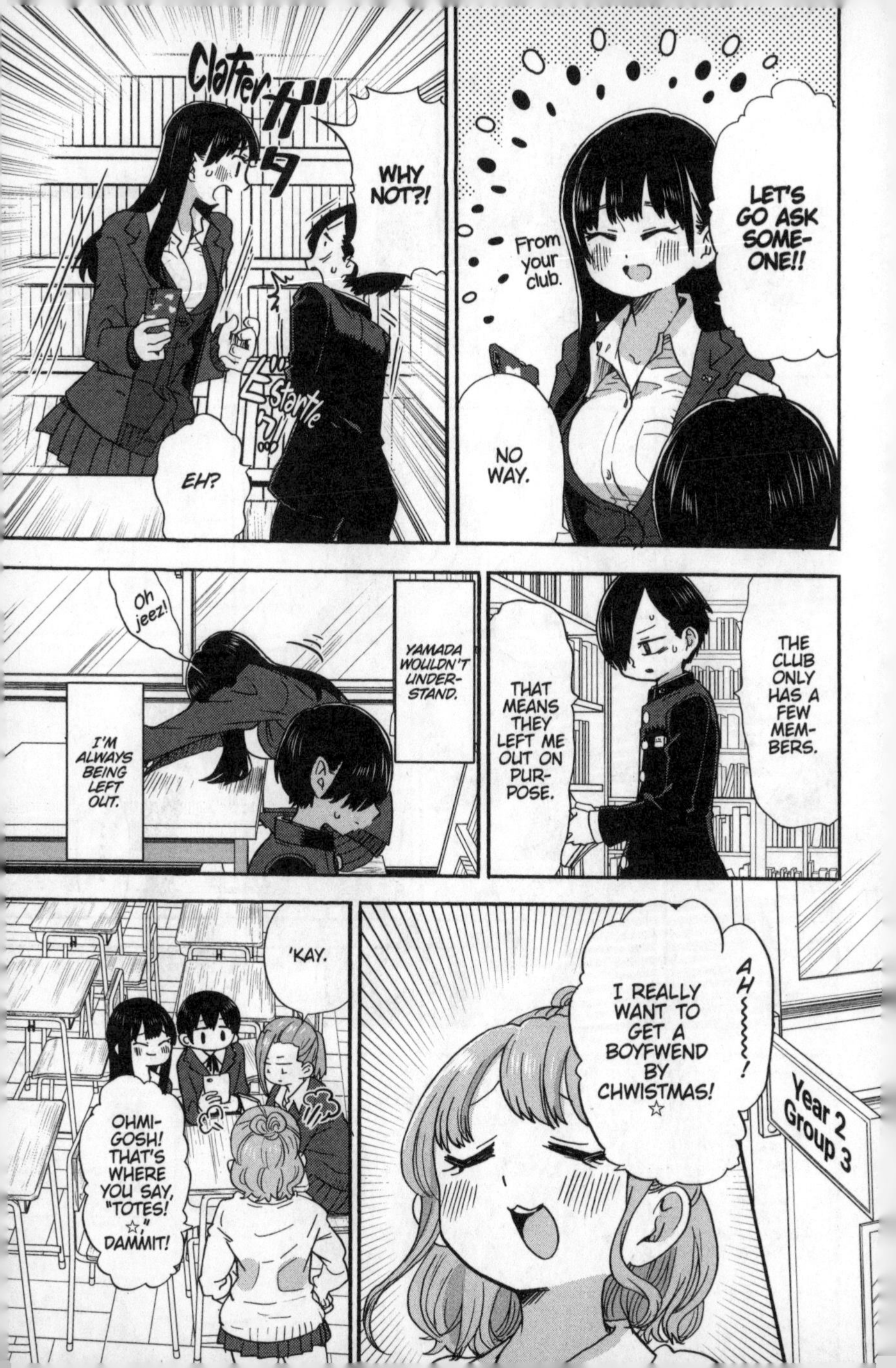

LET'S GO ASK SOMEONE!!
From your club.
NO WAY.
Clatter
WHY NOT?!
Startle
EH?
THE CLUB ONLY HAS A FEW MEMBERS.
THAT MEANS THEY LEFT ME OUT ON PURPOSE.
YAMADA WOULDN'T UNDERSTAND.
Oh jeez!
I'M ALWAYS BEING LEFT OUT.
AH~~~!
I REALLY WANT TO GET A BOYFWEND BY CHWISTMAS! ☆
Year 2 Group 3
'KAY.
OHMIGOSH! THAT'S WHERE YOU SAY, "TOTES! ☆" DAMMIT!

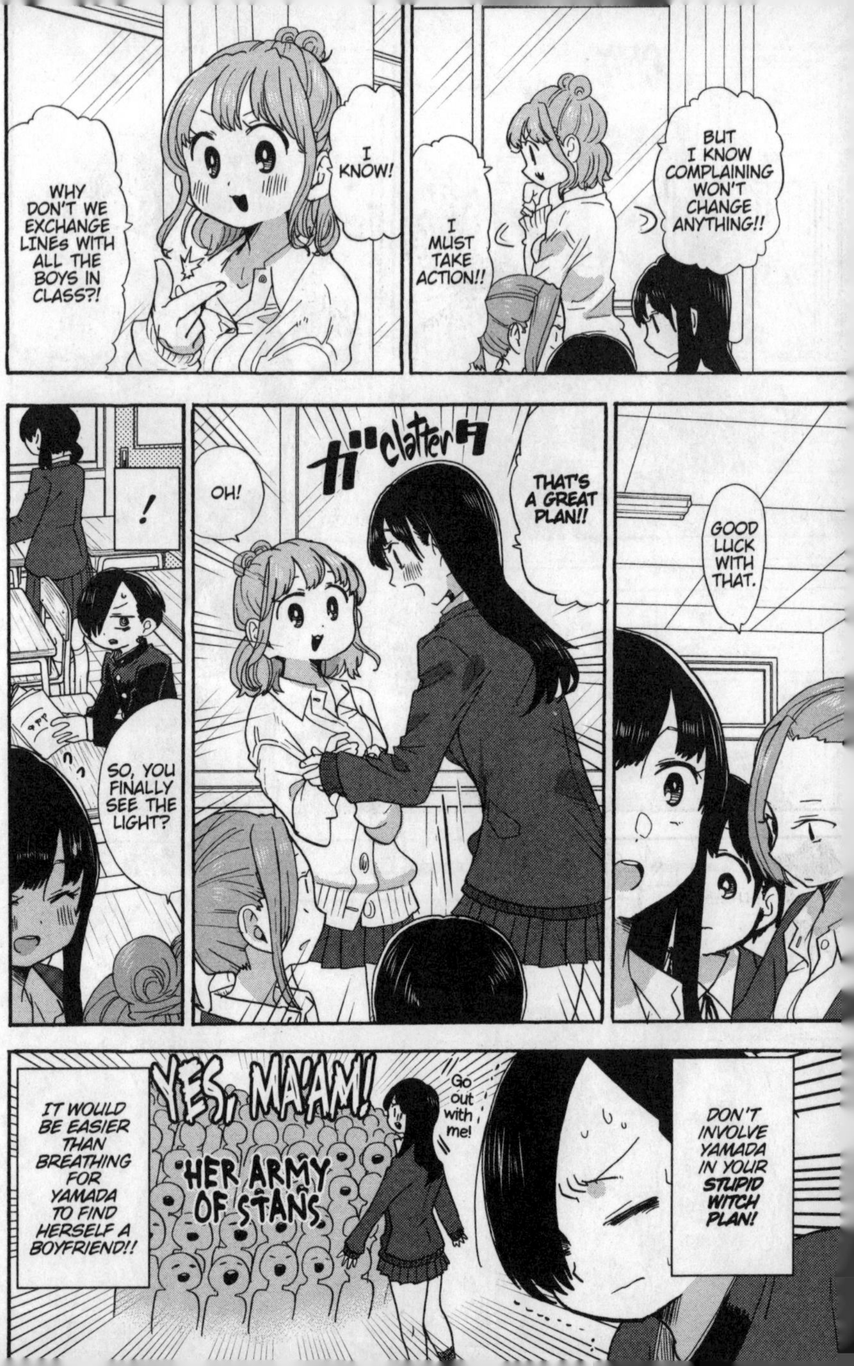
BUT I KNOW COMPLAINING WON'T CHANGE ANYTHING!!
I MUST TAKE ACTION!!
I KNOW!
WHY DON'T WE EXCHANGE LINEs WITH ALL THE BOYS IN CLASS?!
GOOD LUCK WITH THAT.
THAT'S A GREAT PLAN!!
ガ clatter ッ
OH!
!
SO, YOU FINALLY SEE THE LIGHT?
DON'T INVOLVE YAMADA IN YOUR **STUPID WITCH PLAN!**
Go out with me!
YES, MA'AM!
HER ARMY OF STANS
IT WOULD BE EASIER THAN BREATHING FOR YAMADA TO FIND HERSELF A BOYFRIEND!!

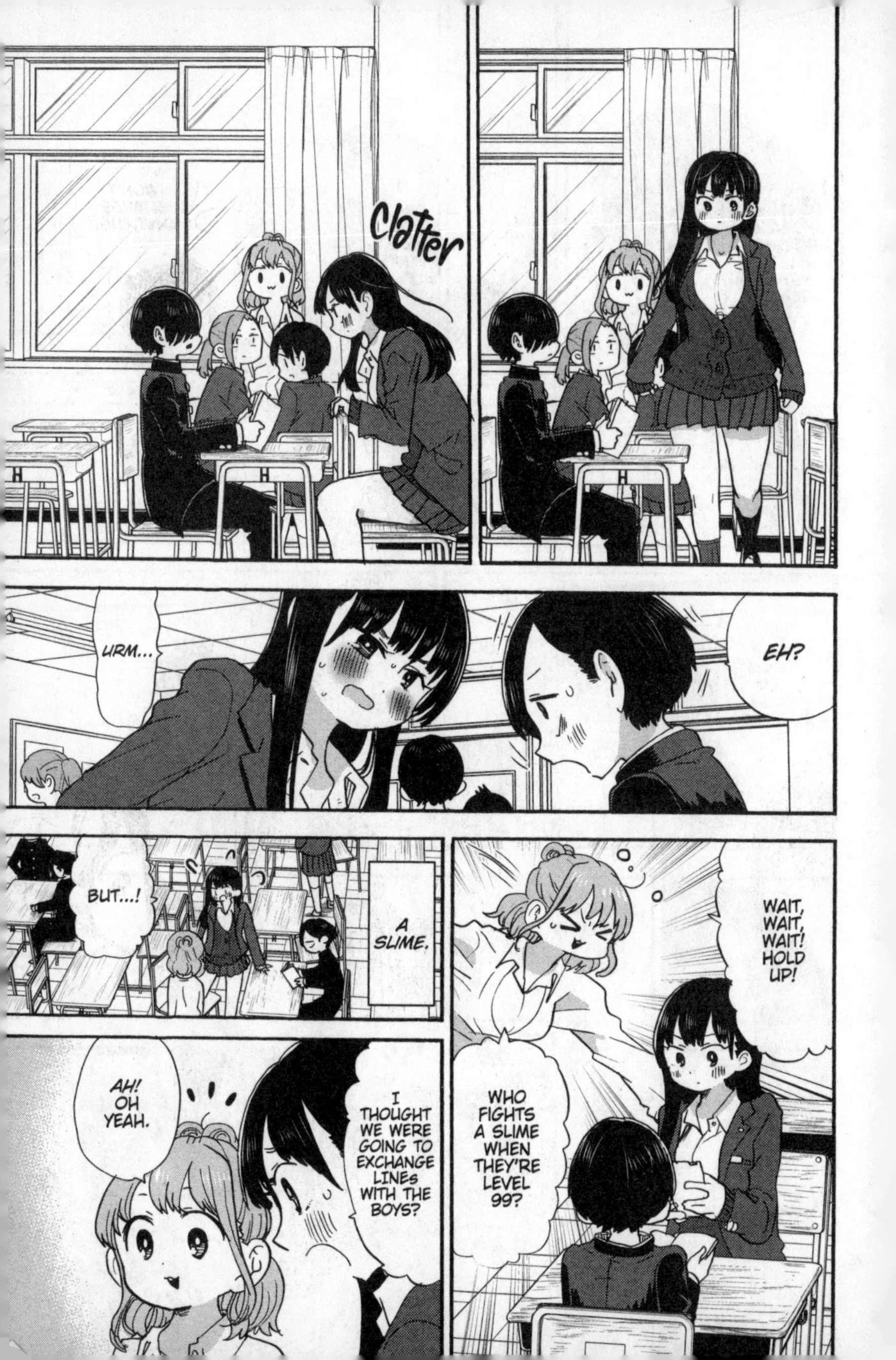
Clatter
EH?
URM...
WAIT, WAIT, WAIT! HOLD UP!
WHO FIGHTS A SLIME WHEN THEY'RE LEVEL 99?
A SLIME.
BUT...!
I THOUGHT WE WERE GOING TO EXCHANGE LINES WITH THE BOYS?
AH! OH YEAH.

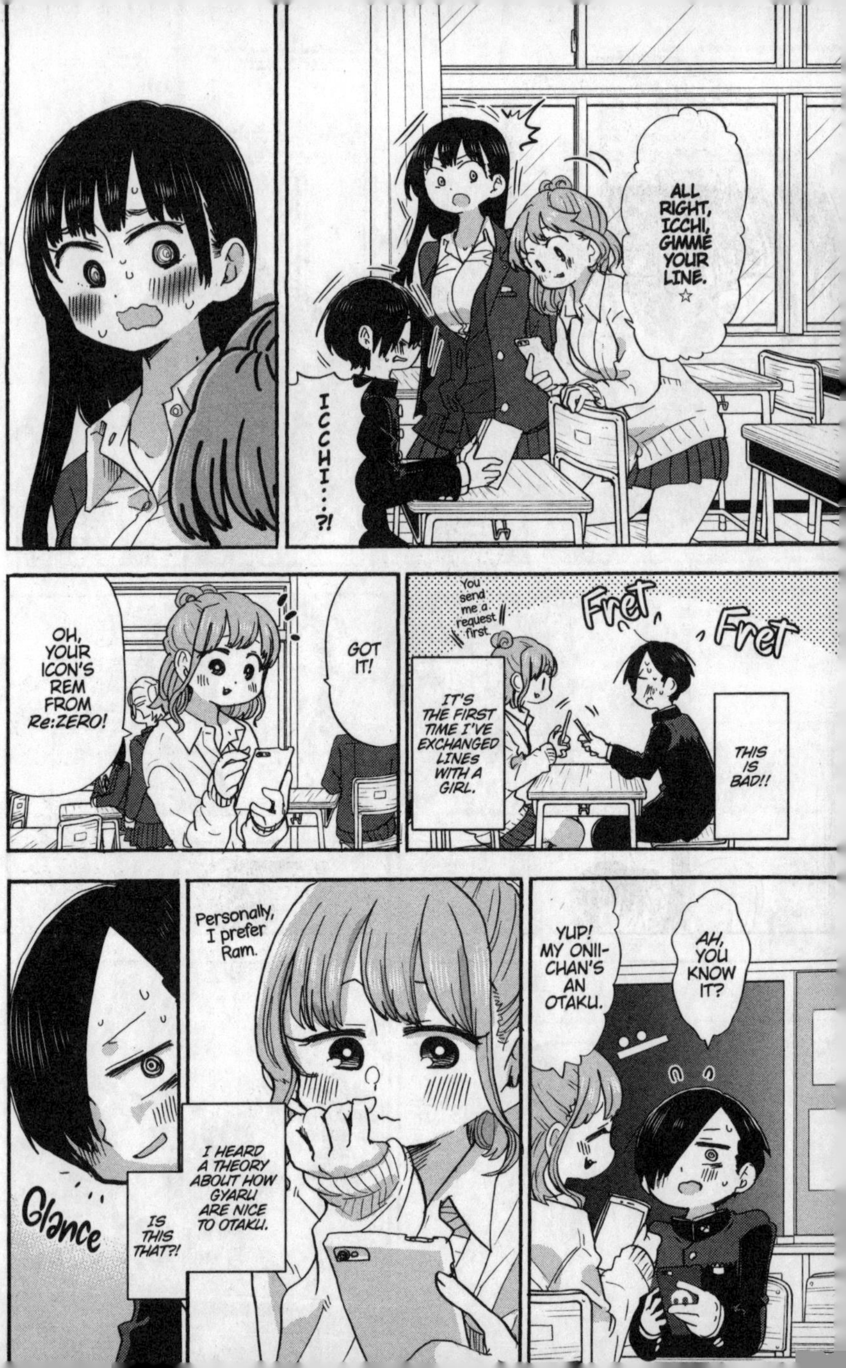
ALL RIGHT, ICCHI, GIMME YOUR LINE. ☆
ICCHI...?!
Fret Fret
You send me a request first.
THIS IS BAD!!
IT'S THE FIRST TIME I'VE EXCHANGED LINES WITH A GIRL.
GOT IT!
OH, YOUR ICON'S REM FROM Re:ZERO!
AH, YOU KNOW IT?
YUP! MY ONII-CHAN'S AN OTAKU.
Personally, I prefer Ram.
I HEARD A THEORY ABOUT HOW GYARU ARE NICE TO OTAKU.
IS THIS THAT?!
Glance

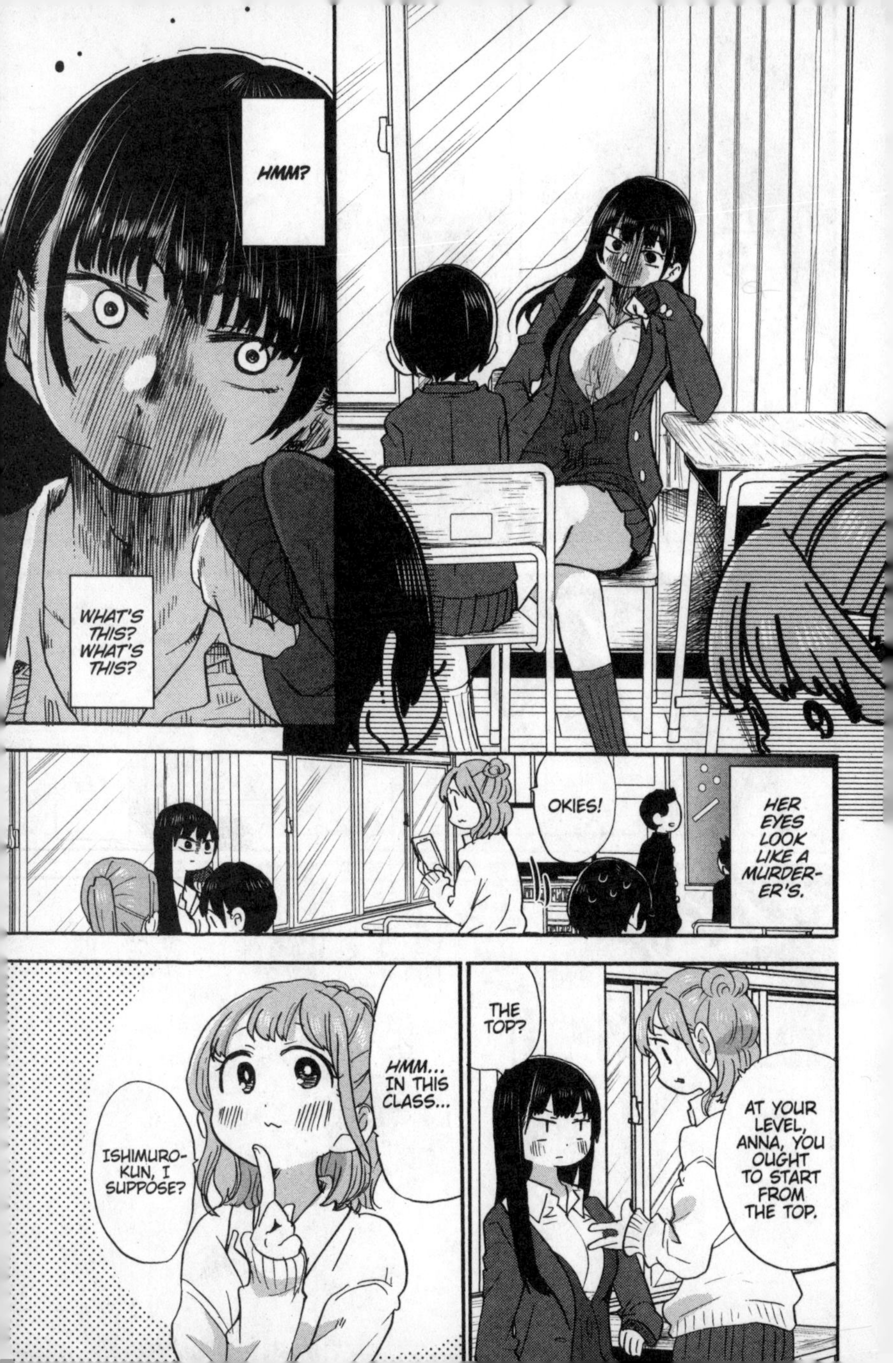
HMM?
WHAT'S THIS? WHAT'S THIS?
HER EYES LOOK LIKE A MURDERER'S.
OKIES!
AT YOUR LEVEL, ANNA, YOU OUGHT TO START FROM THE TOP.
THE TOP?
HMM... IN THIS CLASS...
ISHIMURO-KUN, I SUPPOSE?

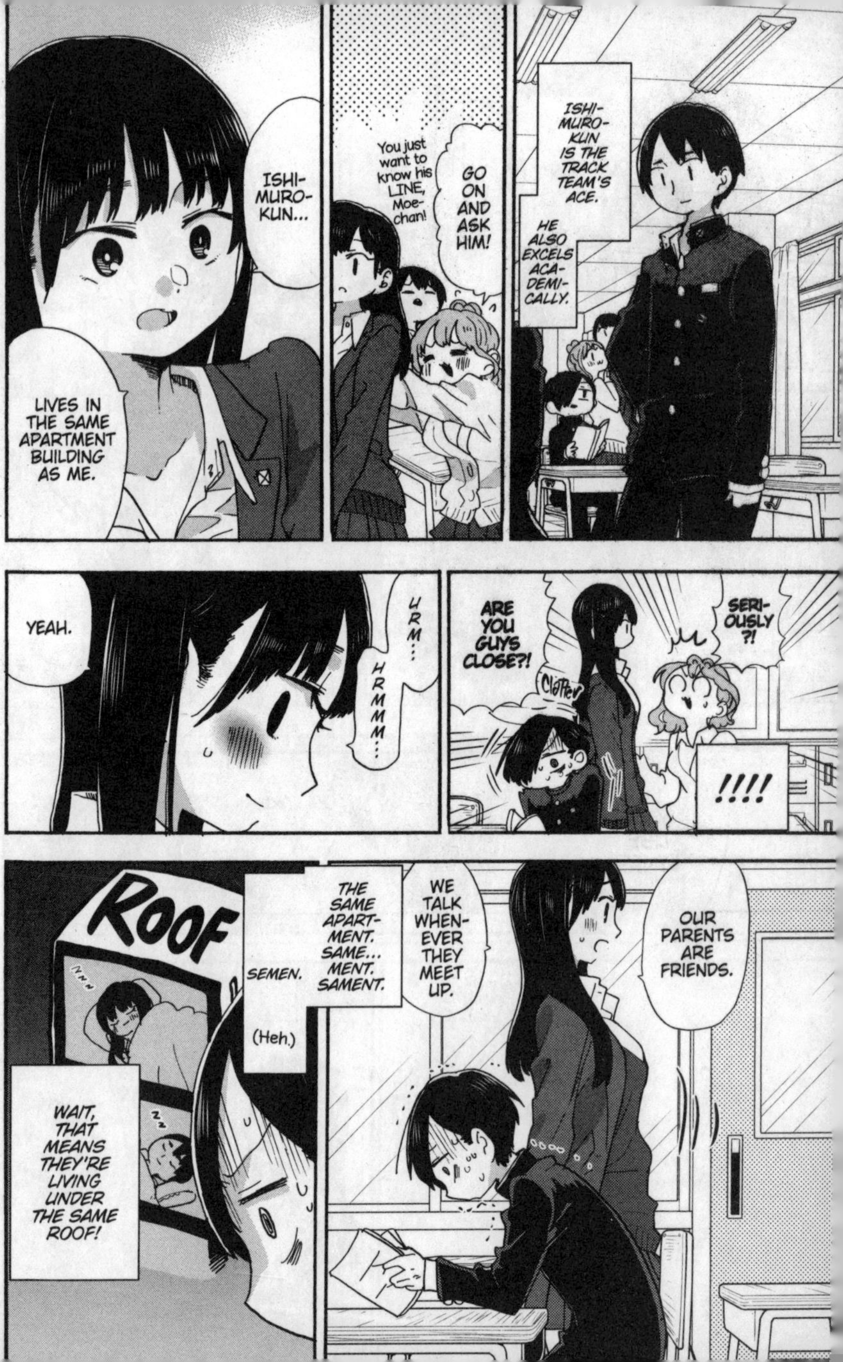
ISHI-MURO-KUN IS THE TRACK TEAM'S ACE.
HE ALSO EXCELS ACA-DEMI-CALLY.
GO ON AND ASK HIM!
You just want to know his LINE, Moe-chan!
ISHI-MURO-KUN...
LIVES IN THE SAME APARTMENT BUILDING AS ME.
SERI-OUSLY?!
ARE YOU GUYS CLOSE?!
Clatter
!!!!
URM... HRMMMM...
YEAH.
OUR PARENTS ARE FRIENDS.
WE TALK WHEN-EVER THEY MEET UP.
THE SAME APART-MENT. SAME... MENT. SAMENT.
SEMEN.
(Heh.)
ROOF
WAIT, THAT MEANS THEY'RE LIVING UNDER THE SAME ROOF!

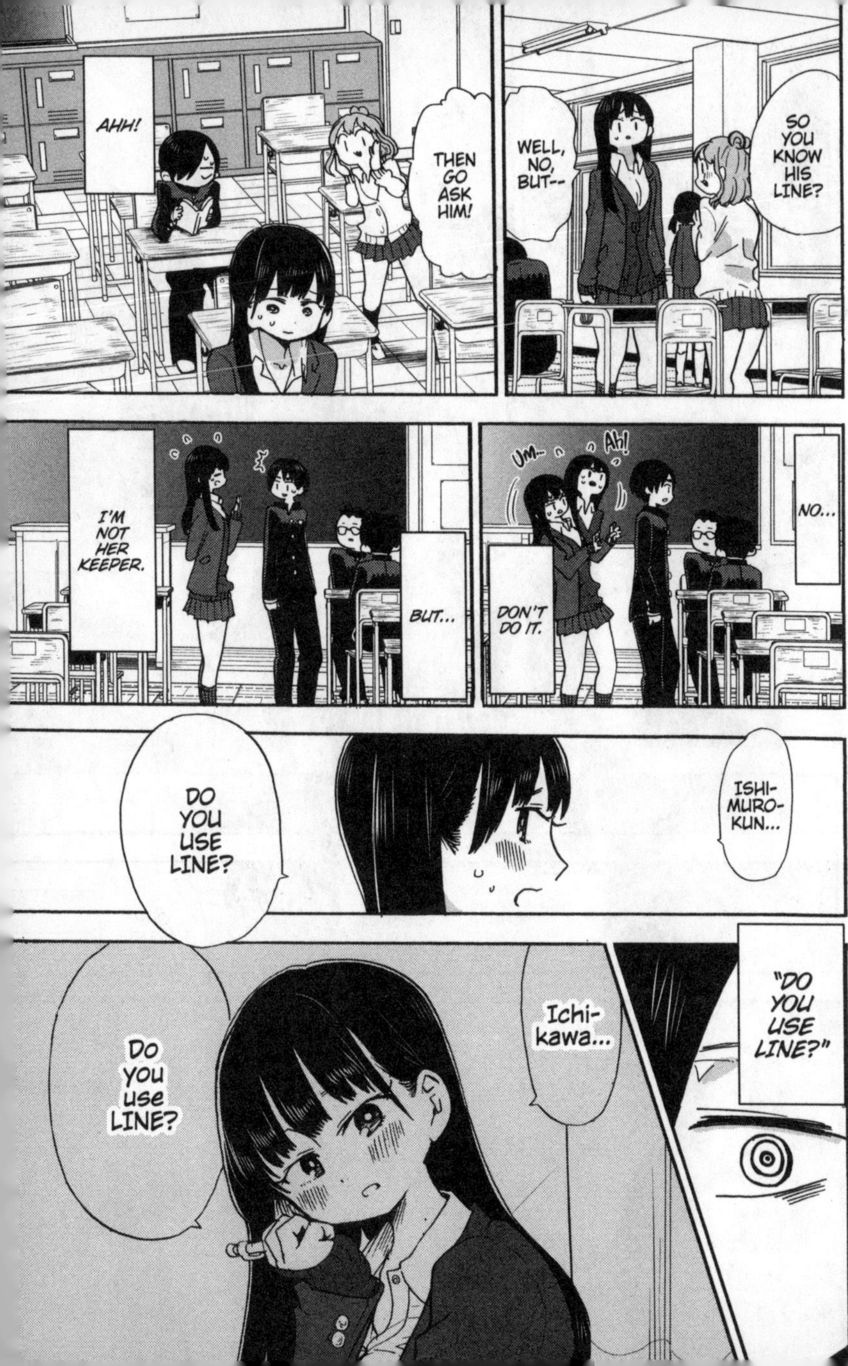
SO YOU KNOW HIS LINE?
WELL, NO, BUT--
THEN GO ASK HIM!
AHH!
NO...
Ah!
Um...
DON'T DO IT.
BUT...
I'M NOT HER KEEPER.
ISHI-MURO-KUN...
DO YOU USE LINE?
"DO YOU USE LINE?"
Ichi-kawa...
Do you use LINE?

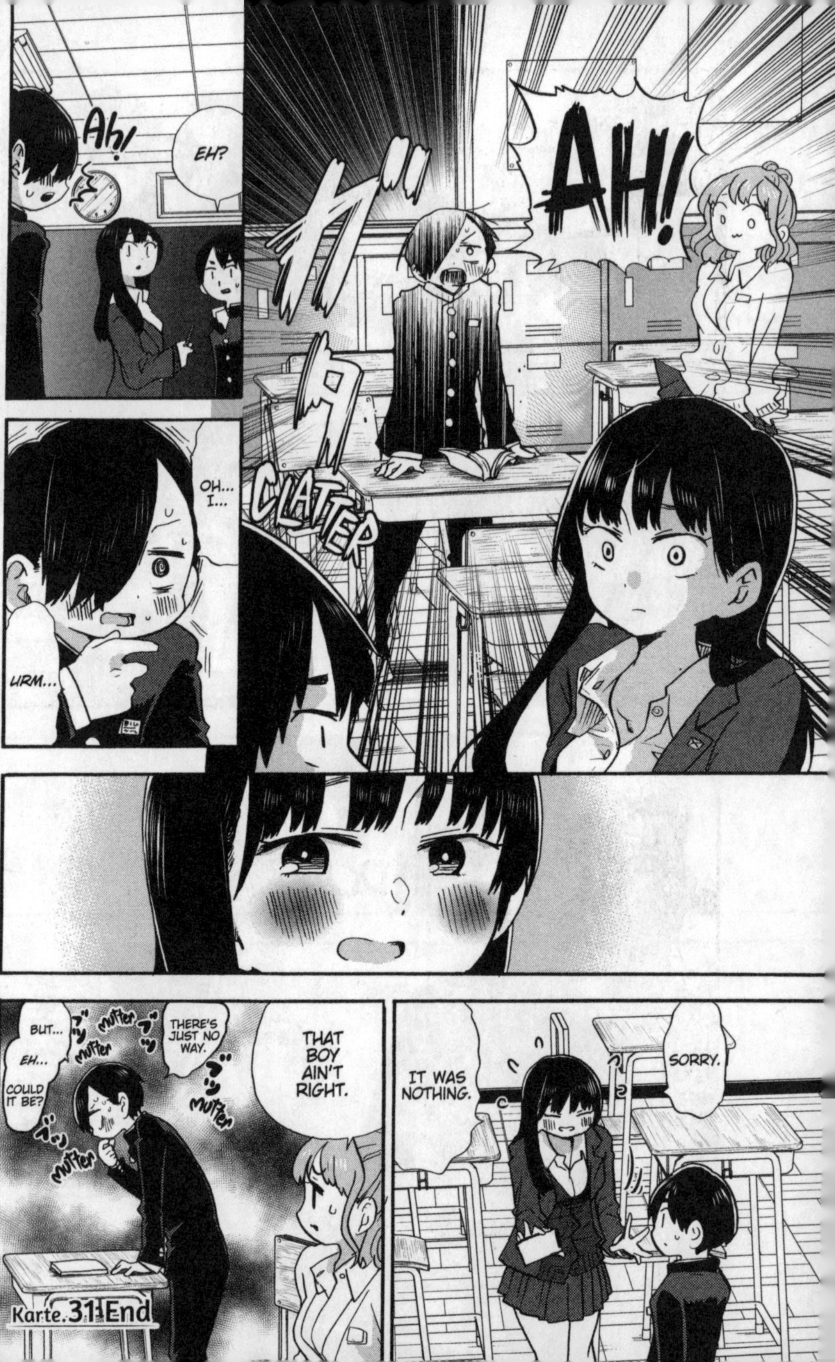

AH!!
CLATTER
Ah!
EH?
OH... I...
URM...
SORRY.
IT WAS NOTHING.
THAT BOY AIN'T RIGHT.
THERE'S JUST NO WAY.
mutter
mutter
BUT...
EH...
mutter
COULD IT BE?
mutter
mutter
Karte. 31 End

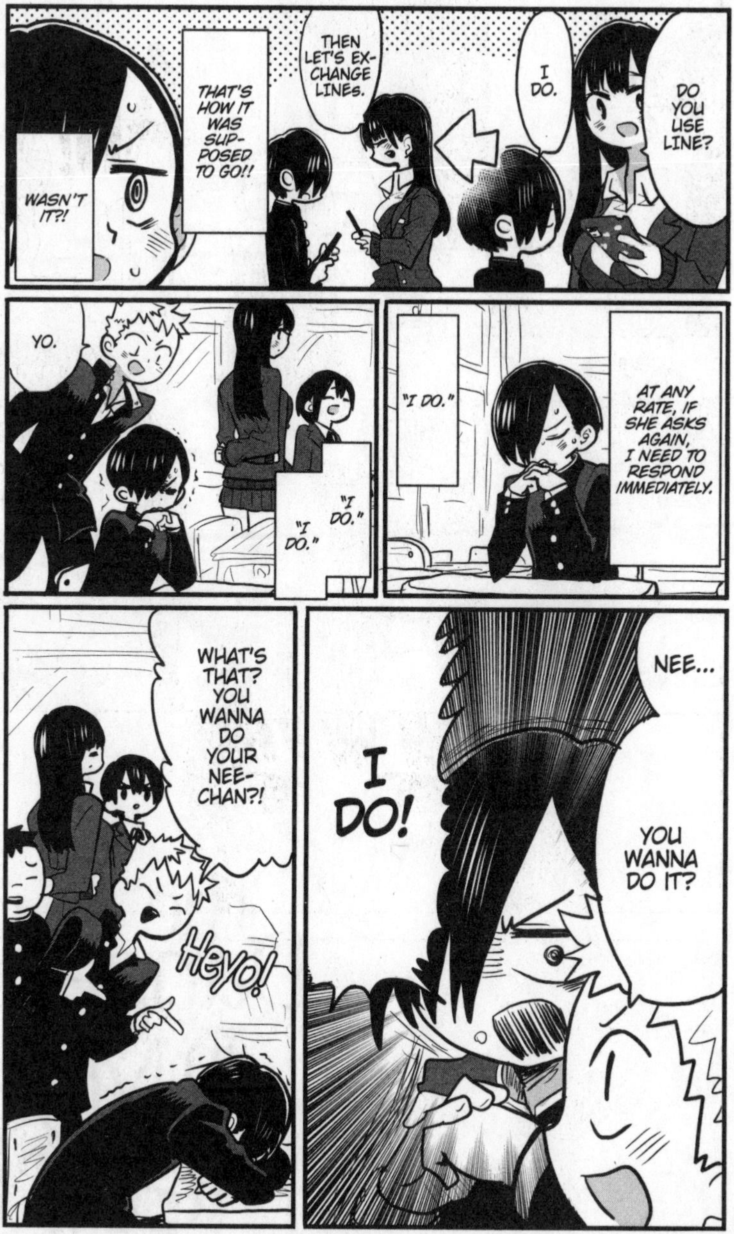
DO YOU USE LINE?
I DO.
THEN LET'S EX-CHANGE LINES.
THAT'S HOW IT WAS SUP-POSED TO GO!!
WASN'T IT?!
AT ANY RATE, IF SHE ASKS AGAIN, I NEED TO RESPOND IMMEDIATELY.
"I DO."
"I DO."
"I DO."
YO.
NEE...
YOU WANNA DO IT?
I DO!
WHAT'S THAT? YOU WANNA DO YOUR NEE-CHAN?!
Heyo!

The
Dangers
in My
Heart

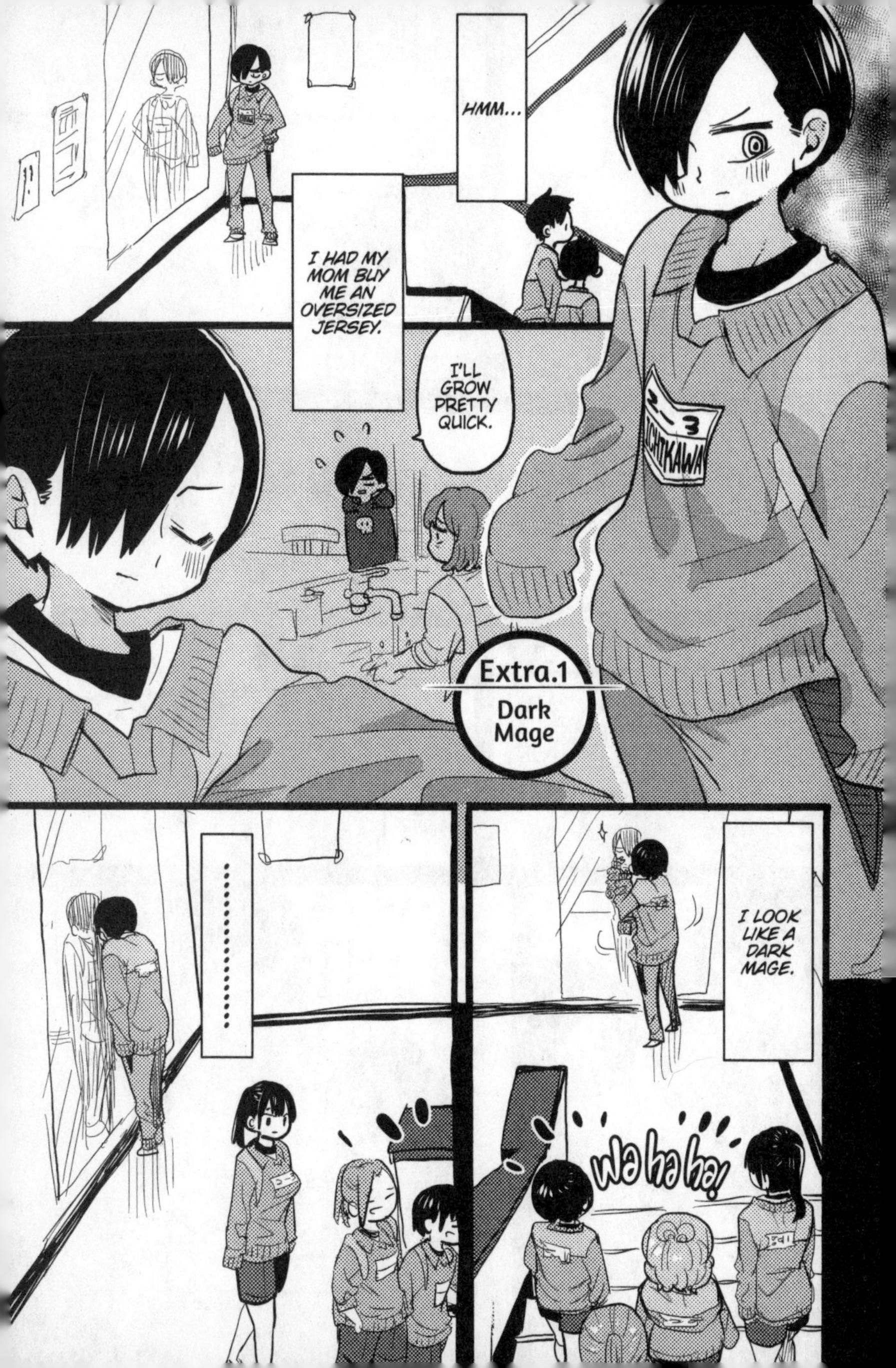
HMM...
I HAD MY MOM BUY ME AN OVERSIZED JERSEY.
I'LL GROW PRETTY QUICK.
2-3 ICHIKAWA
Extra.1
Dark Mage
I LOOK LIKE A DARK MAGE.
WA HA HA!
....

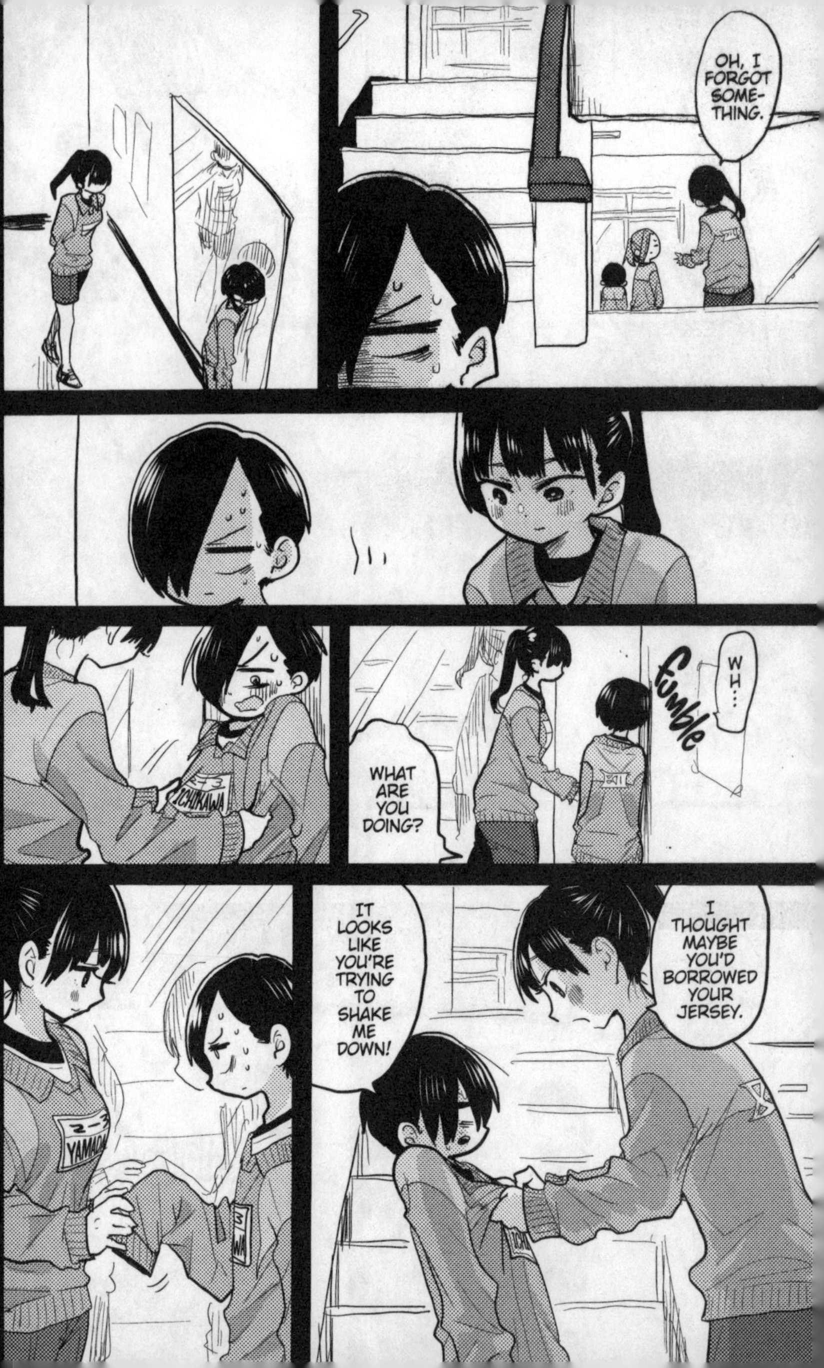
OH, I FORGOT SOMETHING.
WH…
fumble
WHAT ARE YOU DOING?
ICHIKAWA
I THOUGHT MAYBE YOU'D BORROWED YOUR JERSEY.
IT LOOKS LIKE YOU'RE TRYING TO SHAKE ME DOWN!
YAMADA

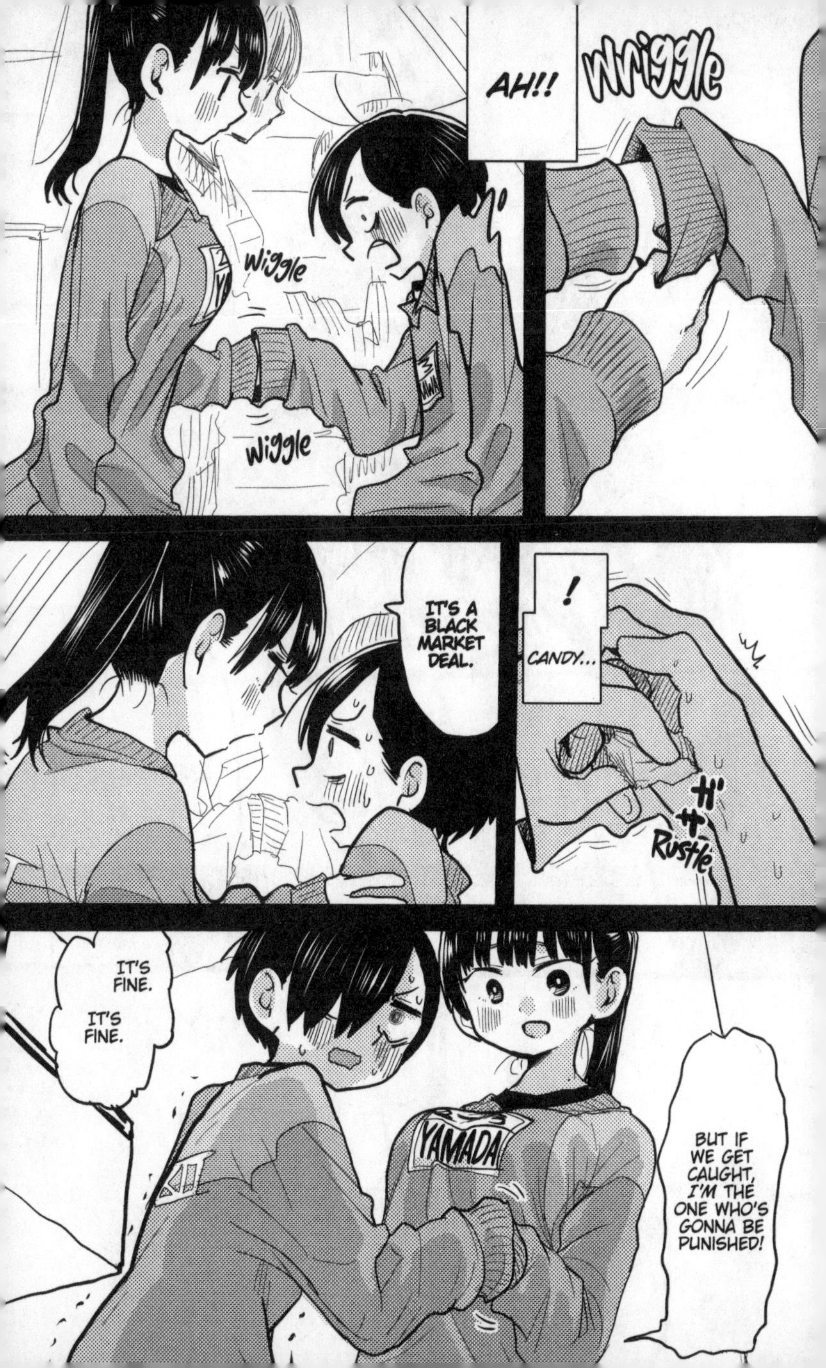
Wriggle
AH!!
wiggle
wiggle
!
CANDY...
Rustle
IT'S A BLACK MARKET DEAL.
BUT IF WE GET CAUGHT, I'M THE ONE WHO'S GONNA BE PUNISHED!
YAMADA
IT'S FINE.
IT'S FINE.

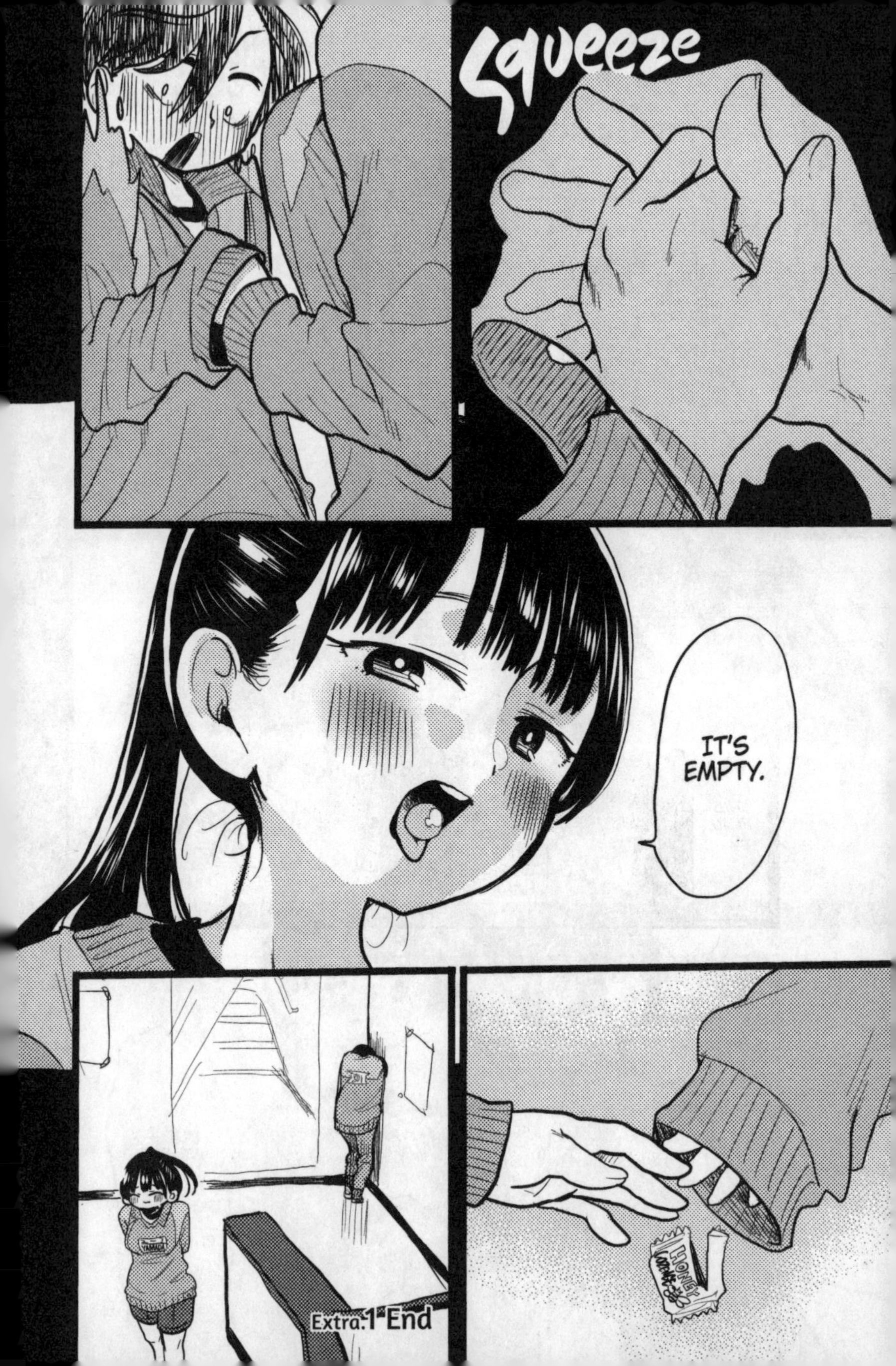
Squeeze
IT'S EMPTY.
Extra.1 End

Karte.32
I Can't Keep My Distance

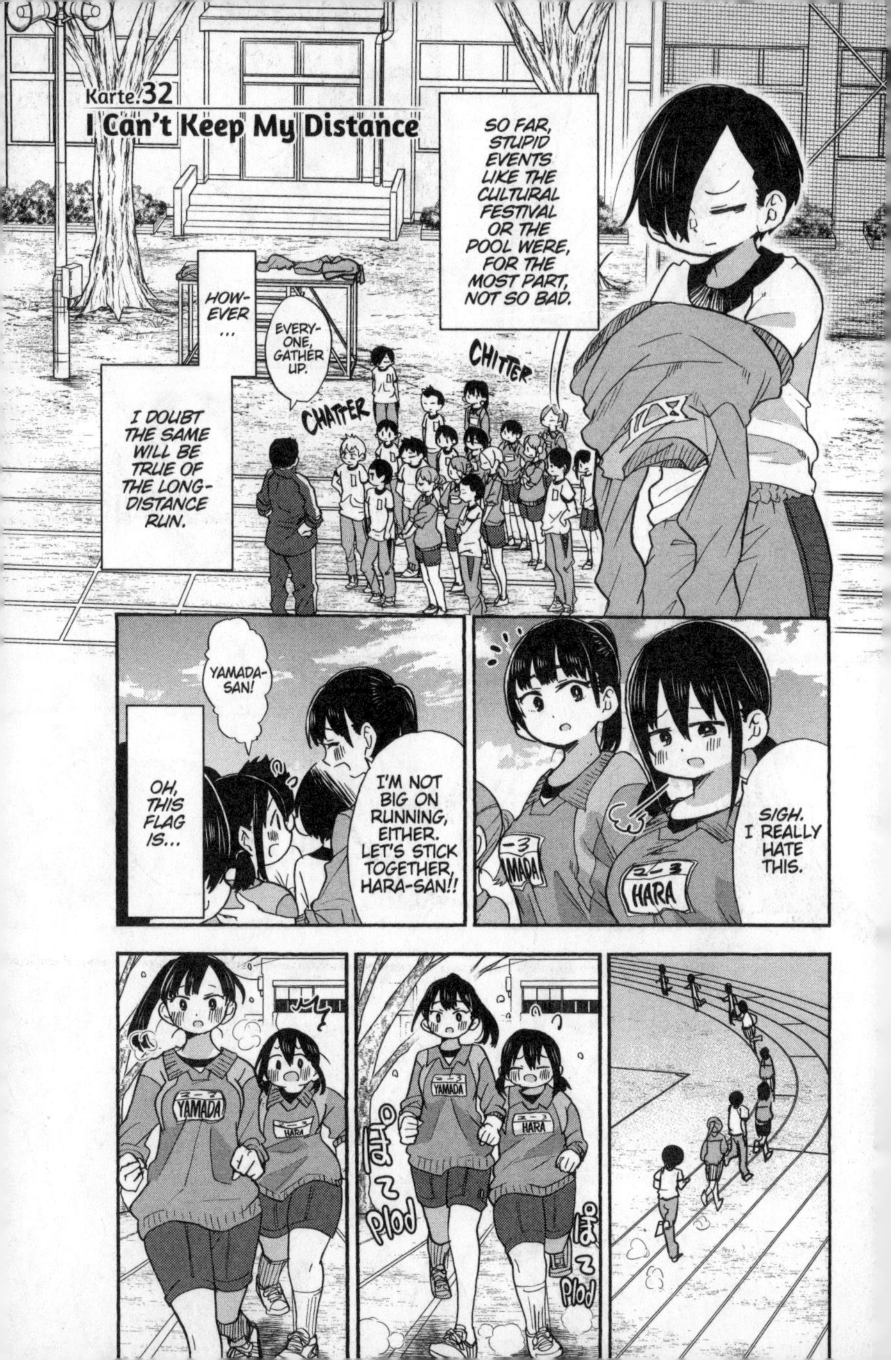

SO FAR, STUPID EVENTS LIKE THE CULTURAL FESTIVAL OR THE POOL WERE, FOR THE MOST PART, NOT SO BAD.
CHITTER
EVERY-ONE, GATHER UP.
HOW-EVER...
CHATTER
I DOUBT THE SAME WILL BE TRUE OF THE LONG-DISTANCE RUN.
SIGH. I REALLY HATE THIS.
HARA
YAMADA
YAMADA-SAN!
I'M NOT BIG ON RUNNING, EITHER. LET'S STICK TOGETHER, HARA-SAN!!
OH, THIS FLAG IS...
ぽて
plod
ぽて
plod
HARA
YAMADA

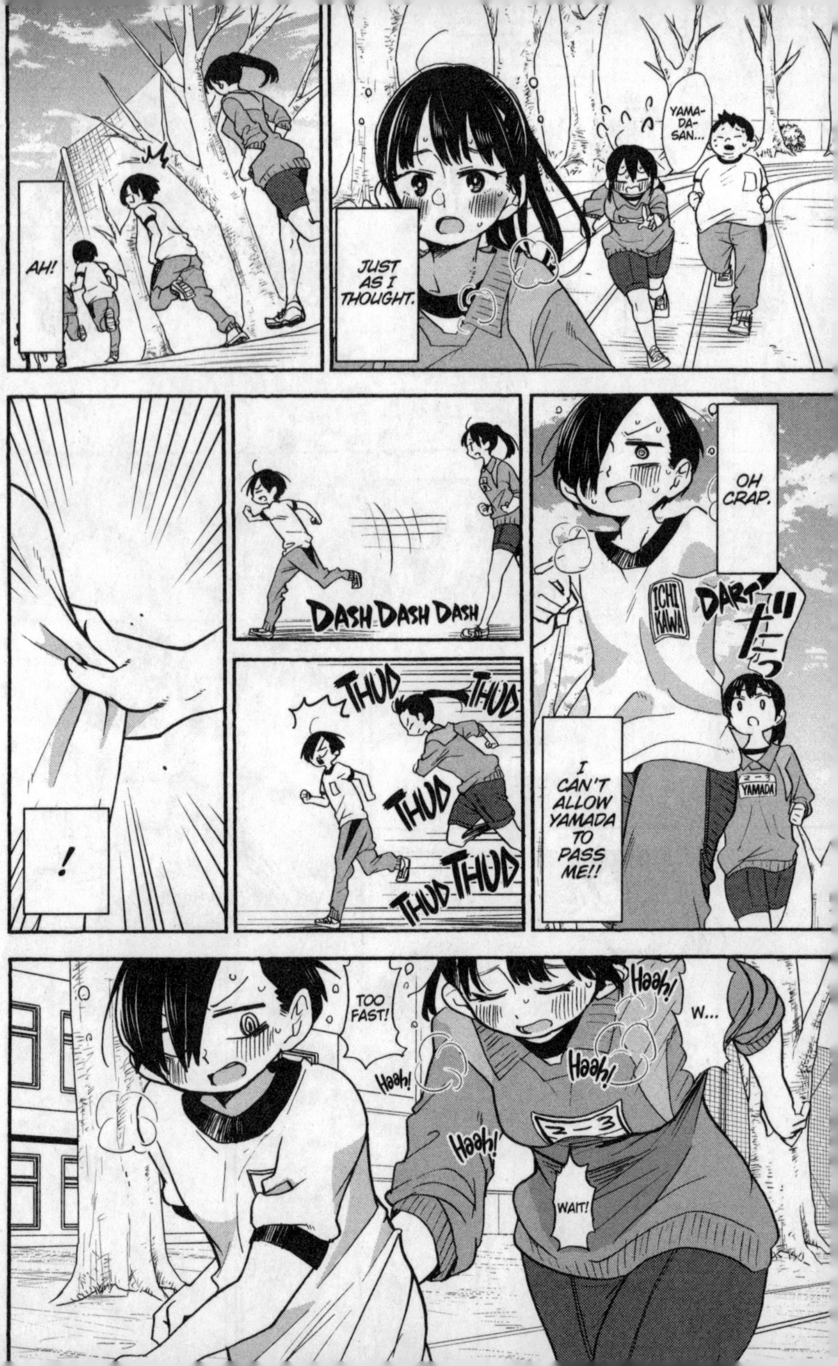

YAMA-DA-SAN...
JUST AS I THOUGHT.
AH!
OH CRAP.
ICHI KAWA
DART
I CAN'T ALLOW YAMADA TO PASS ME!!
2-3 YAMADA
DASH DASH DASH
THUD THUD
THUD
THUD THUD
!
W...
Haah!
Haah!
TOO FAST!
Haah!
Haah!
2-3
WAIT!

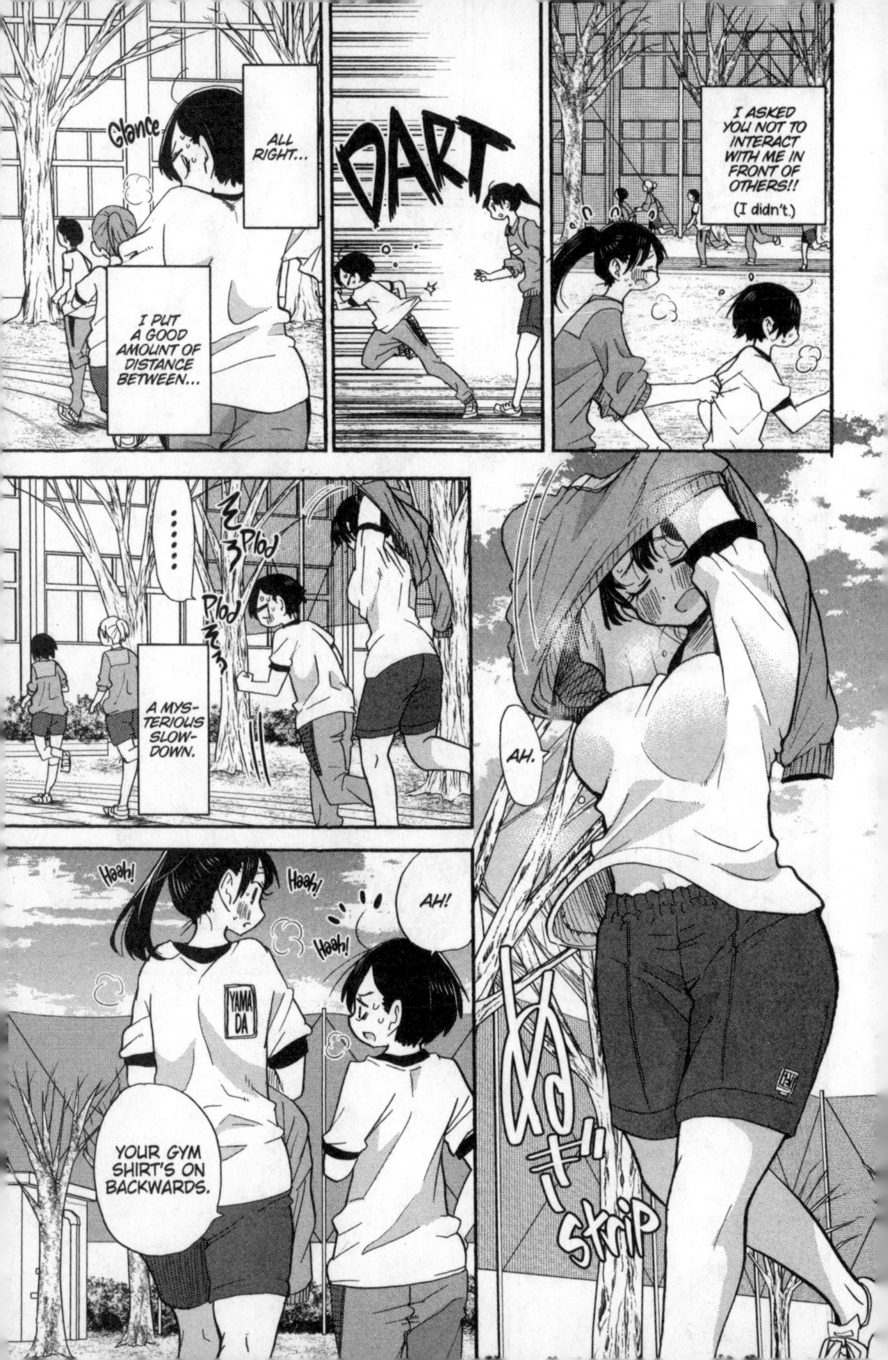

I ASKED YOU NOT TO INTERACT WITH ME IN FRONT OF OTHERS!!
(I didn't.)
DART
Glance
ALL RIGHT...
I PUT A GOOD AMOUNT OF DISTANCE BETWEEN...
AH.
strip
......
Plod
Plod
A MYS-TERIOUS SLOW-DOWN.
AH!
Haah!
Haah!
Haah!
YAMA DA
YOUR GYM SHIRT'S ON BACKWARDS.

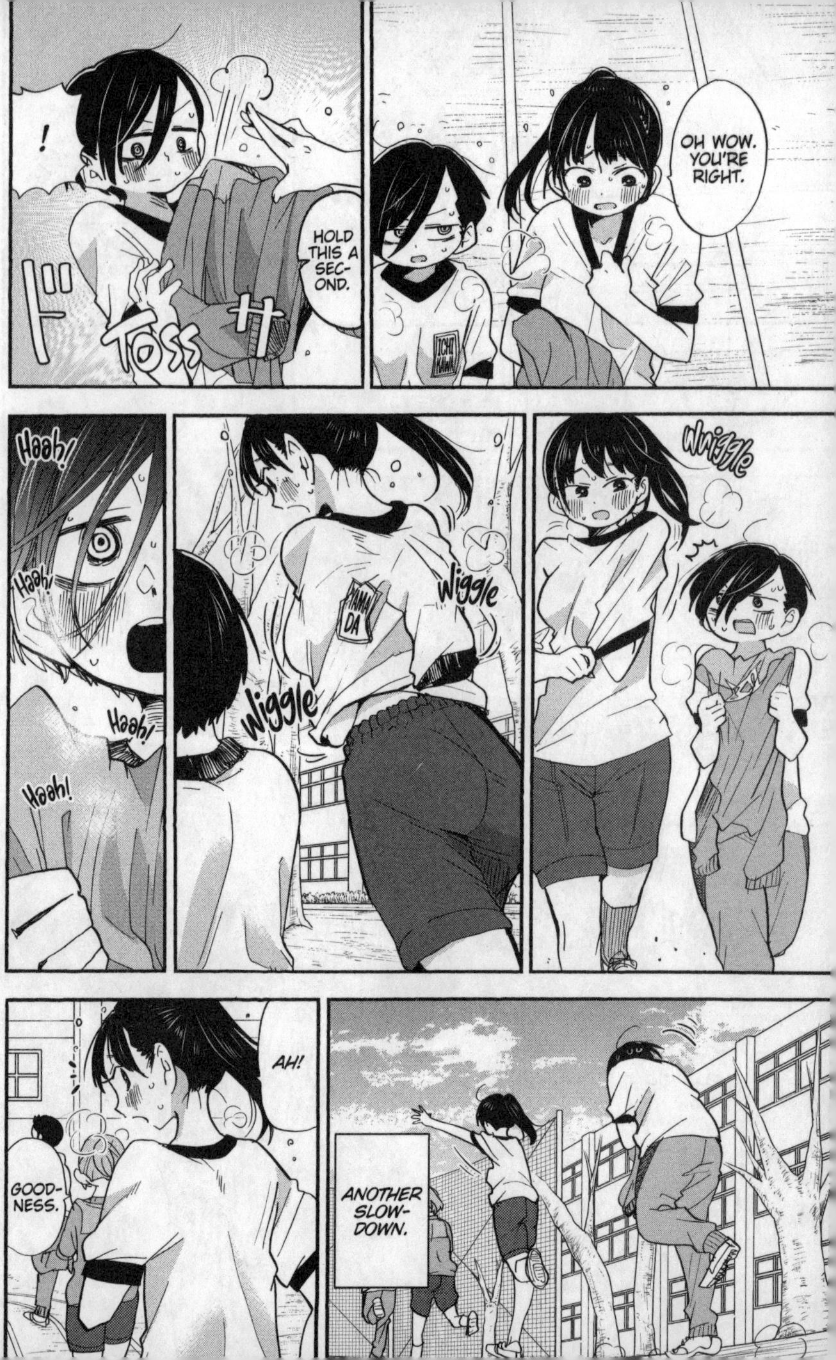
OH WOW. YOU'RE RIGHT.
!
HOLD THIS A SEC-OND.
ドッ
TOSS
サ
Wiggle
Wiggle
Wiggle
Haah!
Haah!
Haah!
Haah!
ANOTHER SLOW-DOWN.
AH!
GOOD-NESS.

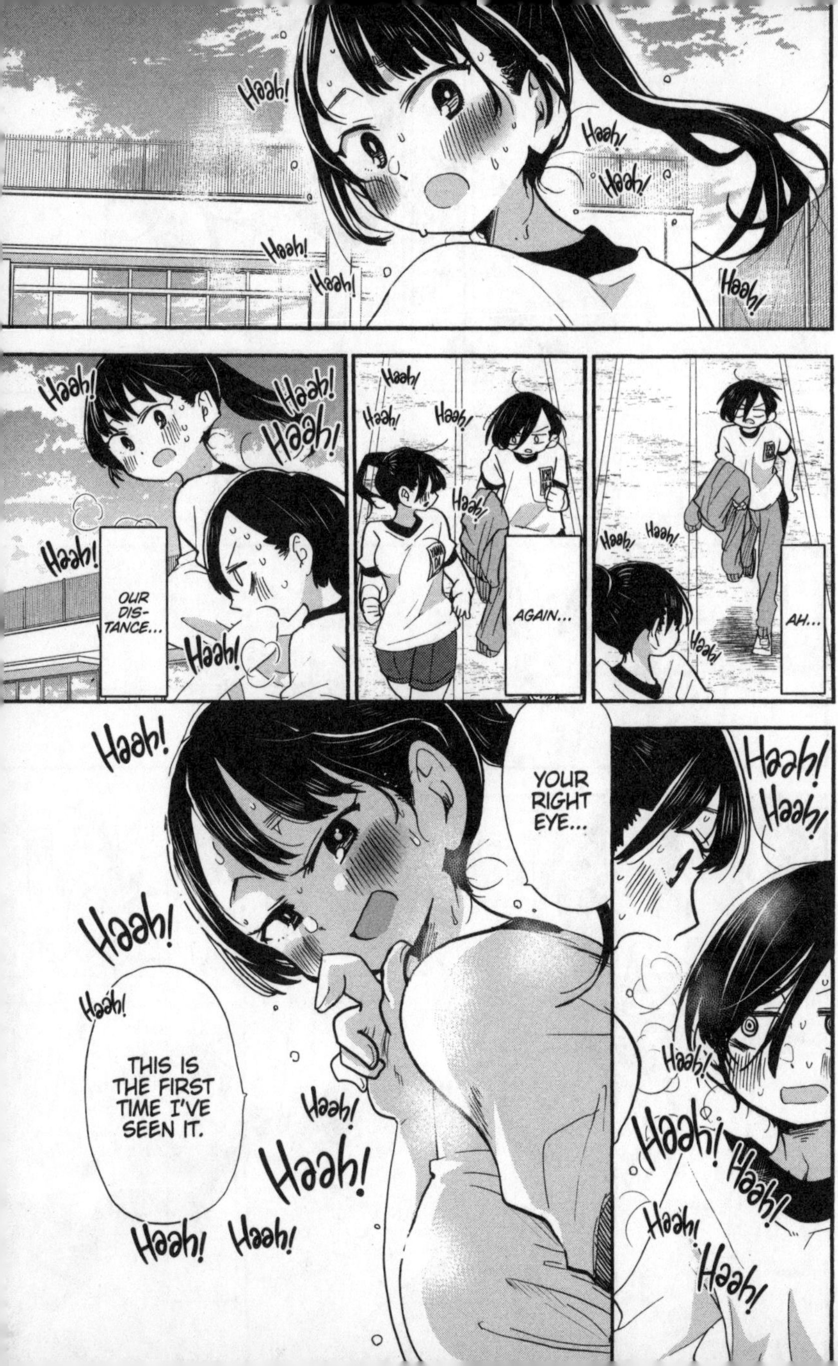
Haah!
Haah!
Haah!
Haah!
Haah!
Haah!
Haah!
Haah!
Haah!
Haah!
AH...
Haah!
Haah!
Haah!
Haah!
Haah!
AGAIN...
Haah!
Haah!
Haah!
Haah!
Haah!
OUR DIS-TANCE...
Haah!
Haah!
Haah!
Haah!
Haah!
Haah!
Haah!
Haah!
YOUR RIGHT EYE...
Haah!
Haah!
Haah!
THIS IS THE FIRST TIME I'VE SEEN IT.
Haah!
Haah!
Haah!
Haah!

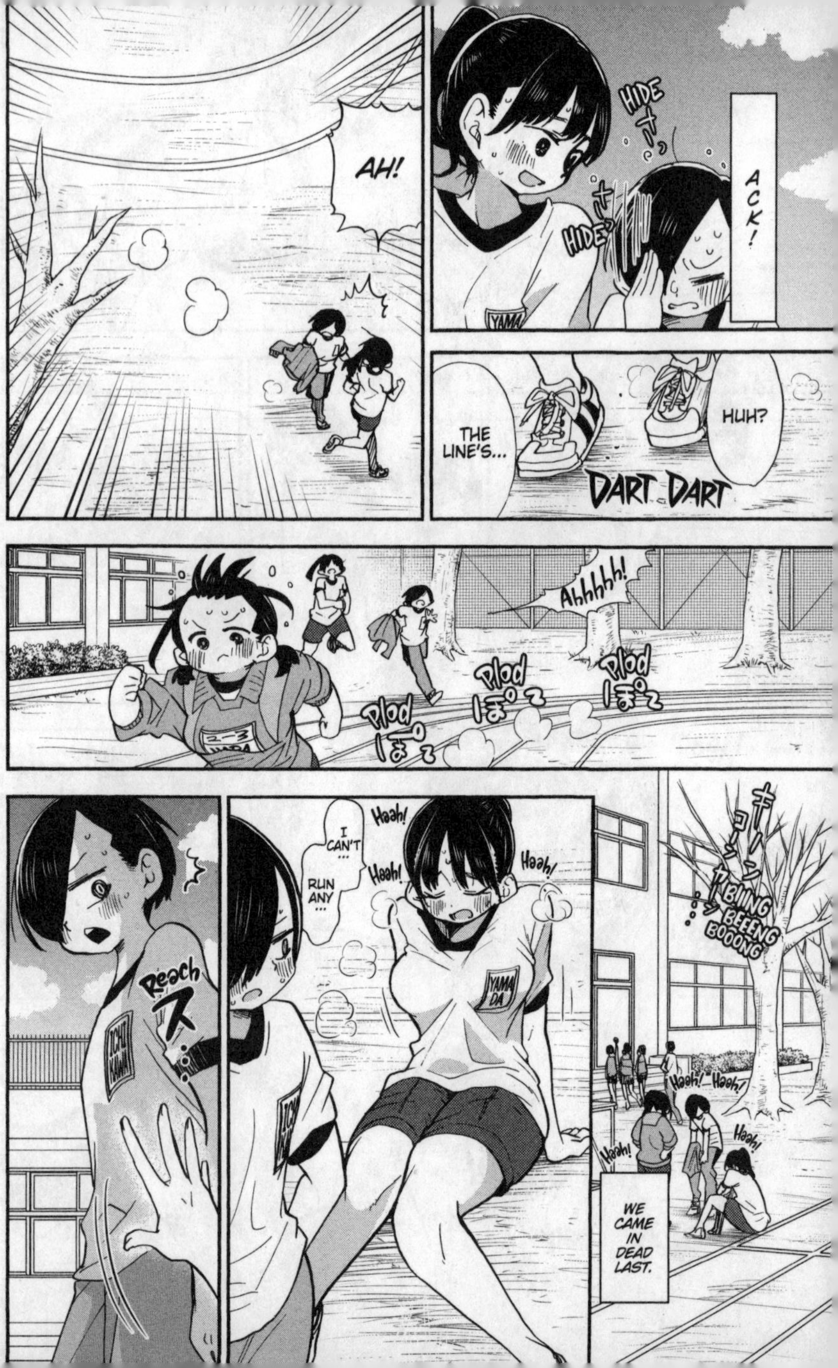
ACK!
HIDE
HIDE
AH!
HUH?
THE LINE'S...
DART DART
Ahhhhh!
Plod
Plod
Plod
BIIING BEEEENG BOOONG
WE CAME IN DEAD LAST.
Haah!
Haah!
Haah!
I CAN'T ... RUN ANY ...
Haah! Haah!
Haah!
Haah!
Reach

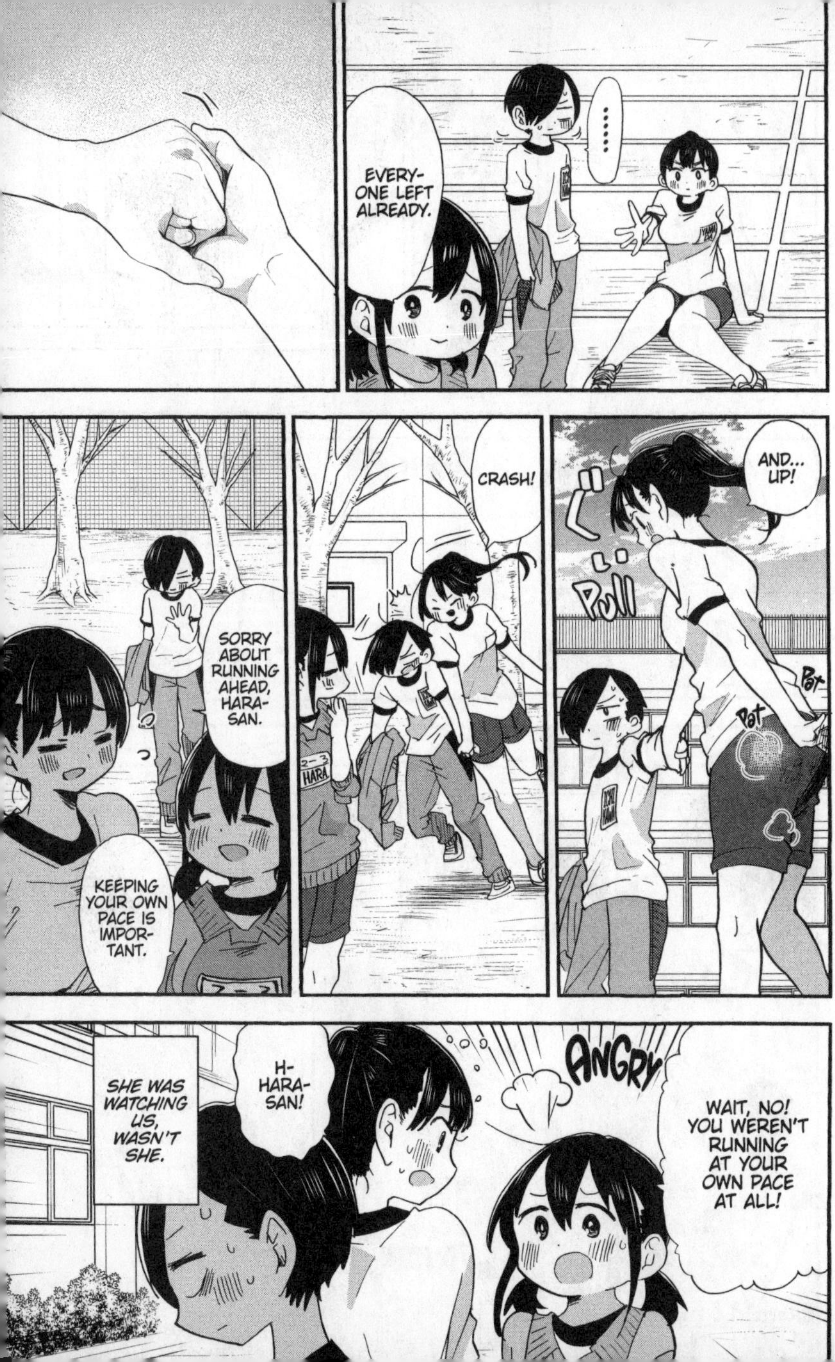
......
EVERY-ONE LEFT ALREADY.
AND... UP!
Pull
Pat
Pat
CRASH!
SORRY ABOUT RUNNING AHEAD, HARA-SAN.
KEEPING YOUR OWN PACE IS IMPORTANT.
ANGRY
WAIT, NO! YOU WEREN'T RUNNING AT YOUR OWN PACE AT ALL!
H- HARA-SAN!
SHE WAS WATCHING US, WASN'T SHE.

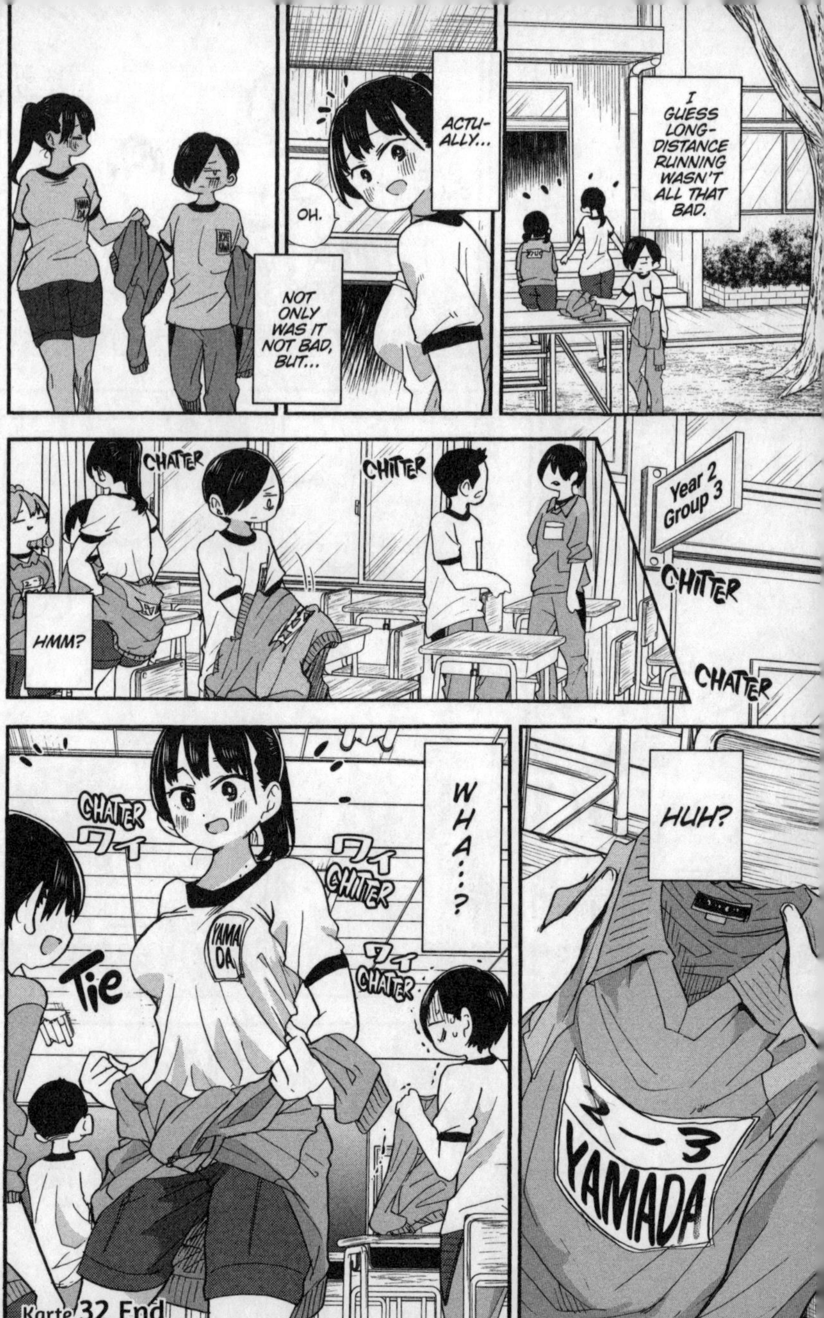
I GUESS LONG-DISTANCE RUNNING WASN'T ALL THAT BAD.
ACTU-ALLY...
OH.
NOT ONLY WAS IT NOT BAD, BUT...
Year 2 Group 3
CHITTER
CHATTER
CHATTER
CHITTER
CHATTER
HMM?
HUH?
2-3
YAMADA
WHA...?
ワイ
CHITTER
ワイ
CHATER
CHATER
ワイ
YAMADA
Tie
Karte.32 End

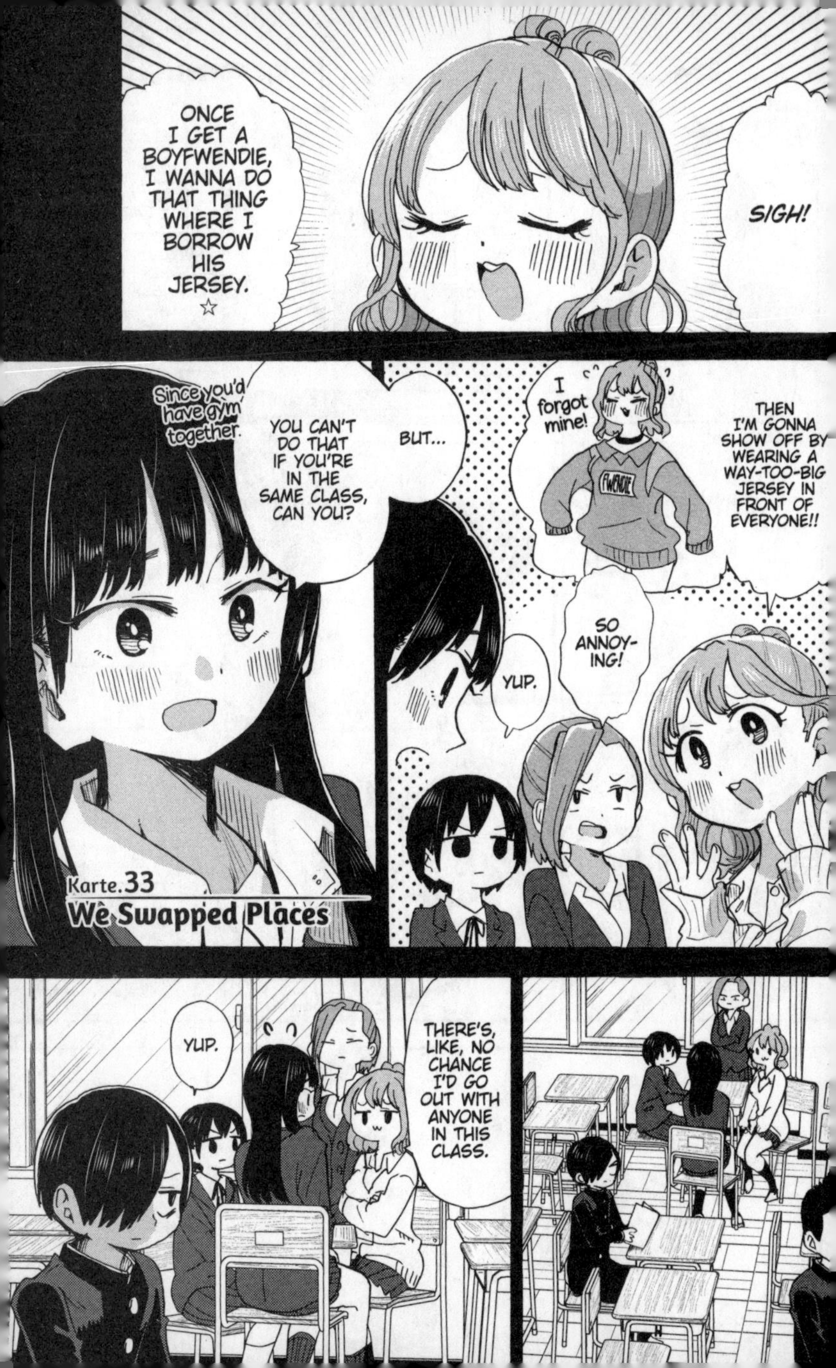
SIGH!
ONCE I GET A BOYFWENDIE, I WANNA DO THAT THING WHERE I BORROW HIS JERSEY. ☆
THEN I'M GONNA SHOW OFF BY WEARING A WAY-TOO-BIG JERSEY IN FRONT OF EVERYONE!!
I forgot mine!
FWENDIE
SO ANNOY-ING!
YUP.
BUT...
YOU CAN'T DO THAT IF YOU'RE IN THE SAME CLASS, CAN YOU?
Since you'd have gym together.
Karte.33
We Swapped Places
THERE'S, LIKE, NO CHANCE I'D GO OUT WITH ANYONE IN THIS CLASS.
YUP.

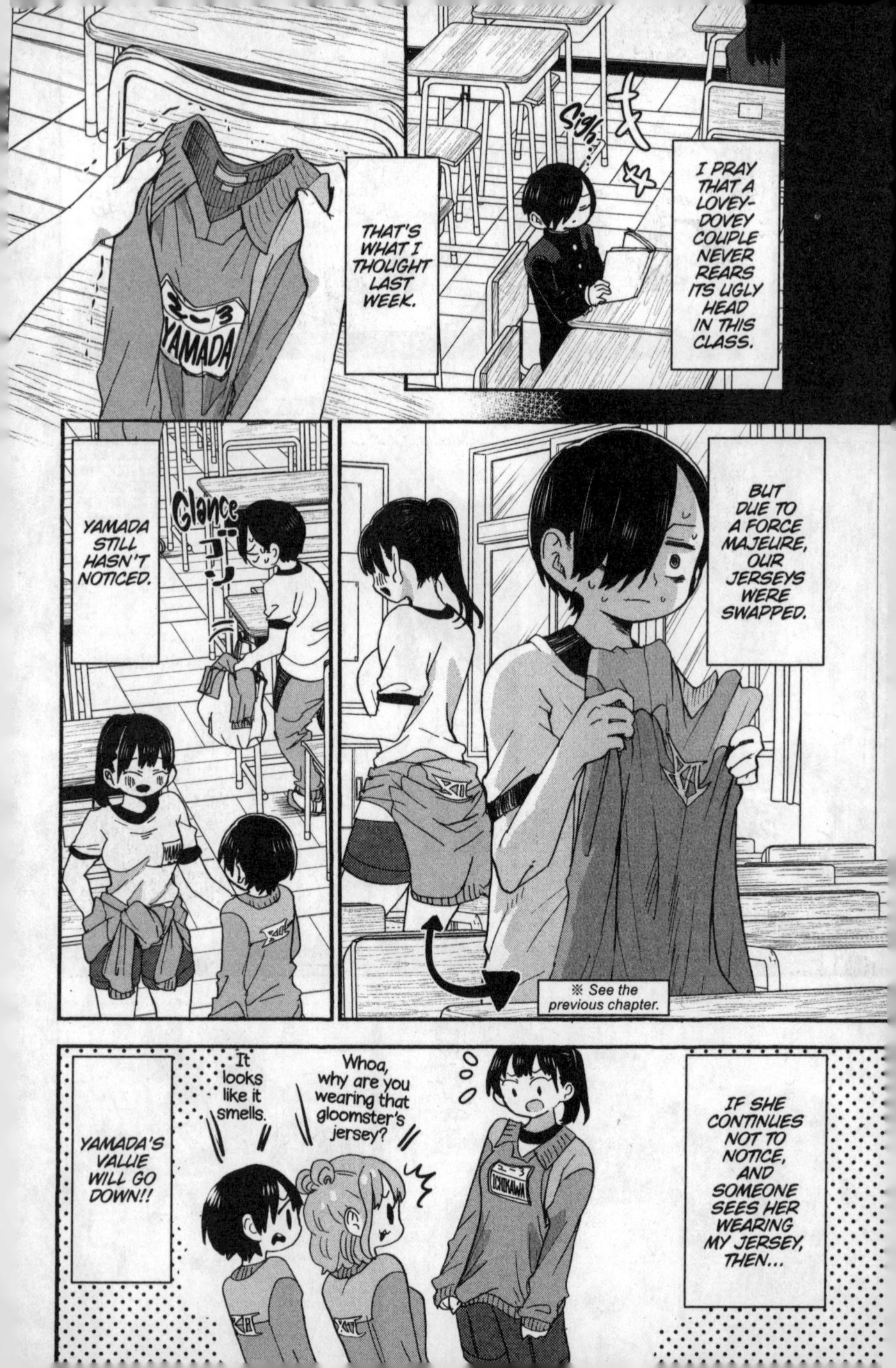

I PRAY THAT A LOVEY-DOVEY COUPLE NEVER REARS ITS UGLY HEAD IN THIS CLASS.
Sigh...
THAT'S WHAT I THOUGHT LAST WEEK.
YAMADA
BUT DUE TO A FORCE MAJEURE, OUR JERSEYS WERE SWAPPED.
※ See the previous chapter.
YAMADA STILL HASN'T NOTICED.
Glance
IF SHE CONTINUES NOT TO NOTICE, AND SOMEONE SEES HER WEARING MY JERSEY, THEN...
ICHIKAWA
Whoa, why are you wearing that gloomster's jersey?
It looks like it smells.
YAMADA'S VALUE WILL GO DOWN!!

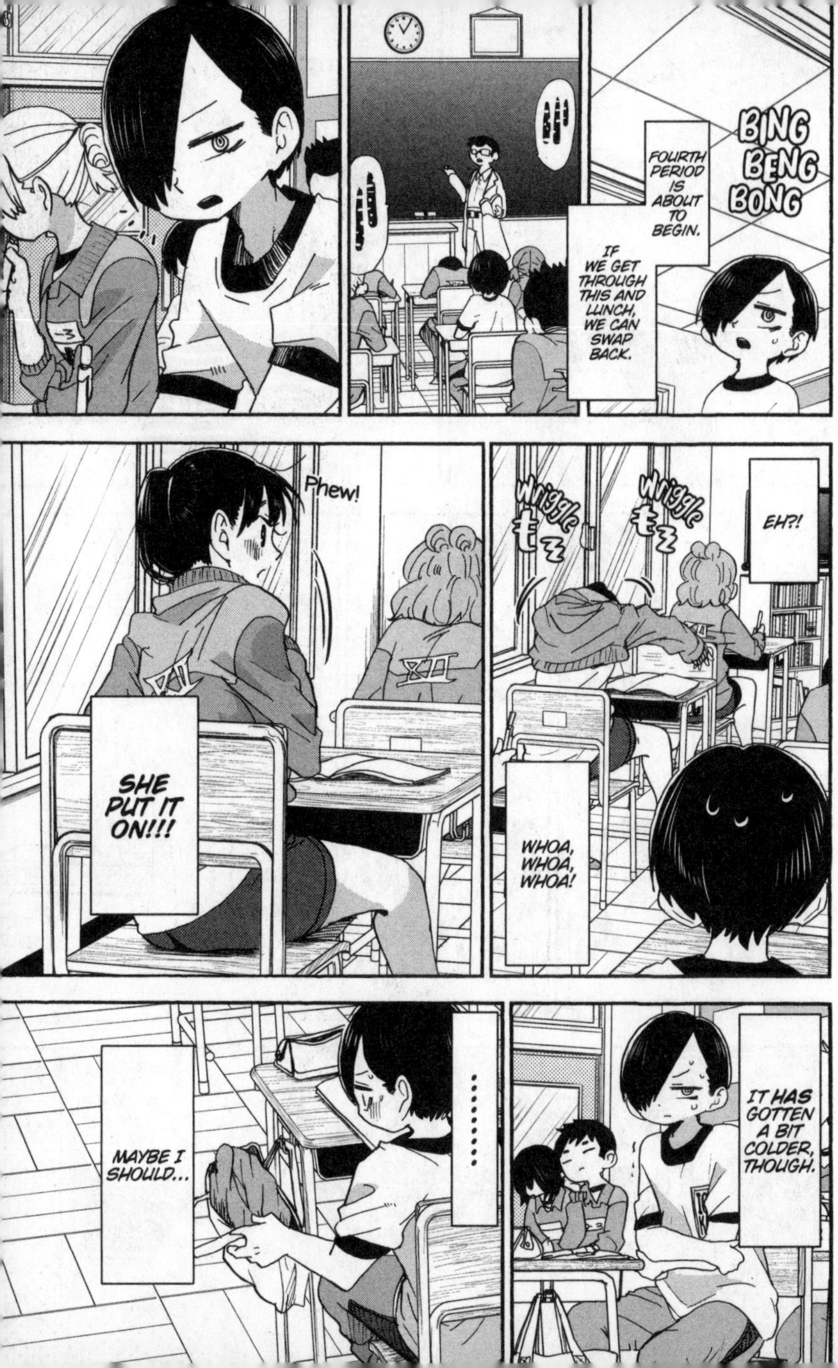

BING BENG BONG
FOURTH PERIOD IS ABOUT TO BEGIN.
IF WE GET THROUGH THIS AND LUNCH, WE CAN SWAP BACK.
EH?!
Wriggle
Wriggle
WHOA, WHOA, WHOA!
Phew!
SHE PUT IT ON!!!
IT HAS GOTTEN A BIT COLDER, THOUGH.
....
MAYBE I SHOULD...

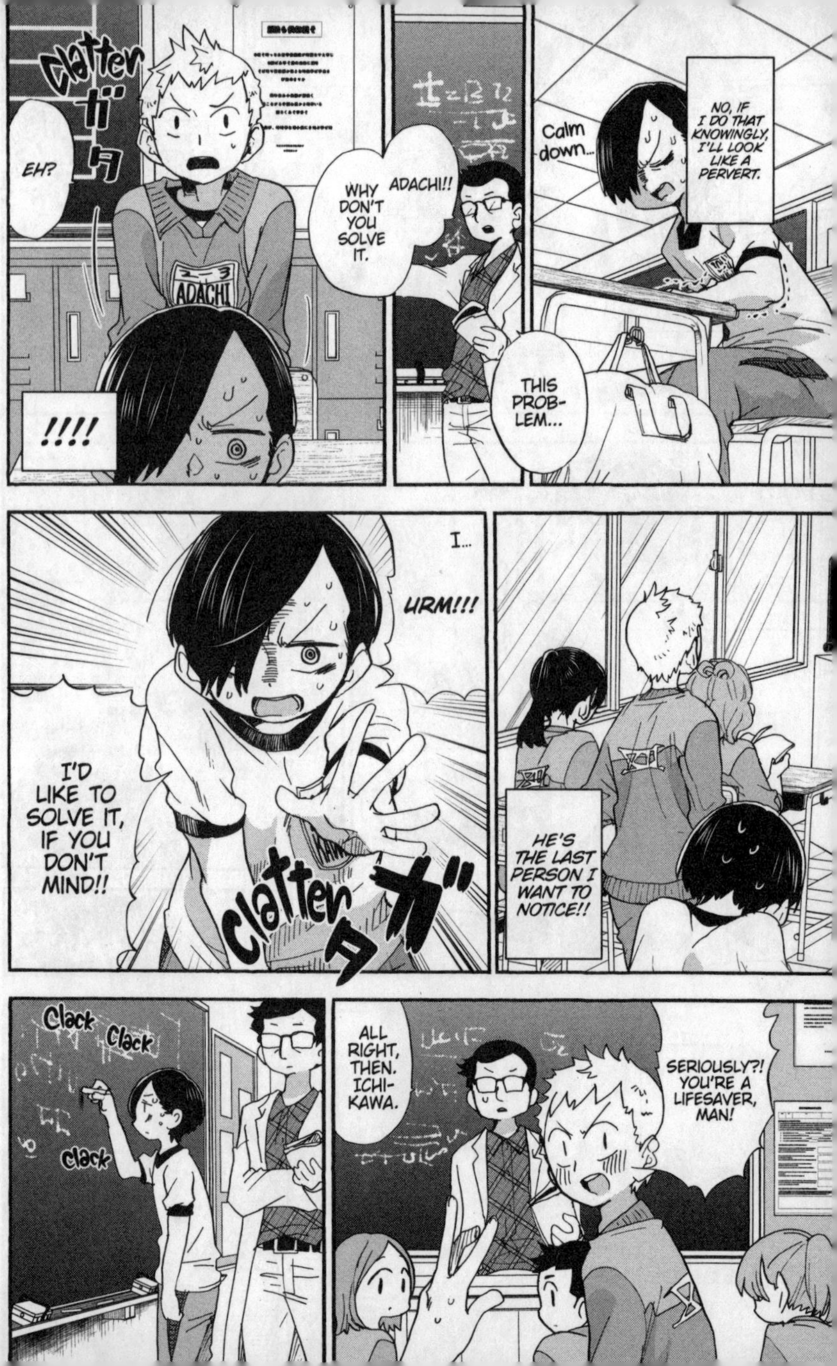
NO, IF I DO THAT KNOWINGLY, I'LL LOOK LIKE A PERVERT.
Calm down...
ADACHI!!
WHY DON'T YOU SOLVE IT.
THIS PROB-LEM...
clatter ガタ
EH?
!!!!
HE'S THE LAST PERSON I WANT TO NOTICE!!
I...
URM!!!
I'D LIKE TO SOLVE IT, IF YOU DON'T MIND!!
clatter ガタ
SERIOUSLY?! YOU'RE A LIFESAVER, MAN!
ALL RIGHT, THEN. ICHI-KAWA.
Clack
Clack
clack

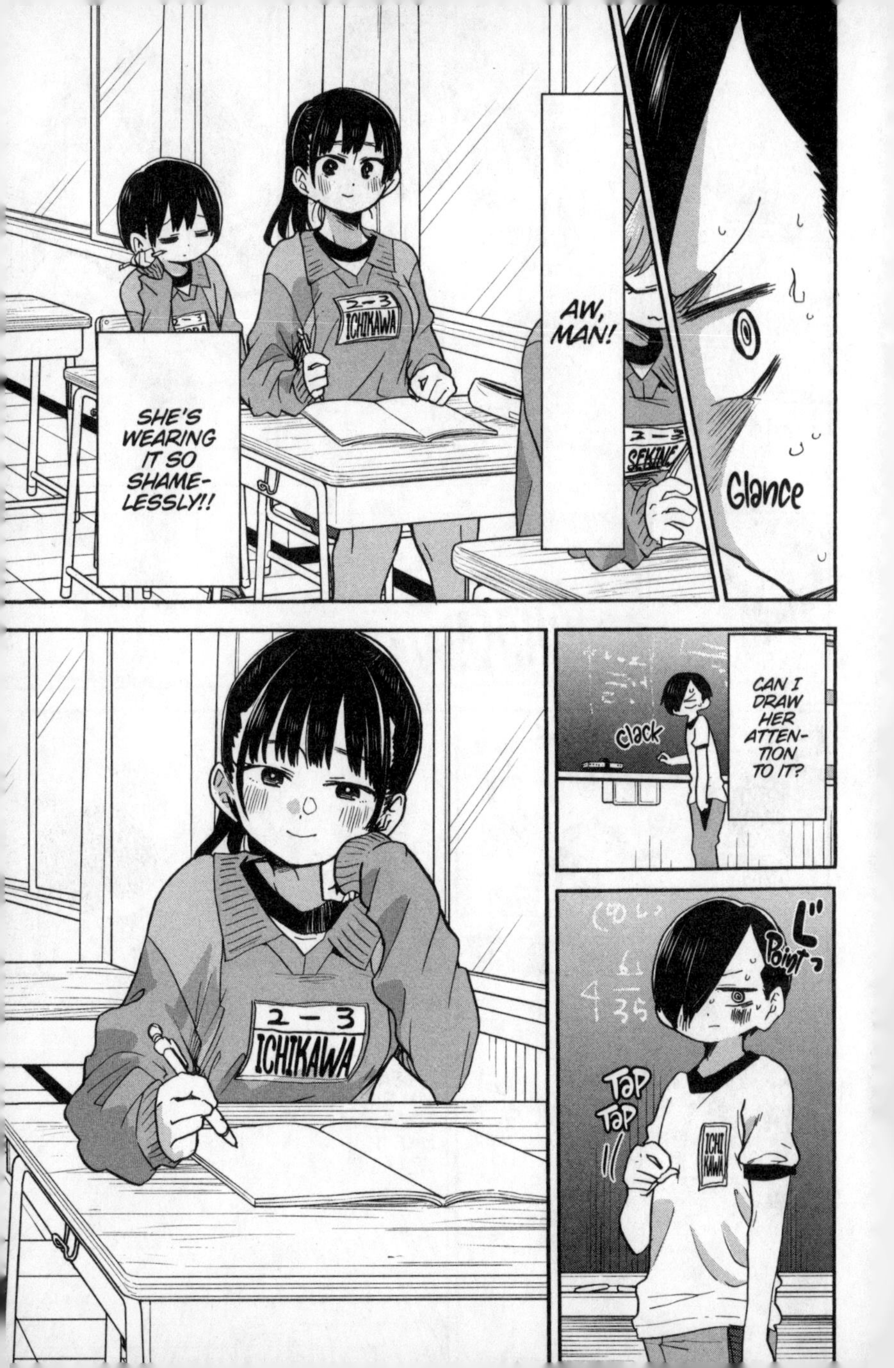
Glance
AW, MAN!
SHE'S WEARING IT SO SHAME-LESSLY!!
CAN I DRAW HER ATTEN-TION TO IT?
clack
じ
Point
Tap Tap
ICHIKAWA
2-3
ICHIKAWA

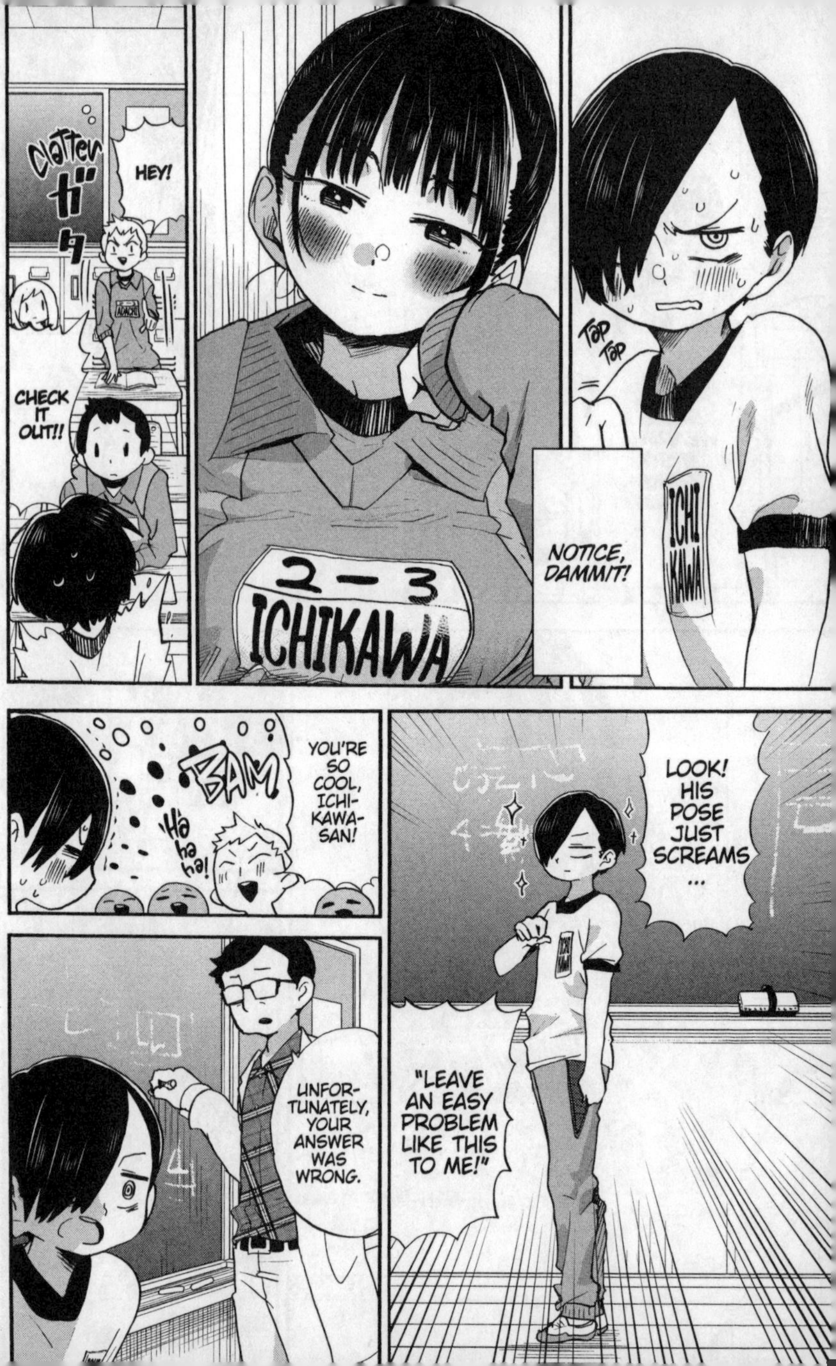

Tap tap
ICHIKAWA
NOTICE, DAMMIT!
2-3 ICHIKAWA
Clatter ガタ
HEY!
ADACHI
CHECK IT OUT!!
LOOK! HIS POSE JUST SCREAMS...
"LEAVE AN EASY PROBLEM LIKE THIS TO ME!"
YOU'RE SO COOL, ICHIKAWA-SAN!
BAM
Ha ha ha!
UNFORTUNATELY, YOUR ANSWER WAS WRONG.

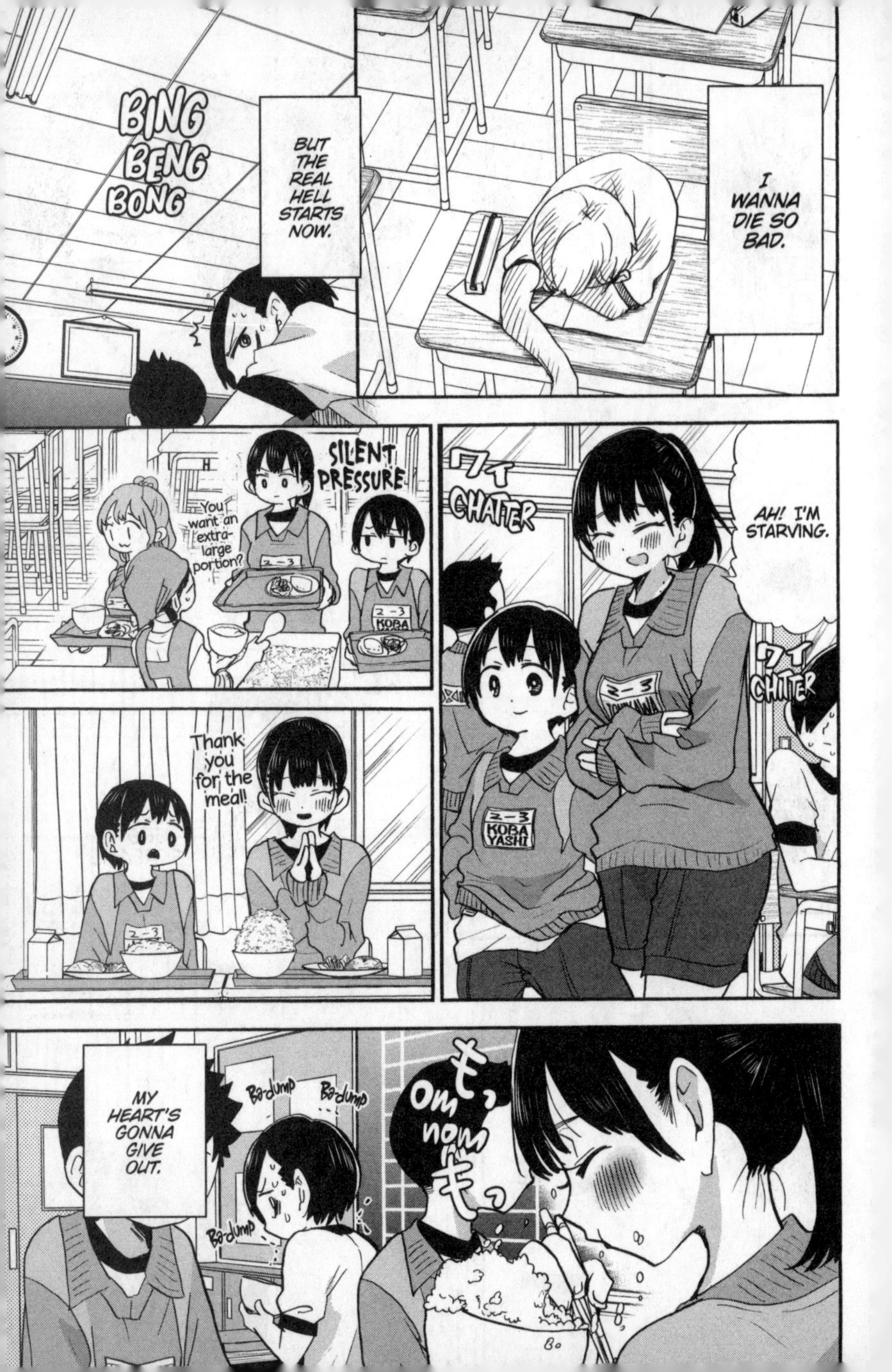
I WANNA DIE SO BAD.
BUT THE REAL HELL STARTS NOW.
BING BENG BONG
ワイ
CHATTER
AH! I'M STARVING.
ワイ
CHITTER
SILENT PRESSURE
You want an extra-large portion?
Thank you for the meal!
もっ
om nom
もっ
Ba-dump
Ba-dump
Ba-dump
MY HEART'S GONNA GIVE OUT.

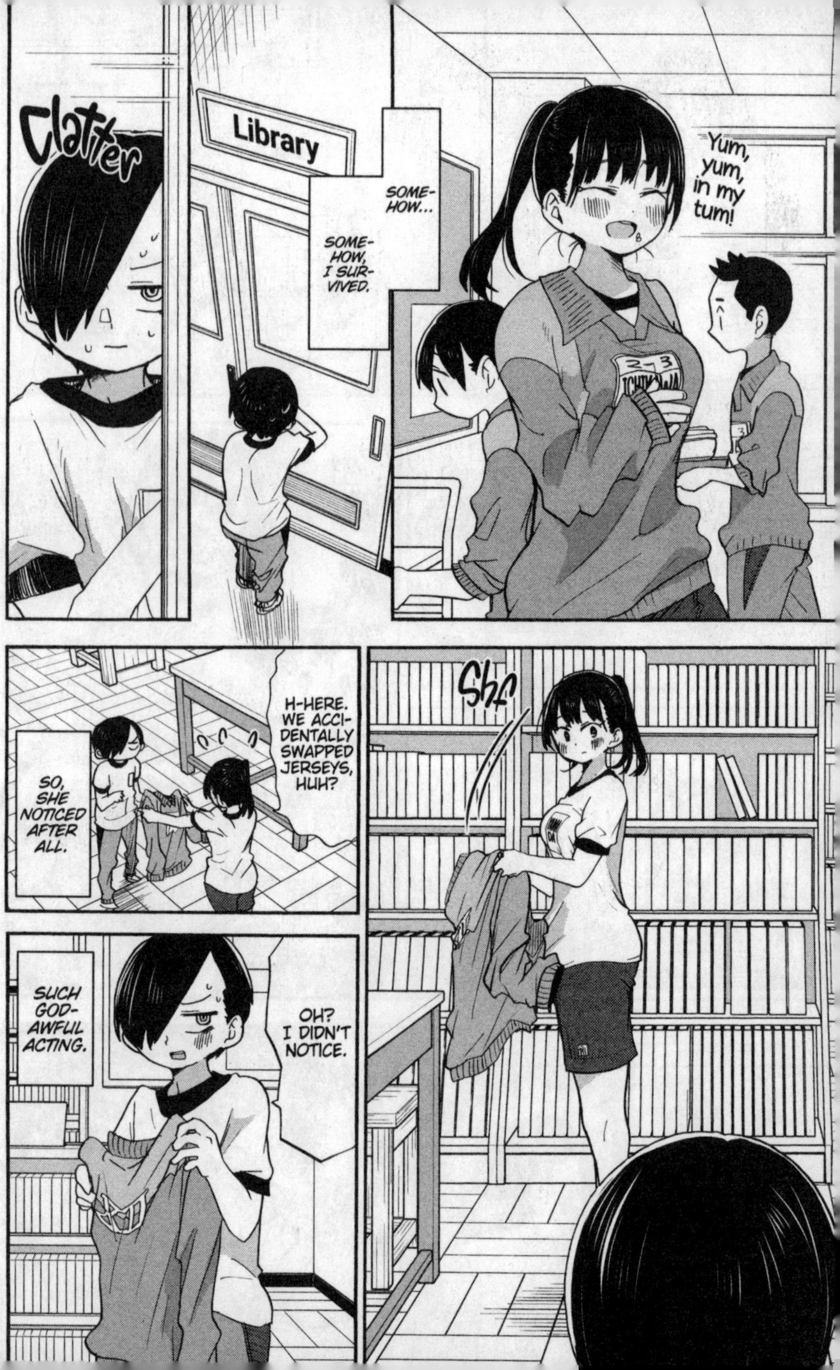
Yum, yum, in my tum!
Library
SOME-HOW...
SOME-HOW, I SUR-VIVED.
Clatter
Shf
H-HERE. WE ACCI-DENTALLY SWAPPED JERSEYS, HUH?
SO, SHE NOTICED AFTER ALL.
OH? I DIDN'T NOTICE.
SUCH GOD-AWFUL ACTING.

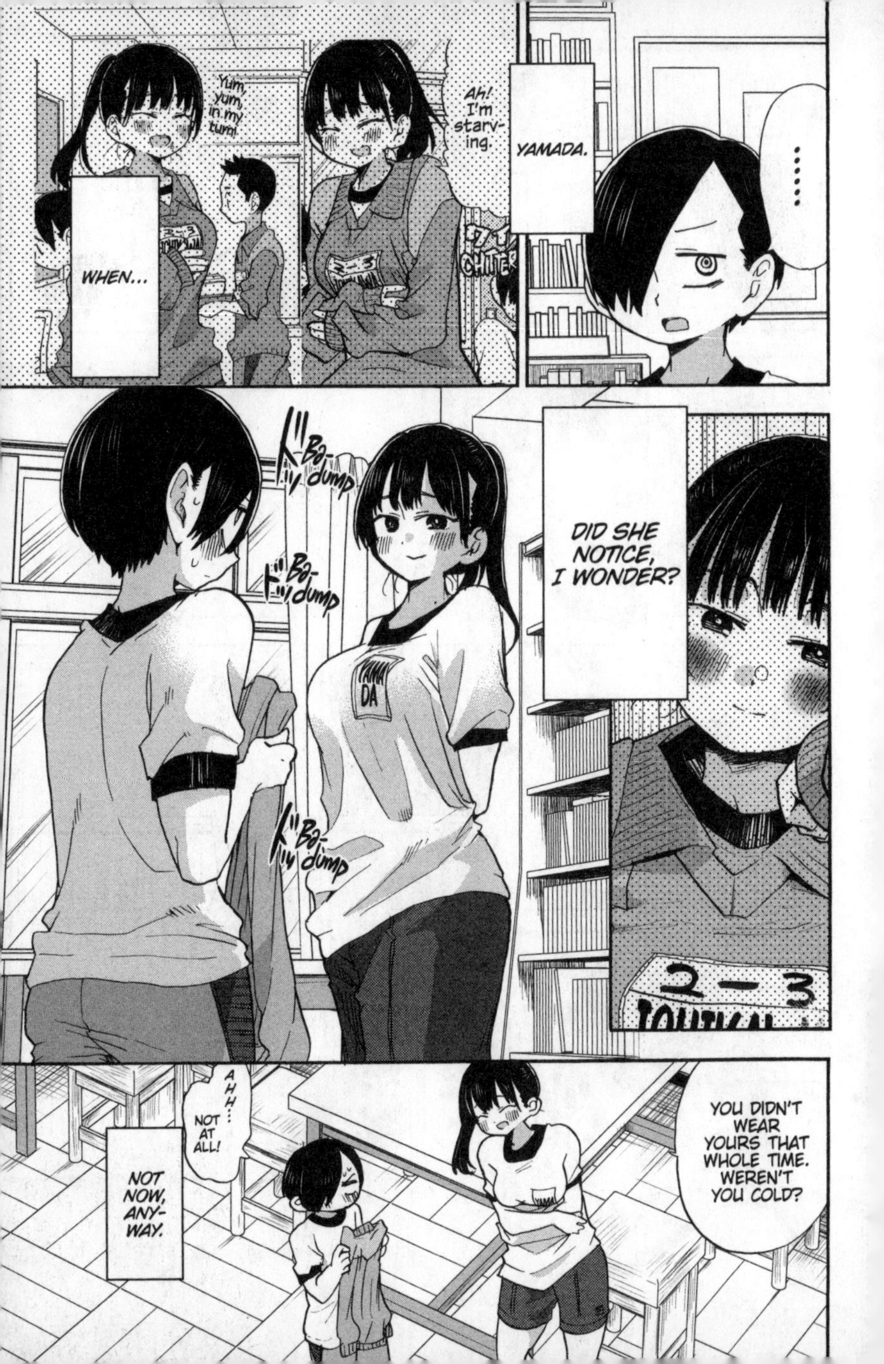
……
YAMADA.
Ah! I'm starving.
CHITTER
Yum, yum, in my tum!
WHEN…
DID SHE NOTICE, I WONDER?
Ba-dump
Ba-dump
Ba-dump
YOU DIDN'T WEAR YOURS THAT WHOLE TIME. WEREN'T YOU COLD?
AHH… NOT AT ALL!
NOT NOW, ANYWAY.

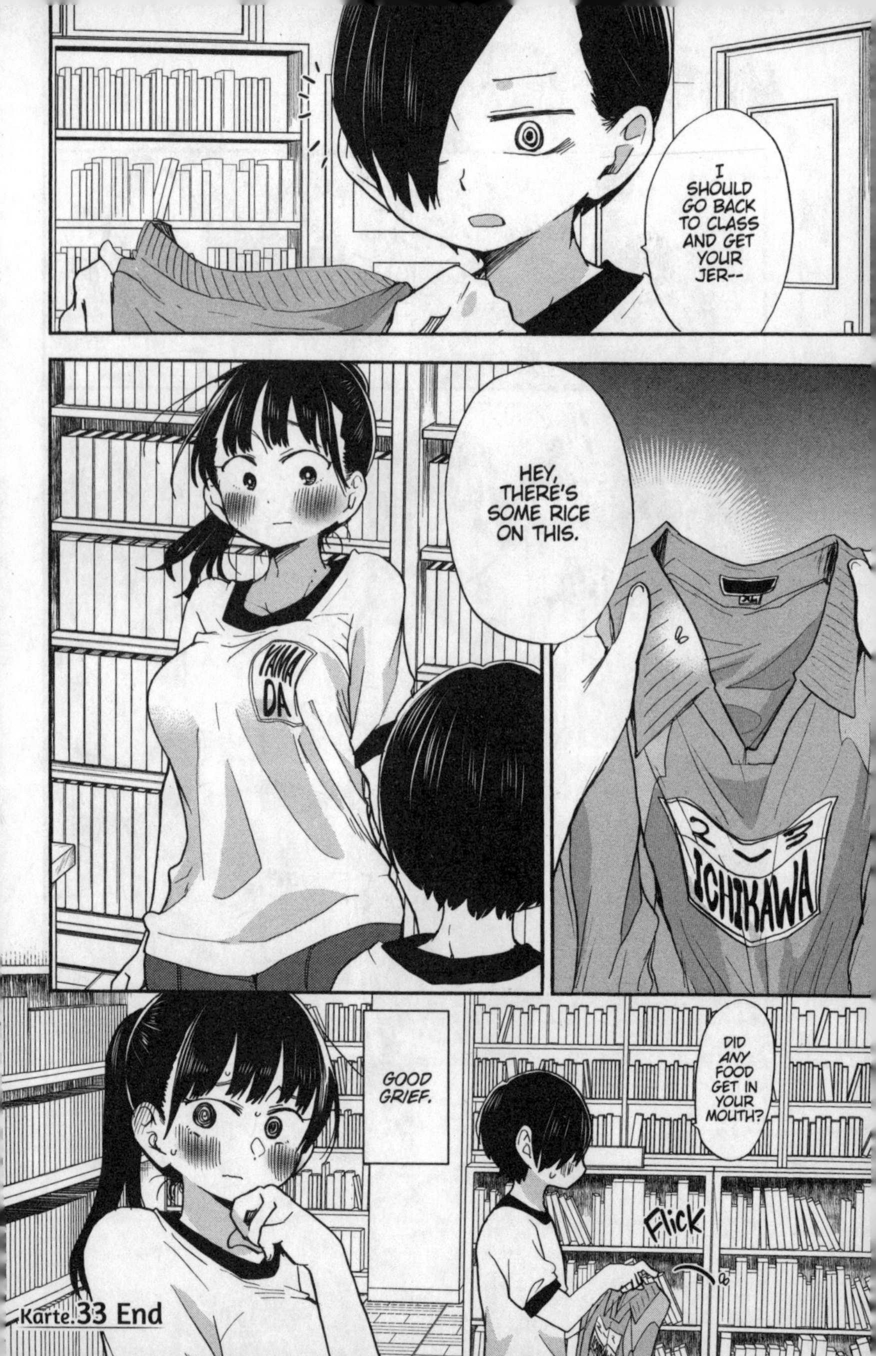
I SHOULD GO BACK TO CLASS AND GET YOUR JER--
HEY, THERE'S SOME RICE ON THIS.
ICHIKAWA
DID ANY FOOD GET IN YOUR MOUTH?
FLICK
GOOD GRIEF.
Karte.33 End

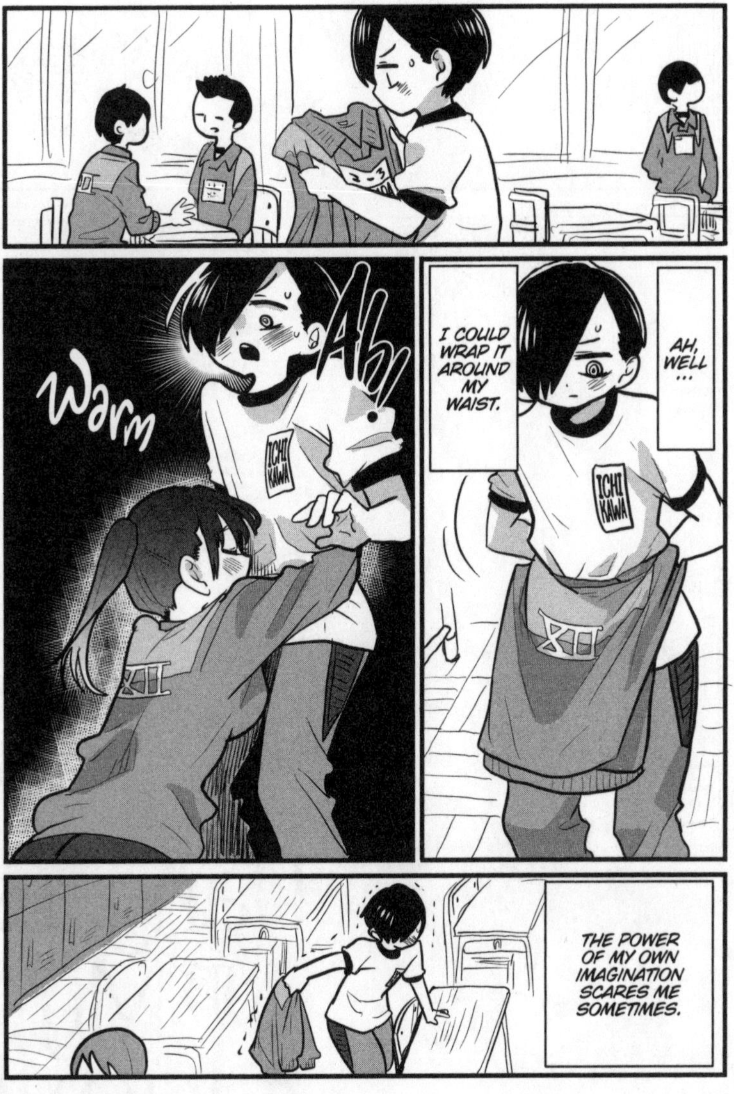
AH, WELL ...
I COULD WRAP IT AROUND MY WAIST.
ICHIKAWA
Ah!!
warm
ICHIKAWA
THE POWER OF MY OWN IMAGINATION SCARES ME SOMETIMES.

The
Dangers
in My
Heart

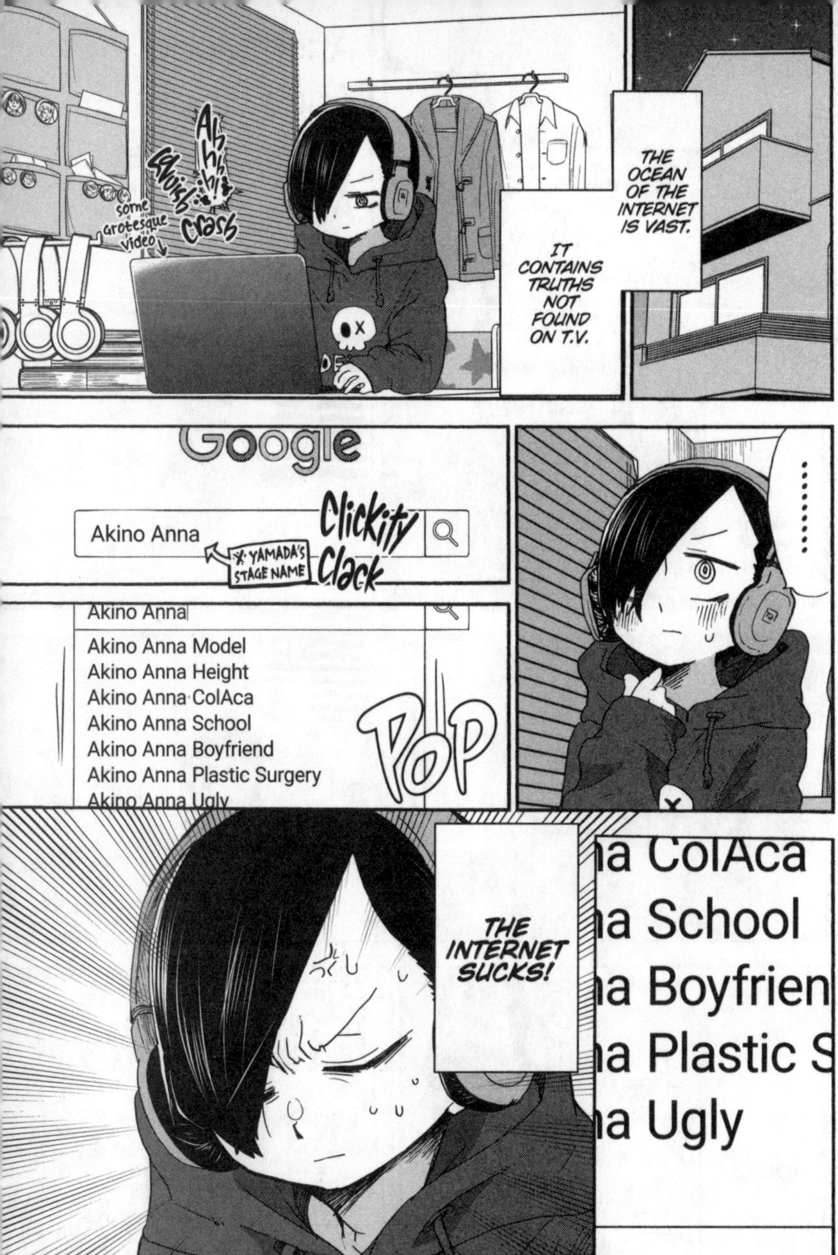
THE OCEAN OF THE INTERNET IS VAST.
IT CONTAINS TRUTHS NOT FOUND ON T.V.
Ahhhh!
Swish
Crash
some grotesque video
....
Google
Akino Anna
Clickity Clack
※YAMADA'S STAGE NAME
Akino Anna
Akino Anna Model
Akino Anna Height
Akino Anna ColAca
Akino Anna School
Akino Anna Boyfriend
Akino Anna Plastic Surgery
Akino Anna Ugly
POP
THE INTERNET SUCKS!
na ColAca
na School
na Boyfrien
na Plastic S
na Ugly

Karte.34
I Tuned In

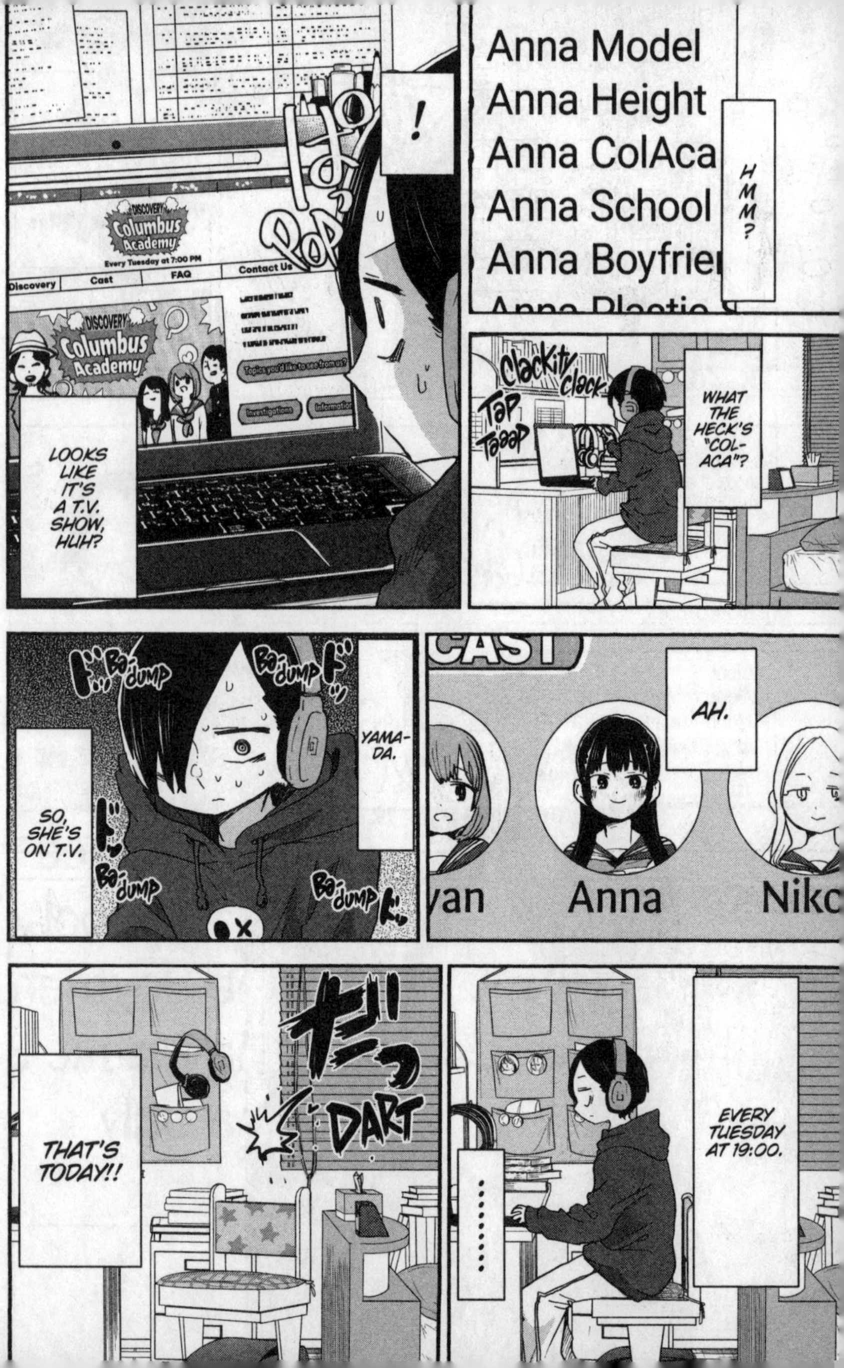
Anna Model
Anna Height
Anna ColAca
Anna School
Anna Boyfrie
HMM?
Clackity clack
Tap Taaap
WHAT THE HECK'S "COL-ACA"?
!
POP
DISCOVERY
Columbus Academy
Every Tuesday at 7:00 PM
Discovery
Cast
FAQ
Contact Us
Topics you'd like to see from us?
Investigations
Information
LOOKS LIKE IT'S A T.V. SHOW, HUH?
CAST
AH.
Anna
YAMA-DA.
Ba-dump
Ba-dump
Ba-dump
Ba-dump
SO, SHE'S ON T.V.
EVERY TUESDAY AT 19:00.
....
DART
THAT'S TODAY!!

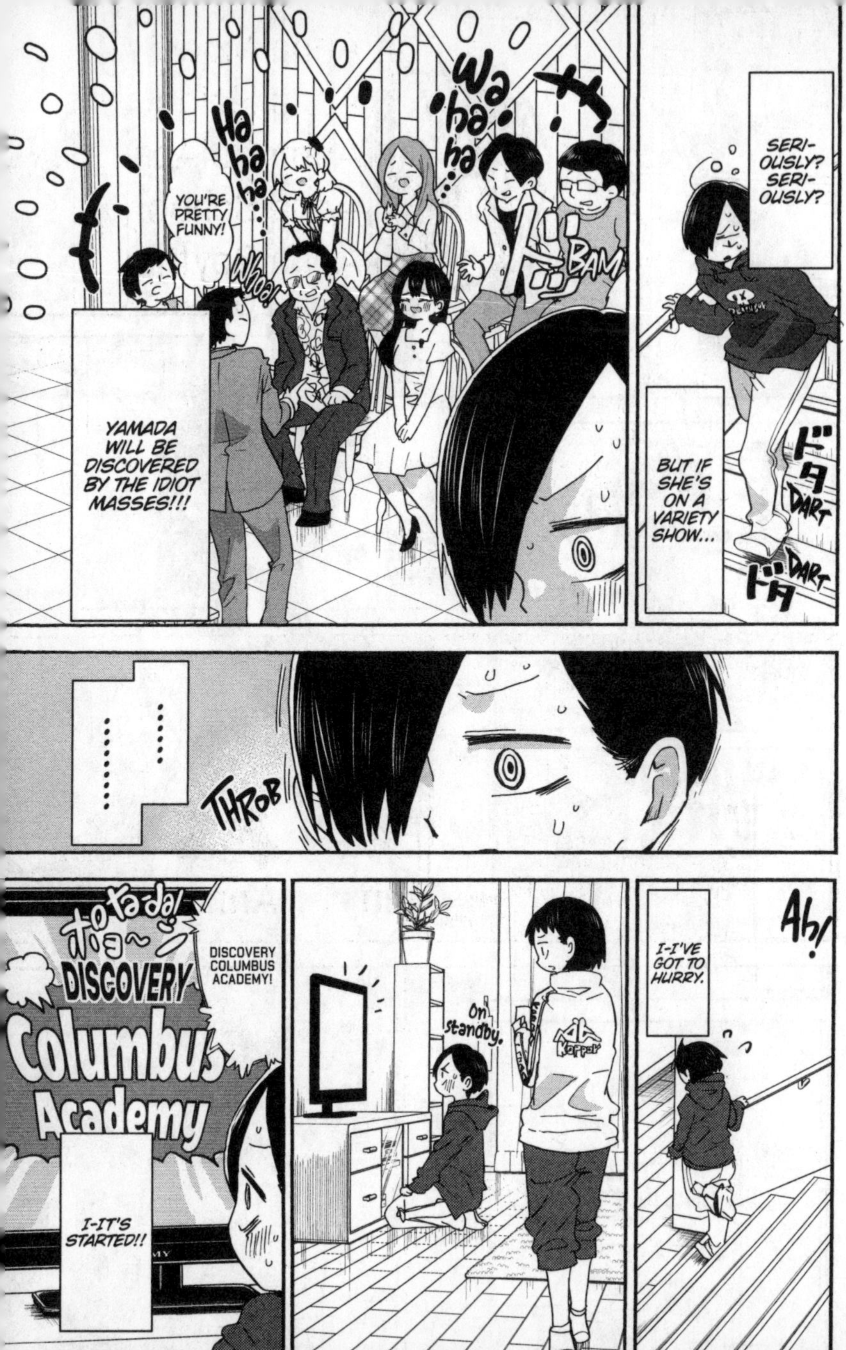
SERI-OUSLY? SERI-OUSLY?
BUT IF SHE'S ON A VARIETY SHOW...
ドタ DART
ドタ DART
Wa ha ha ha...
Ha ha ha...
YOU'RE PRETTY FUNNY!
Whoa!
BAM
YAMADA WILL BE DISCOVERED BY THE IDIOT MASSES!!!
......
......
THROB
Ah!
I-I'VE GOT TO HURRY.
On standby.
ta-da!
DISCOVERY COLUMBUS ACADEMY!
DISCOVERY Columbus Academy
I-IT'S STARTED!!

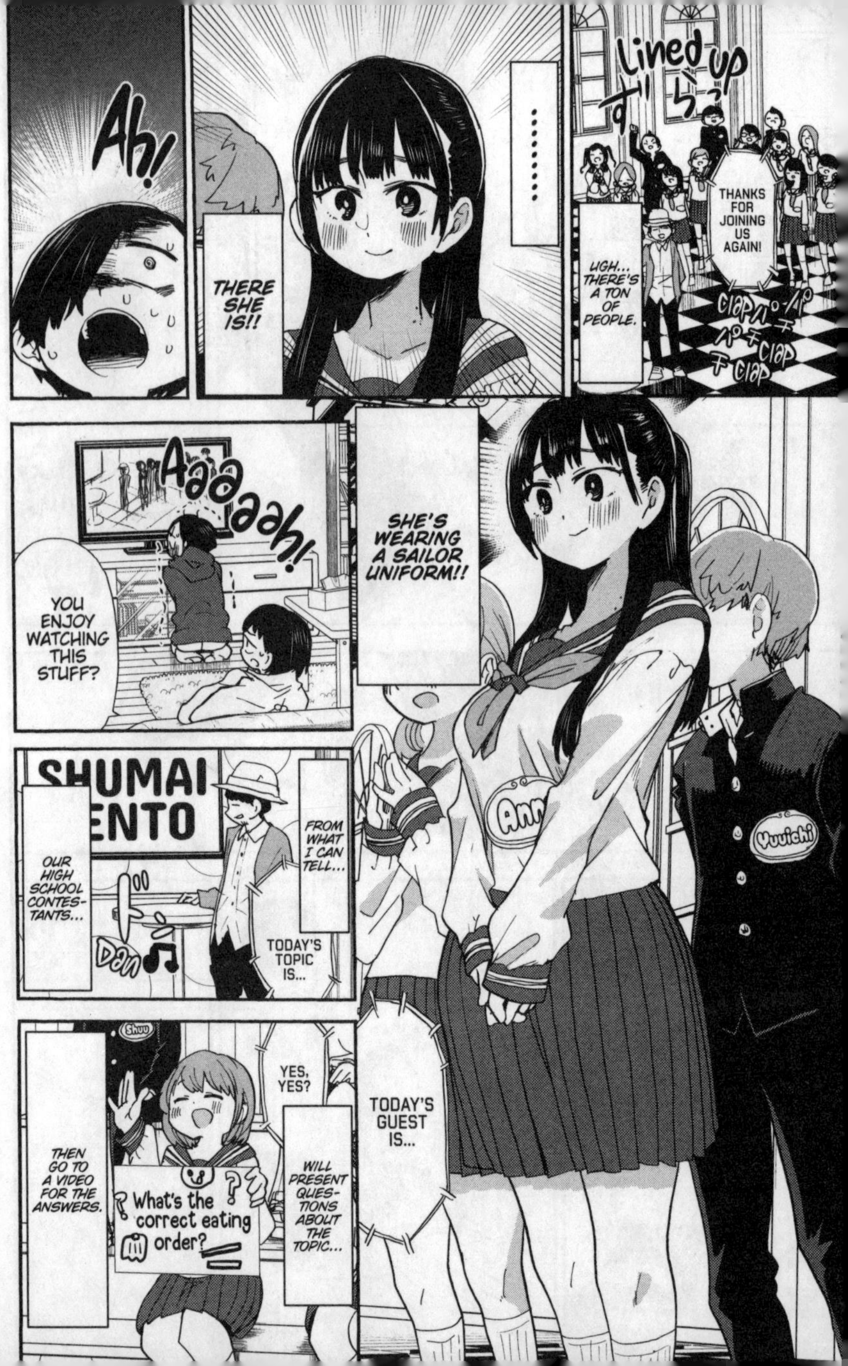
Lined up
ずらっ
THANKS FOR JOINING US AGAIN!
UGH... THERE'S A TON OF PEOPLE.
clap パチ
パチ clap
clap
......
THERE SHE IS!!
Ah!
SHE'S WEARING A SAILOR UNIFORM!!
Ann
Yuuichi
TODAY'S GUEST IS...
Aaaaaah!
YOU ENJOY WATCHING THIS STUFF?
SHUMAI
ENTO
TODAY'S TOPIC IS...
FROM WHAT I CAN TELL...
OUR HIGH SCHOOL CONTESTANTS...
Dan
Shuu
YES, YES?
WILL PRESENT QUESTIONS ABOUT THE TOPIC...
THEN GO TO A VIDEO FOR THE ANSWERS.
What's the correct eating order?

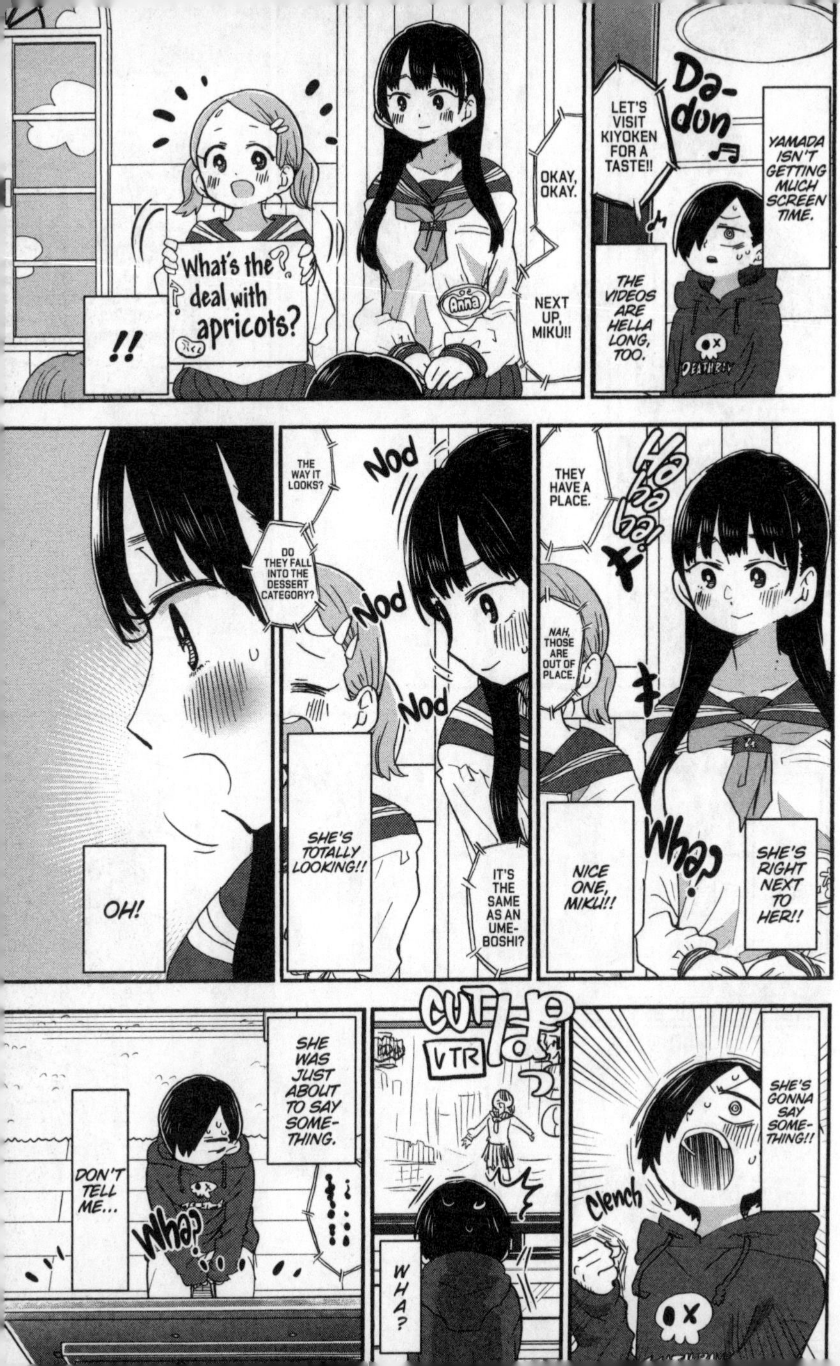
Da-dun
YAMADA ISN'T GETTING MUCH SCREEN TIME.
LET'S VISIT KIYOKEN FOR A TASTE!!
THE VIDEOS ARE HELLA LONG, TOO.
OKAY, OKAY.
NEXT UP, MIKU!!
What's the deal with apricots?
!!
Ha ha ha!
THEY HAVE A PLACE.
NAH, THOSE ARE OUT OF PLACE.
SHE'S RIGHT NEXT TO HER!!
Wha?
NICE ONE, MIKU!!
Nod
THE WAY IT LOOKS?
DO THEY FALL INTO THE DESSERT CATEGORY?
Nod
Nod
IT'S THE SAME AS AN UMEBOSHI?
SHE'S TOTALLY LOOKING!!
OH!
SHE'S GONNA SAY SOMETHING!!
Clench
CUT
ぱっ
VTR
WHA?
SHE WAS JUST ABOUT TO SAY SOMETHING.
...!
DON'T TELL ME...
Wha?

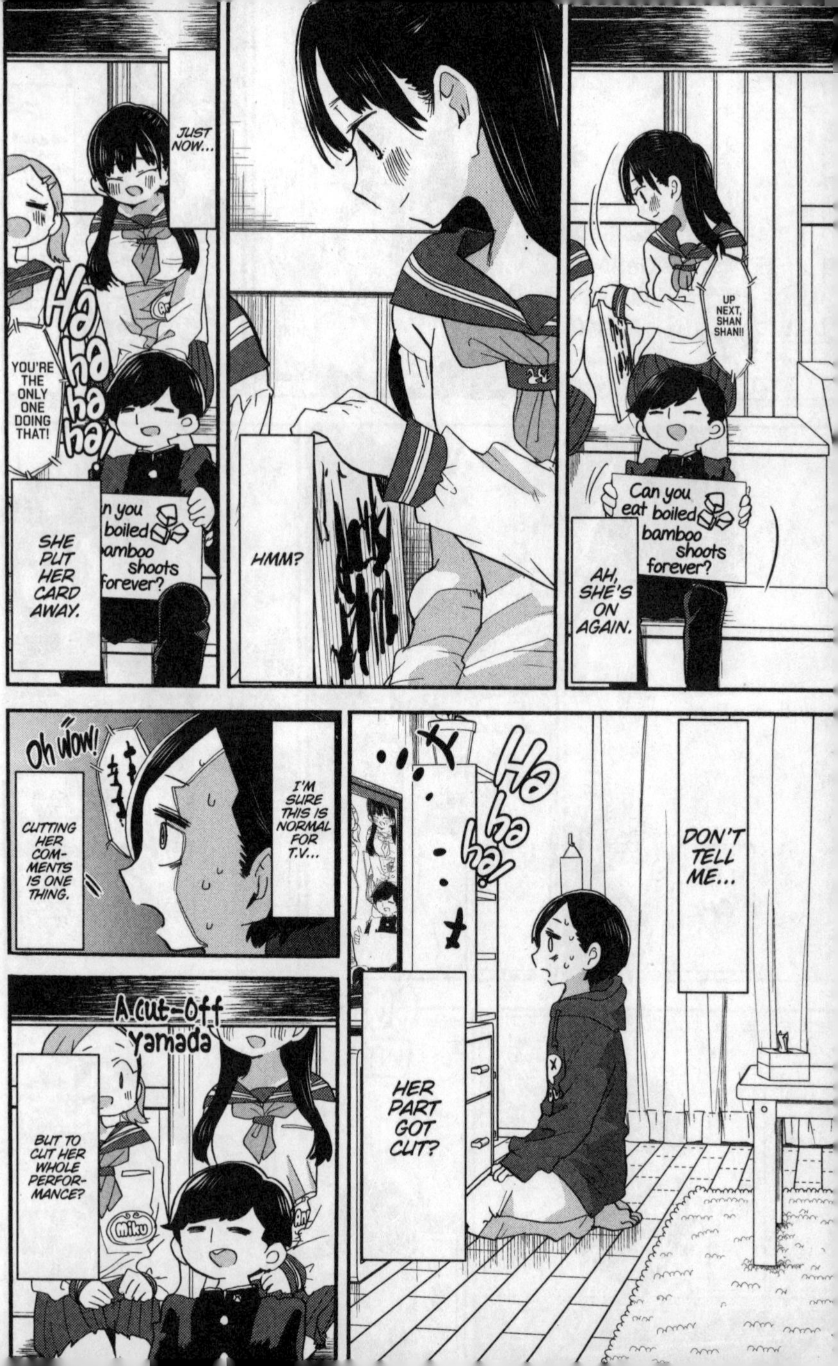
UP NEXT, SHAN SHAN!!
Can you eat boiled bamboo shoots forever?
AH, SHE'S ON AGAIN.
HMM?
JUST NOW...
Ha ha ha ha!
YOU'RE THE ONLY ONE DOING THAT!
n you boiled bamboo shoots forever?
SHE PUT HER CARD AWAY.
Ha ha ha!
DON'T TELL ME...
HER PART GOT CUT?
I'M SURE THIS IS NORMAL FOR T.V...
Oh wow!
CUTTING HER COMMENTS IS ONE THING.
A cut-off Yamada
BUT TO CUT HER WHOLE PERFORMANCE?
Miku

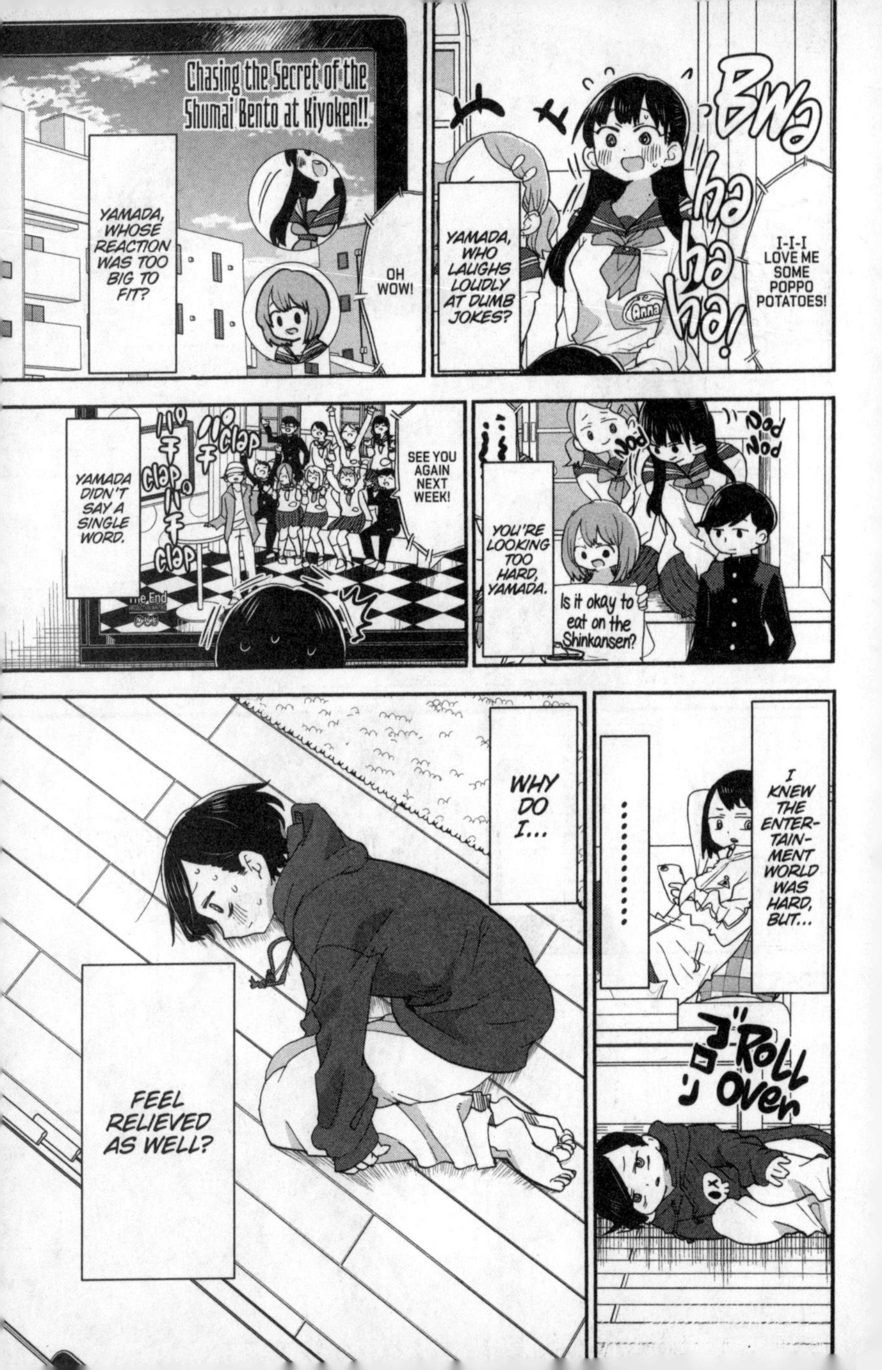

I-I-I LOVE ME SOME POPPO POTATOES!
Bwa ha ha ha!
YAMADA, WHO LAUGHS LOUDLY AT DUMB JOKES?
Anna
Chasing the Secret of the Shumai Bento at Kiyoken!!
OH WOW!
YAMADA, WHOSE REACTION WAS TOO BIG TO FIT?
Nod nod
Nod
YOU'RE LOOKING TOO HARD, YAMADA.
Is it okay to eat on the Shinkansen?
SEE YOU AGAIN NEXT WEEK!
clap clap
clap
YAMADA DIDN'T SAY A SINGLE WORD.
The End
I KNEW THE ENTERTAINMENT WORLD WAS HARD, BUT...
......
Roll over
WHY DO I...
FEEL RELIEVED AS WELL?

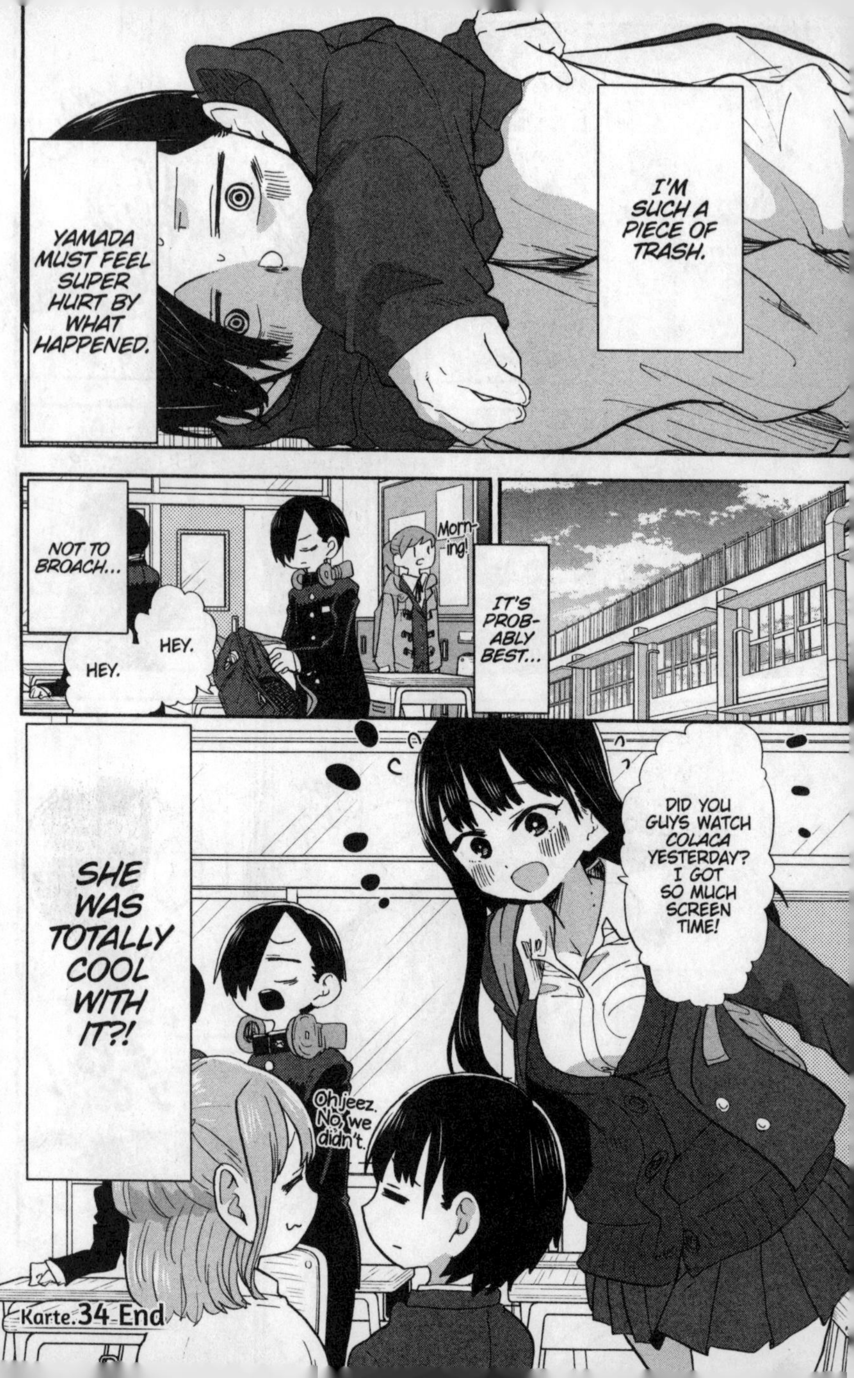
I'M SUCH A PIECE OF TRASH.
YAMADA MUST FEEL SUPER HURT BY WHAT HAPPENED.
IT'S PROBABLY BEST...
Morning!
NOT TO BROACH...
HEY.
HEY.
DID YOU GUYS WATCH COLACA YESTERDAY? I GOT SO MUCH SCREEN TIME!
SHE WAS TOTALLY COOL WITH IT?!
Oh jeez. No, we didn't.
Karte. 34 End

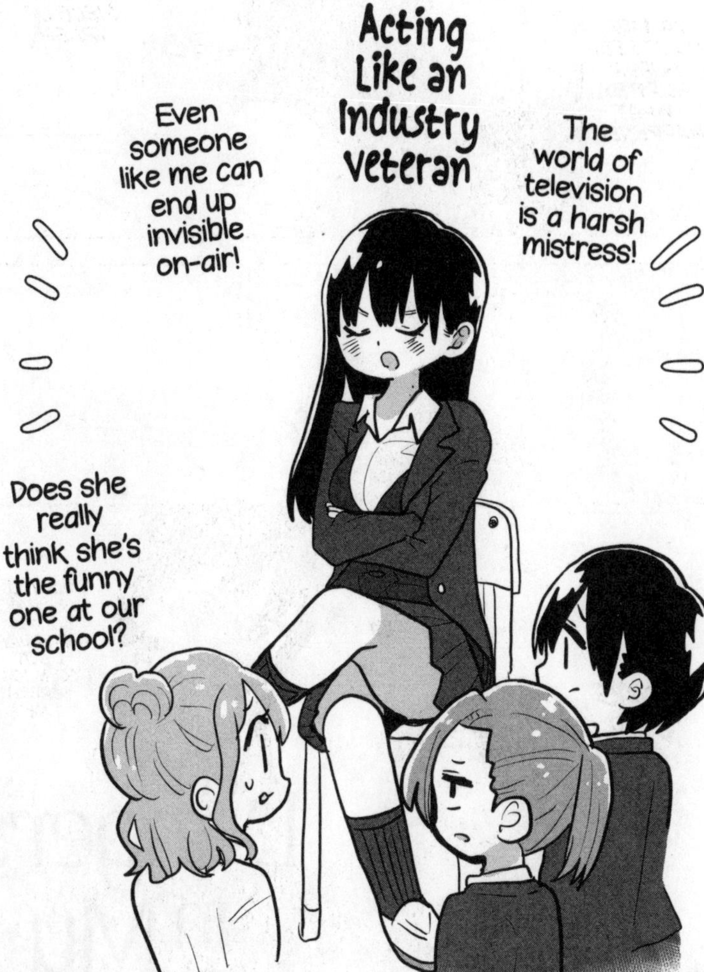
Acting Like an Industry veteran
The world of television is a harsh mistress!
Even someone like me can end up invisible on-air!
Does she really think she's the funny one at our school?

The
Dangers
in My
Heart

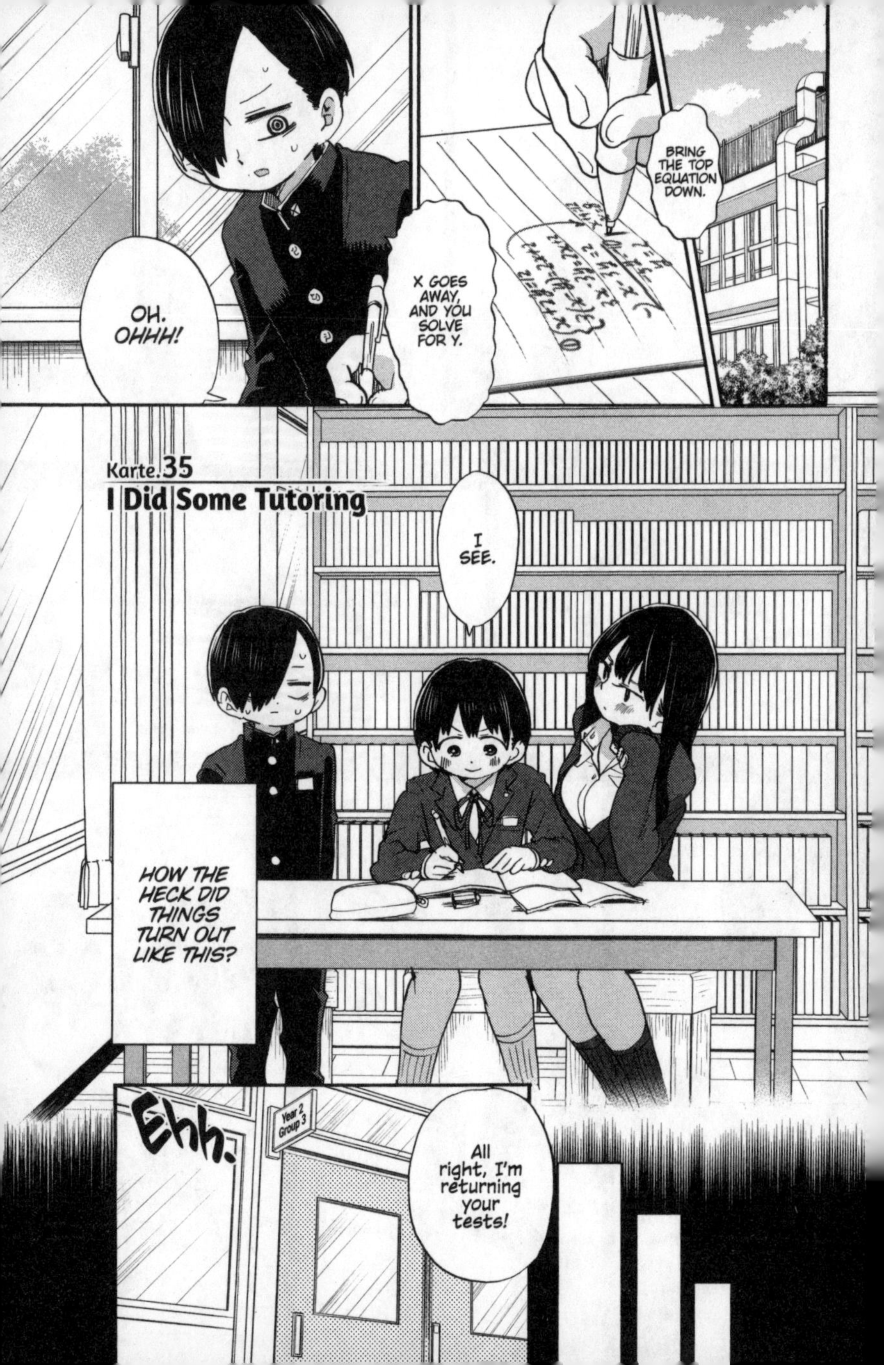
BRING THE TOP EQUATION DOWN.
X GOES AWAY, AND YOU SOLVE FOR Y.
OH. OHHH!
I SEE.
Karte. 35
I Did Some Tutoring
HOW THE HECK DID THINGS TURN OUT LIKE THIS?
All right, I'm returning your tests!
Year 2 Group 3
Ehh.

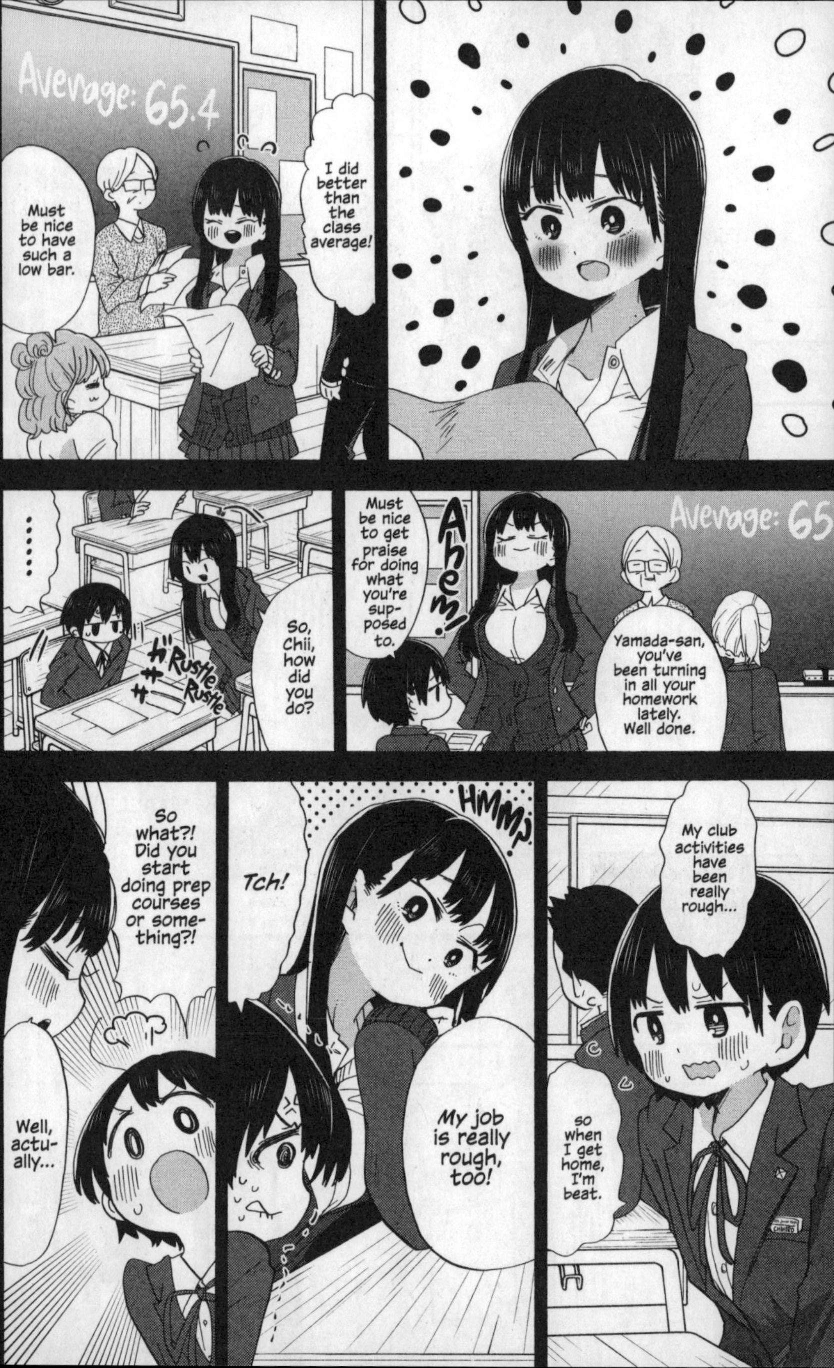
I did better than the class average!
Average: 65.4
Must be nice to have such a low bar.
Average: 65
Yamada-san, you've been turning in all your homework lately. Well done.
Ahem!
Must be nice to get praise for doing what you're supposed to.
So, Chii, how did you do?
Rustle Rustle
......
My club activities have been really rough...
so when I get home, I'm beat.
HMM?
Tch!
My job is really rough, too!
So what?! Did you start doing prep courses or something?!
Well, actually...

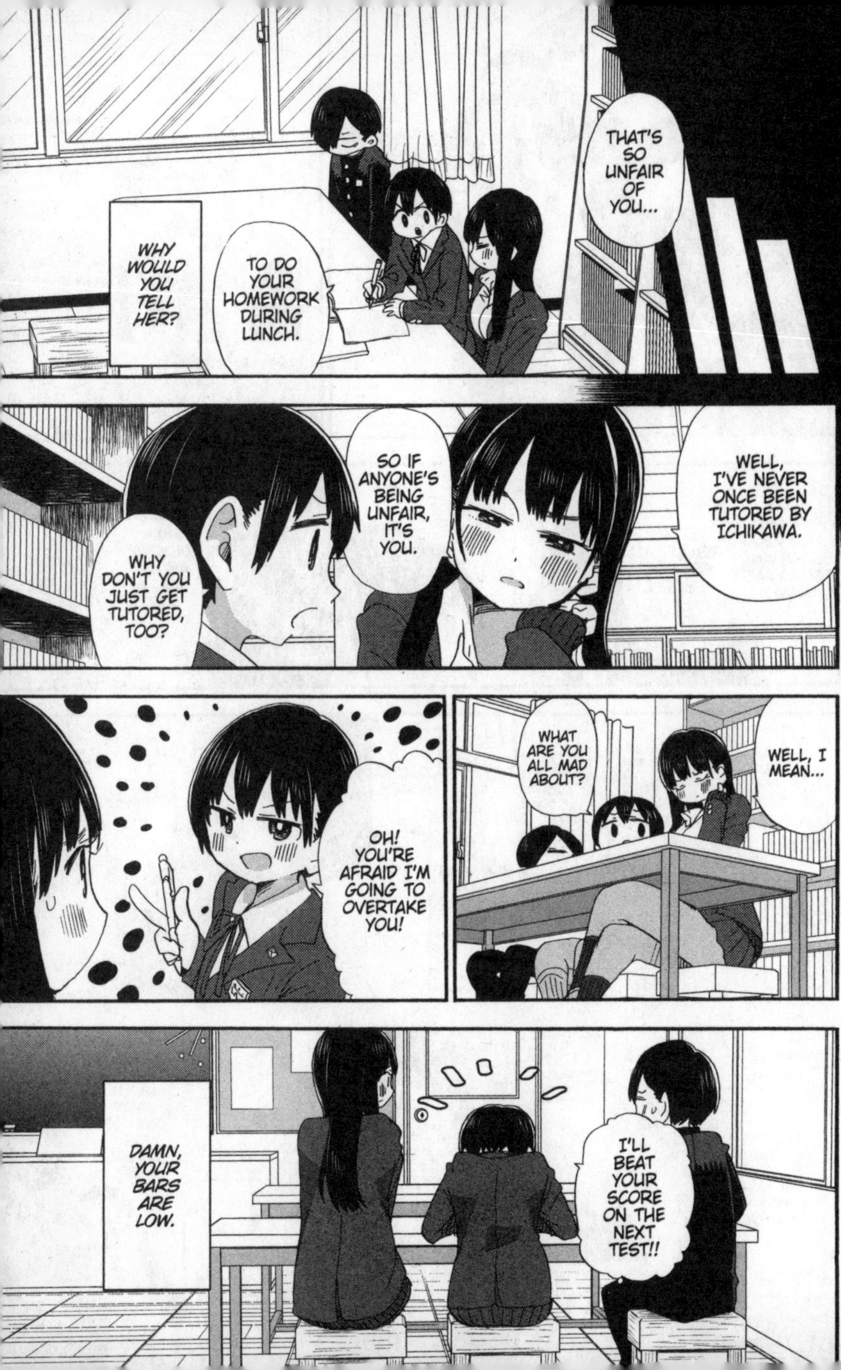
THAT'S SO UNFAIR OF YOU...
TO DO YOUR HOMEWORK DURING LUNCH.
WHY WOULD YOU TELL HER?
WELL, I'VE NEVER ONCE BEEN TUTORED BY ICHIKAWA.
SO IF ANYONE'S BEING UNFAIR, IT'S YOU.
WHY DON'T YOU JUST GET TUTORED, TOO?
WELL, I MEAN...
WHAT ARE YOU ALL MAD ABOUT?
OH! YOU'RE AFRAID I'M GOING TO OVERTAKE YOU!
I'LL BEAT YOUR SCORE ON THE NEXT TEST!!
DAMN, YOUR BARS ARE LOW.

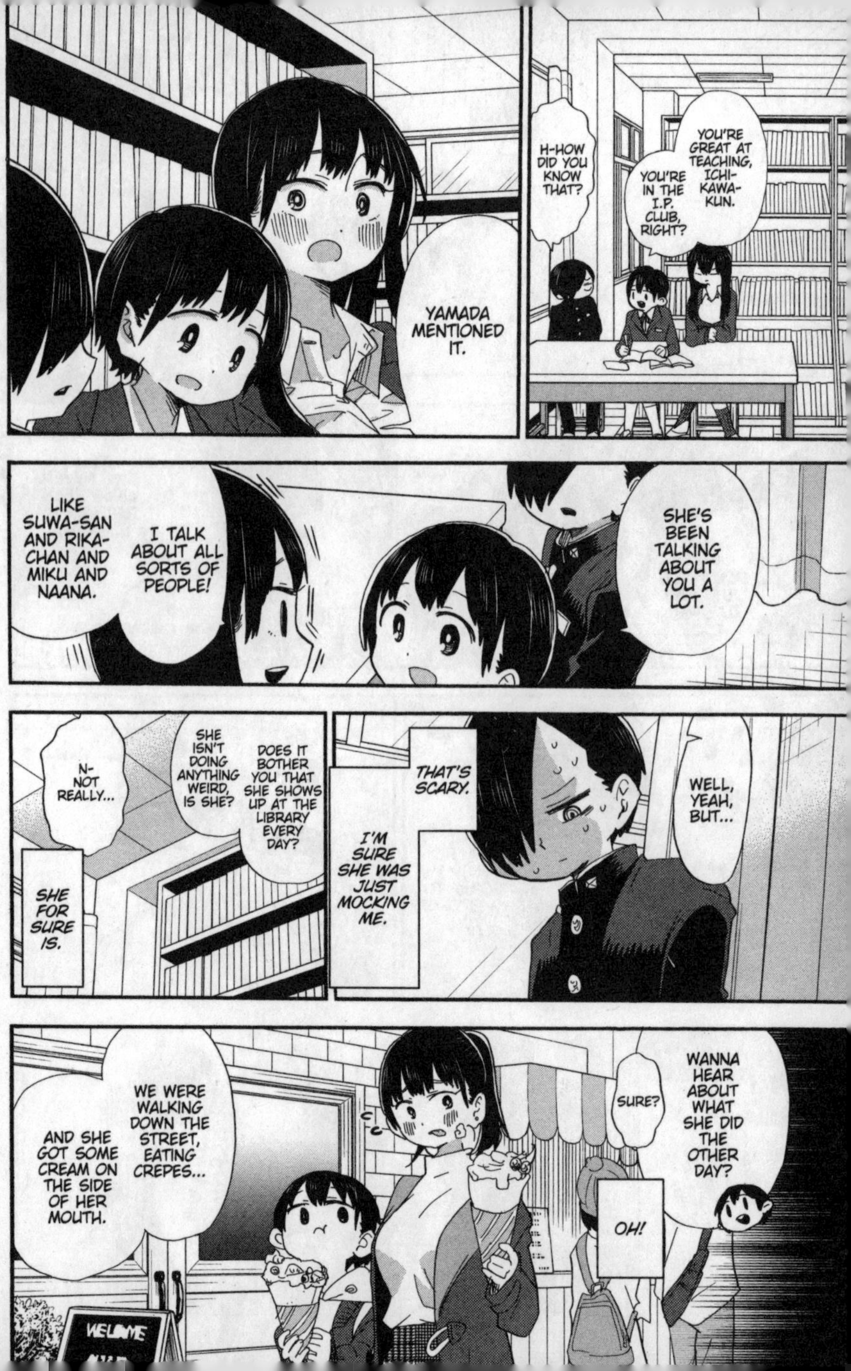

YOU'RE GREAT AT TEACHING, ICHI-KAWA-KUN.
YOU'RE IN THE I.P. CLUB, RIGHT?
H-HOW DID YOU KNOW THAT?
YAMADA MENTIONED IT.
SHE'S BEEN TALKING ABOUT YOU A LOT.
I TALK ABOUT ALL SORTS OF PEOPLE!
LIKE SUWA-SAN AND RIKA-CHAN AND MIKU AND NAANA.
WELL, YEAH, BUT...
THAT'S SCARY.
I'M SURE SHE WAS JUST MOCKING ME.
DOES IT BOTHER YOU THAT SHE SHOWS UP AT THE LIBRARY EVERY DAY?
SHE ISN'T DOING ANYTHING WEIRD, IS SHE?
N-NOT REALLY...
SHE FOR SURE IS.
WANNA HEAR ABOUT WHAT SHE DID THE OTHER DAY?
SURE?
OH!
WE WERE WALKING DOWN THE STREET, EATING CREPES...
AND SHE GOT SOME CREAM ON THE SIDE OF HER MOUTH.

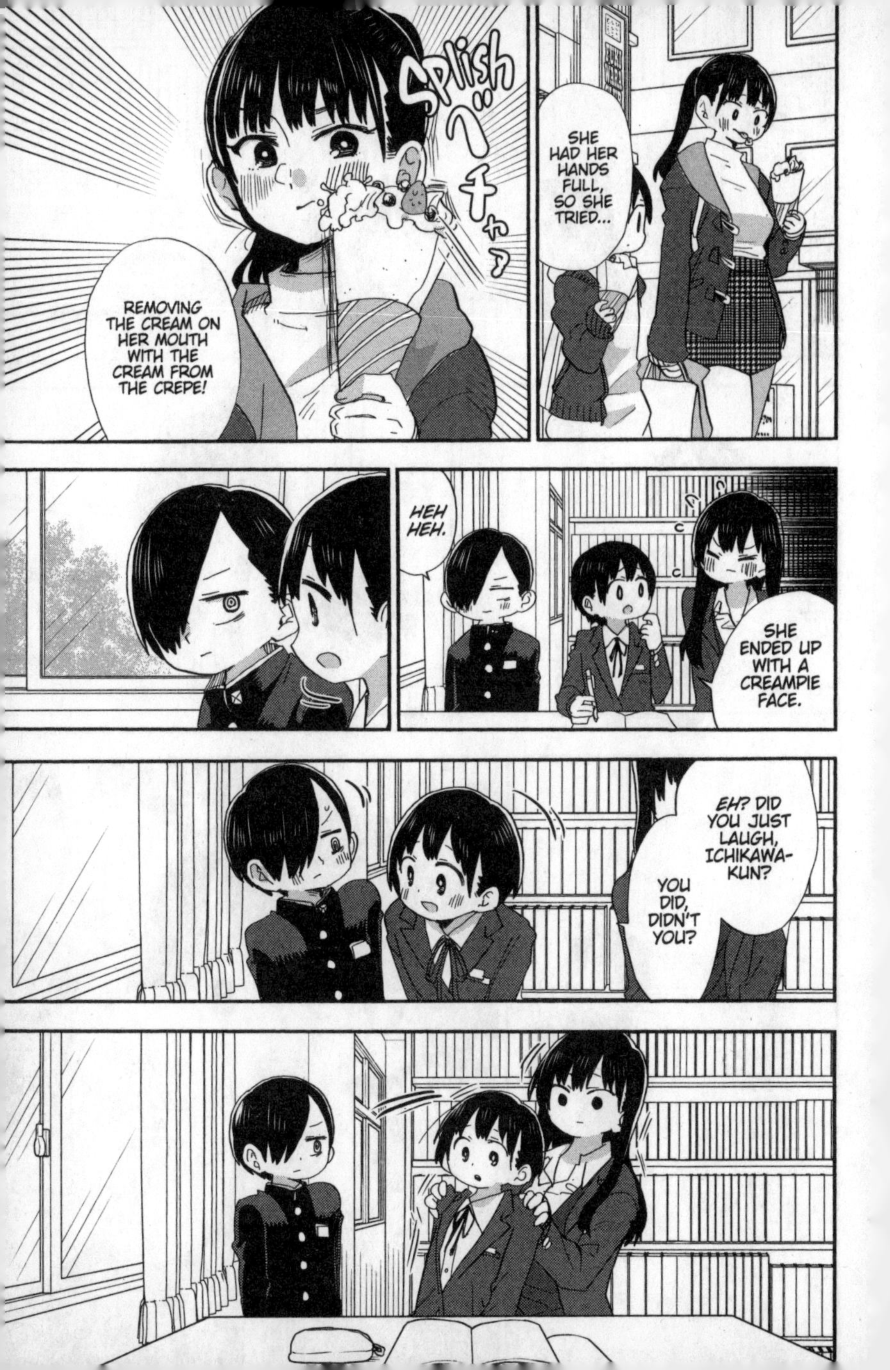
SHE HAD HER HANDS FULL, SO SHE TRIED...
Splish
REMOVING THE CREAM ON HER MOUTH WITH THE CREAM FROM THE CREPE!
SHE ENDED UP WITH A CREAMPIE FACE.
HEH HEH.
EH? DID YOU JUST LAUGH, ICHIKAWA-KUN?
YOU DID, DIDN'T YOU?

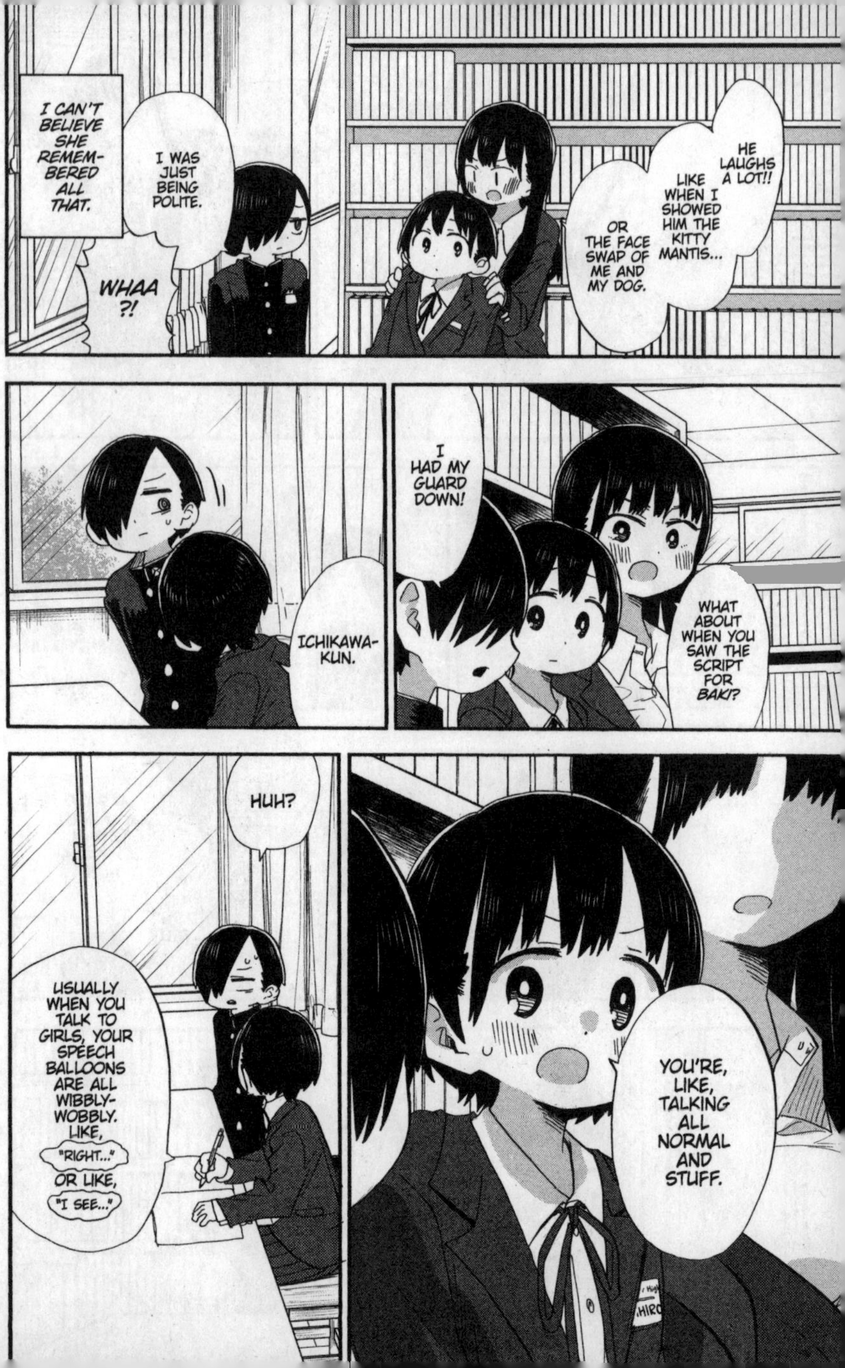
HE LAUGHS A LOT!!
LIKE WHEN I SHOWED HIM THE KITTY MANTIS...
OR THE FACE SWAP OF ME AND MY DOG.
I WAS JUST BEING POLITE.
I CAN'T BELIEVE SHE REMEMBERED ALL THAT.
WHAA ?!
WHAT ABOUT WHEN YOU SAW THE SCRIPT FOR *BAKI*?
I HAD MY GUARD DOWN!
ICHIKAWA-KUN.
YOU'RE, LIKE, TALKING ALL NORMAL AND STUFF.
HUH?
USUALLY WHEN YOU TALK TO GIRLS, YOUR SPEECH BALLOONS ARE ALL WIBBLY-WOBBLY. LIKE, "RIGHT..." OR LIKE, "I SEE..."

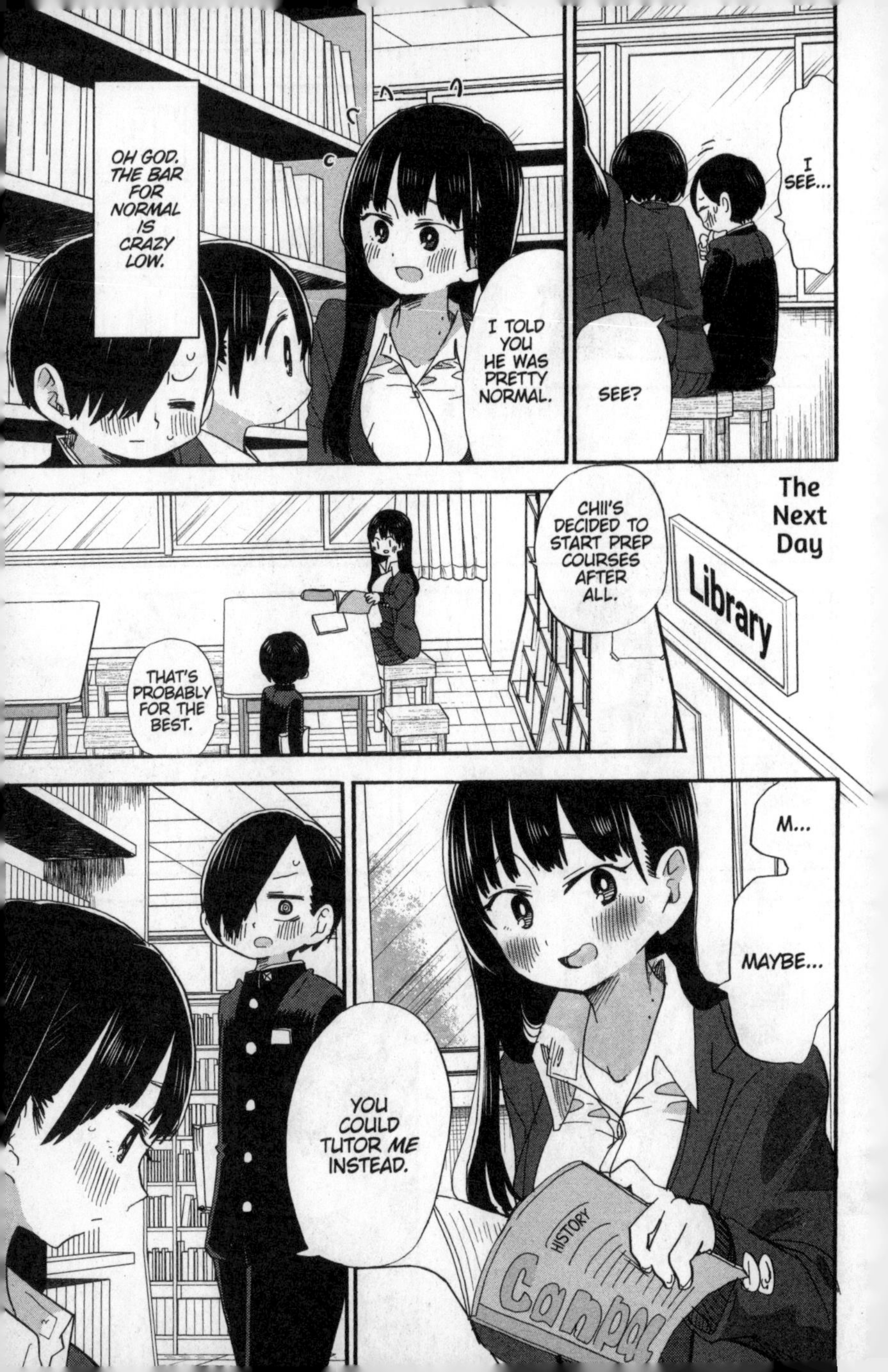
I SEE...
SEE?
I TOLD YOU HE WAS PRETTY NORMAL.
OH GOD. THE BAR FOR NORMAL IS CRAZY LOW.
The Next Day
Library
CHII'S DECIDED TO START PREP COURSES AFTER ALL.
THAT'S PROBABLY FOR THE BEST.
M...
MAYBE...
YOU COULD TUTOR ME INSTEAD.
HISTORY

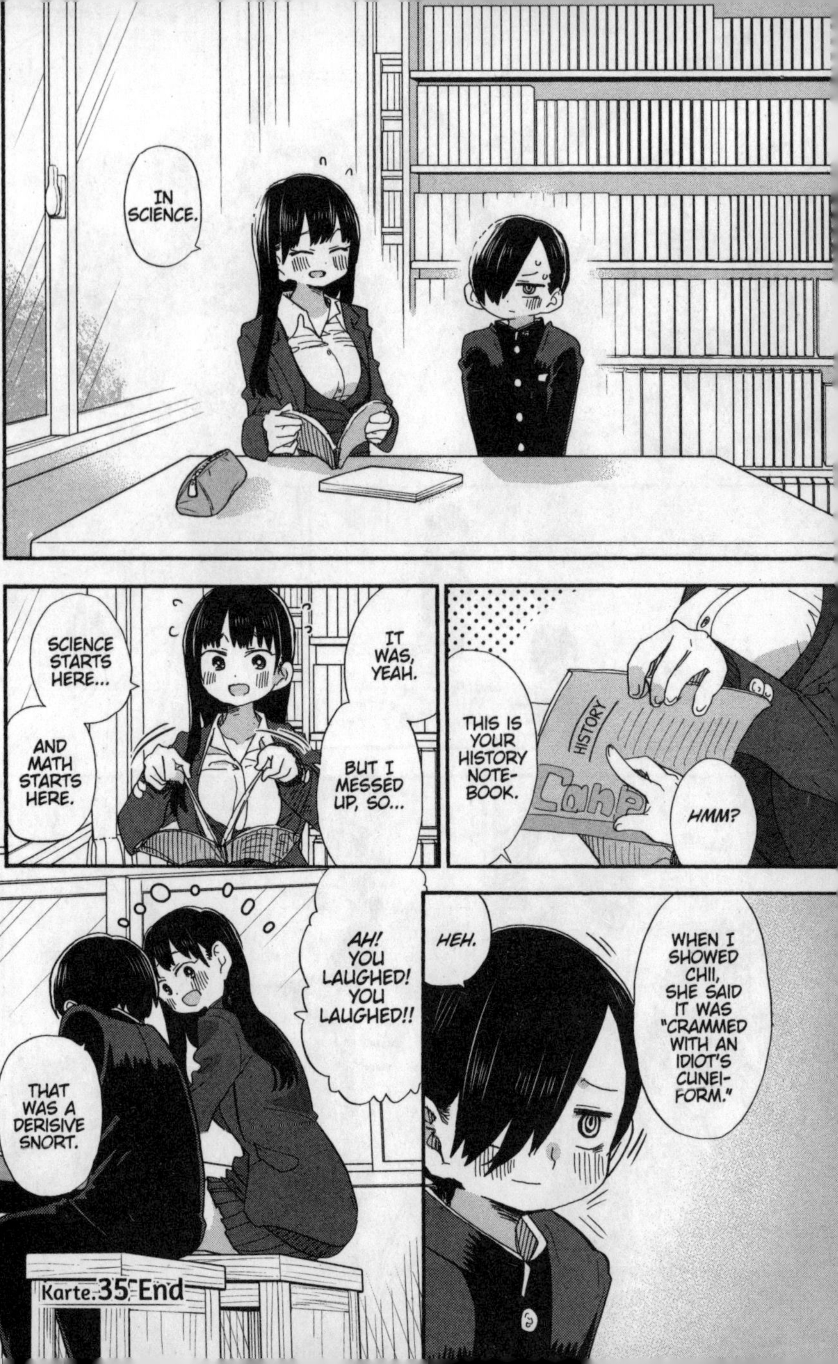
IN SCIENCE.
THIS IS YOUR HISTORY NOTEBOOK.
HISTORY
HMM?
IT WAS, YEAH.
BUT I MESSED UP, SO...
SCIENCE STARTS HERE...
AND MATH STARTS HERE.
WHEN I SHOWED CHII, SHE SAID IT WAS "CRAMMED WITH AN IDIOT'S CUNEIFORM."
HEH.
AH! YOU LAUGHED! YOU LAUGHED!!
THAT WAS A DERISIVE SNORT.
Karte.35 End

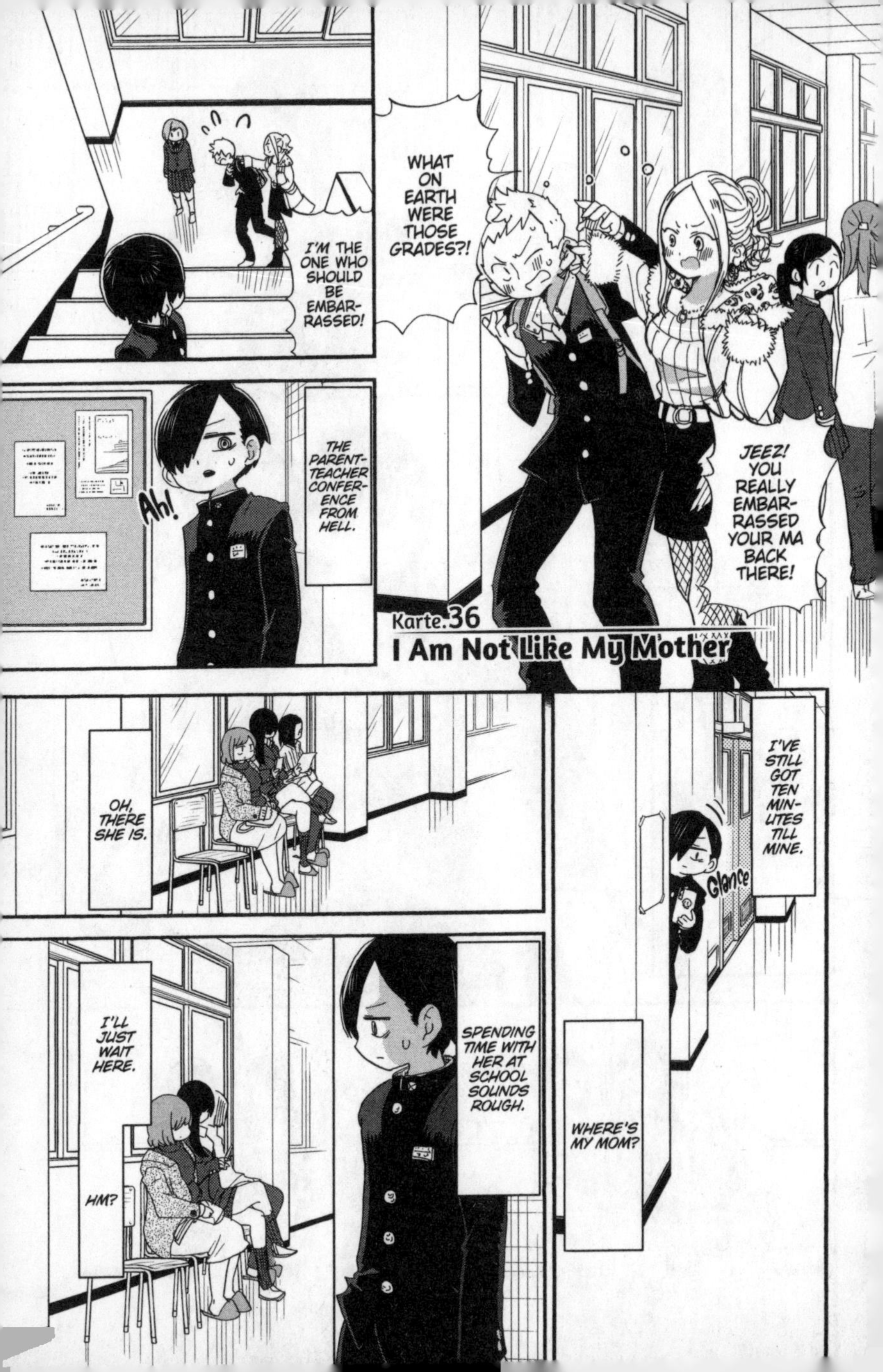
WHAT ON EARTH WERE THOSE GRADES?!
JEEZ! YOU REALLY EMBARRASSED YOUR MA BACK THERE!
Karte.36
I Am Not Like My Mother
I'M THE ONE WHO SHOULD BE EMBARRASSED!
THE PARENT-TEACHER CONFERENCE FROM HELL.
Ah!
I'VE STILL GOT TEN MINUTES TILL MINE.
Glance
WHERE'S MY MOM?
OH, THERE SHE IS.
SPENDING TIME WITH HER AT SCHOOL SOUNDS ROUGH.
I'LL JUST WAIT HERE.
HM?

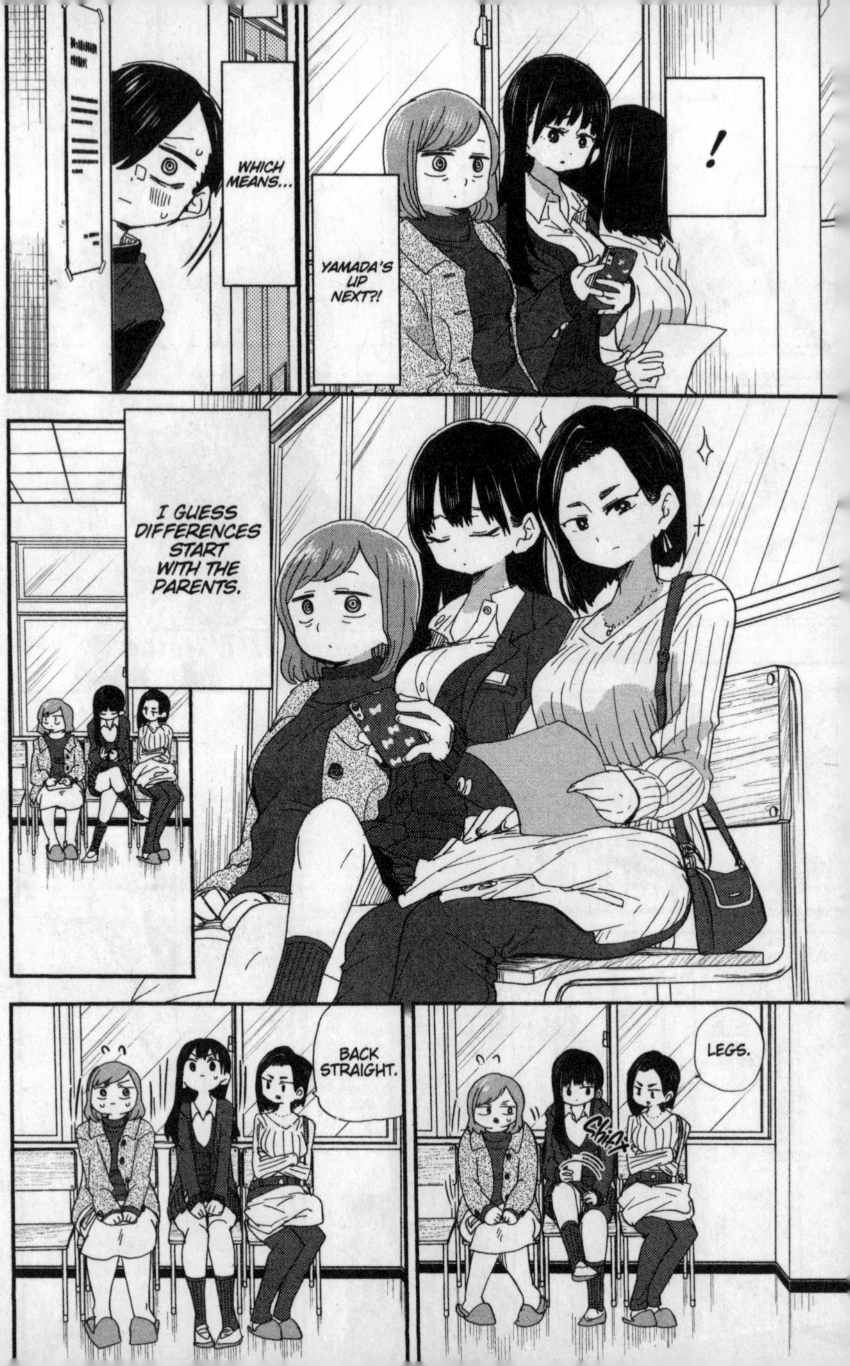
!
WHICH MEANS...
YAMADA'S UP NEXT?!
I GUESS DIFFERENCES START WITH THE PARENTS.
LEGS.
SHIFT
BACK STRAIGHT.

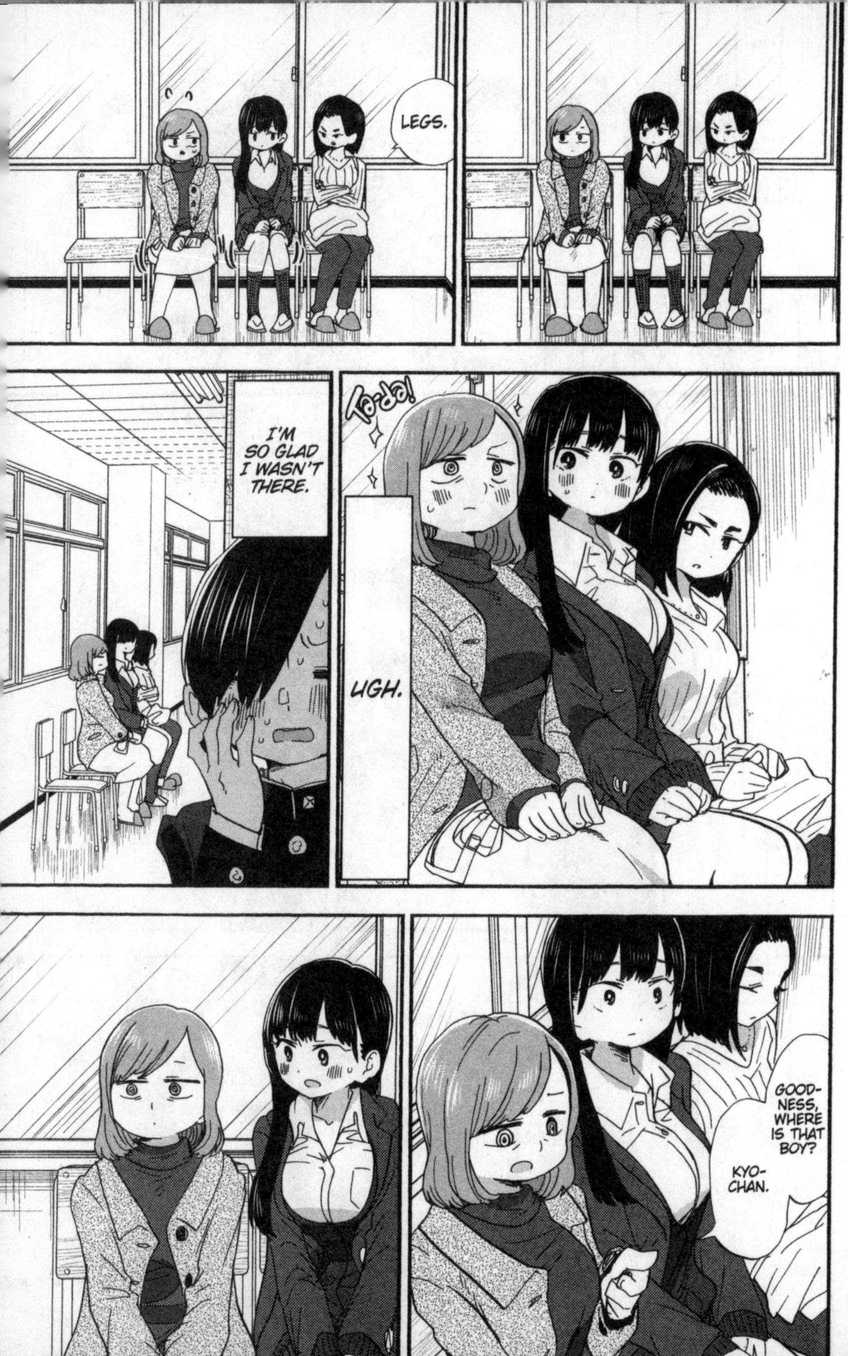
LEGS.
TA-DA!
UGH.
I'M SO GLAD I WASN'T THERE.
GOOD-NESS, WHERE IS THAT BOY?
KYO-CHAN.

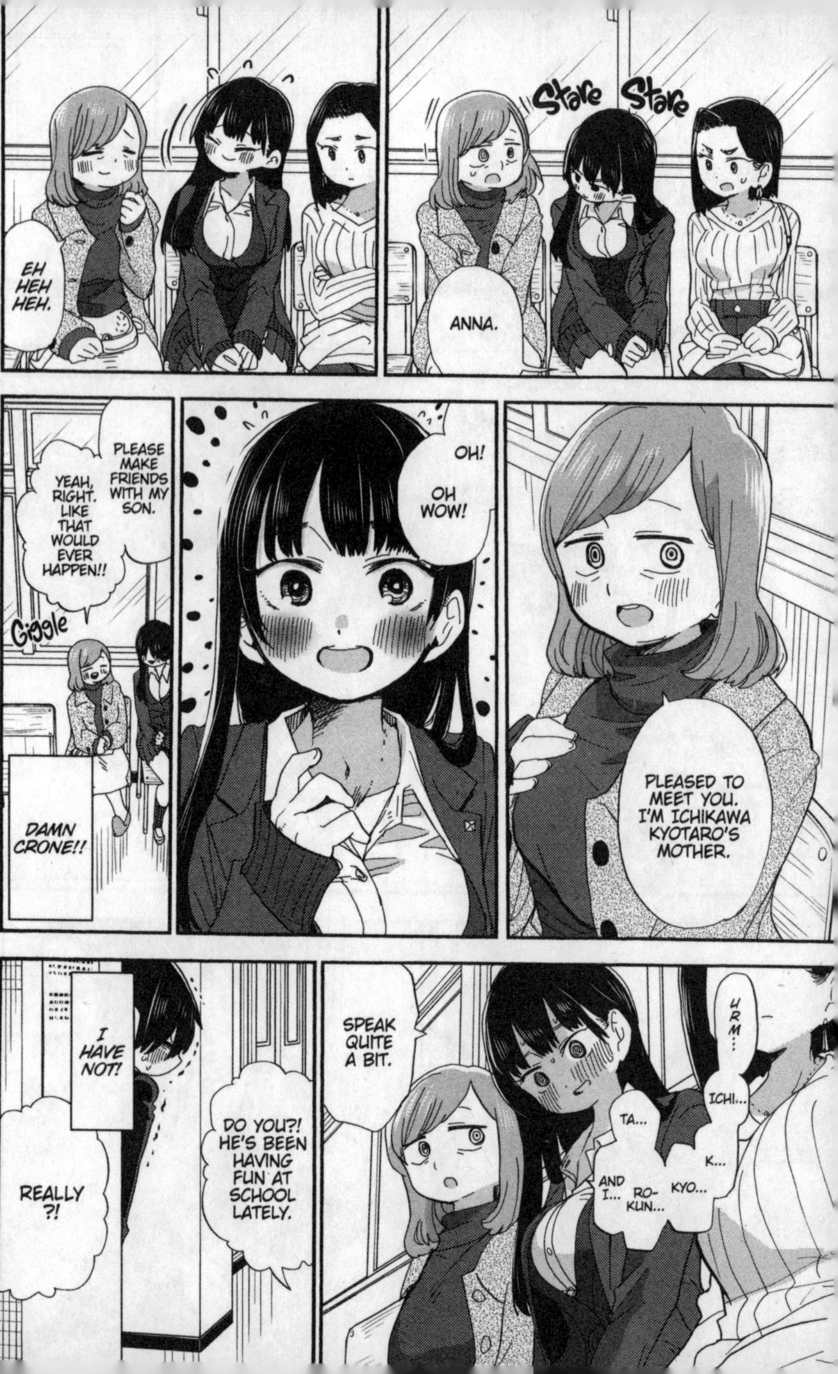

Stare Stare
ANNA.
EH HEH HEH.
PLEASED TO MEET YOU. I'M ICHIKAWA KYOTARO'S MOTHER.
OH!
OH WOW!
PLEASE MAKE FRIENDS WITH MY SON.
YEAH, RIGHT. LIKE THAT WOULD EVER HAPPEN!!
Giggle
DAMN CRONE!!
URM...
ICHI...
TA...
K...
KYO...
RO-KUN...
AND I...
SPEAK QUITE A BIT.
DO YOU?! HE'S BEEN HAVING FUN AT SCHOOL LATELY.
I HAVE NOT!
REALLY?!

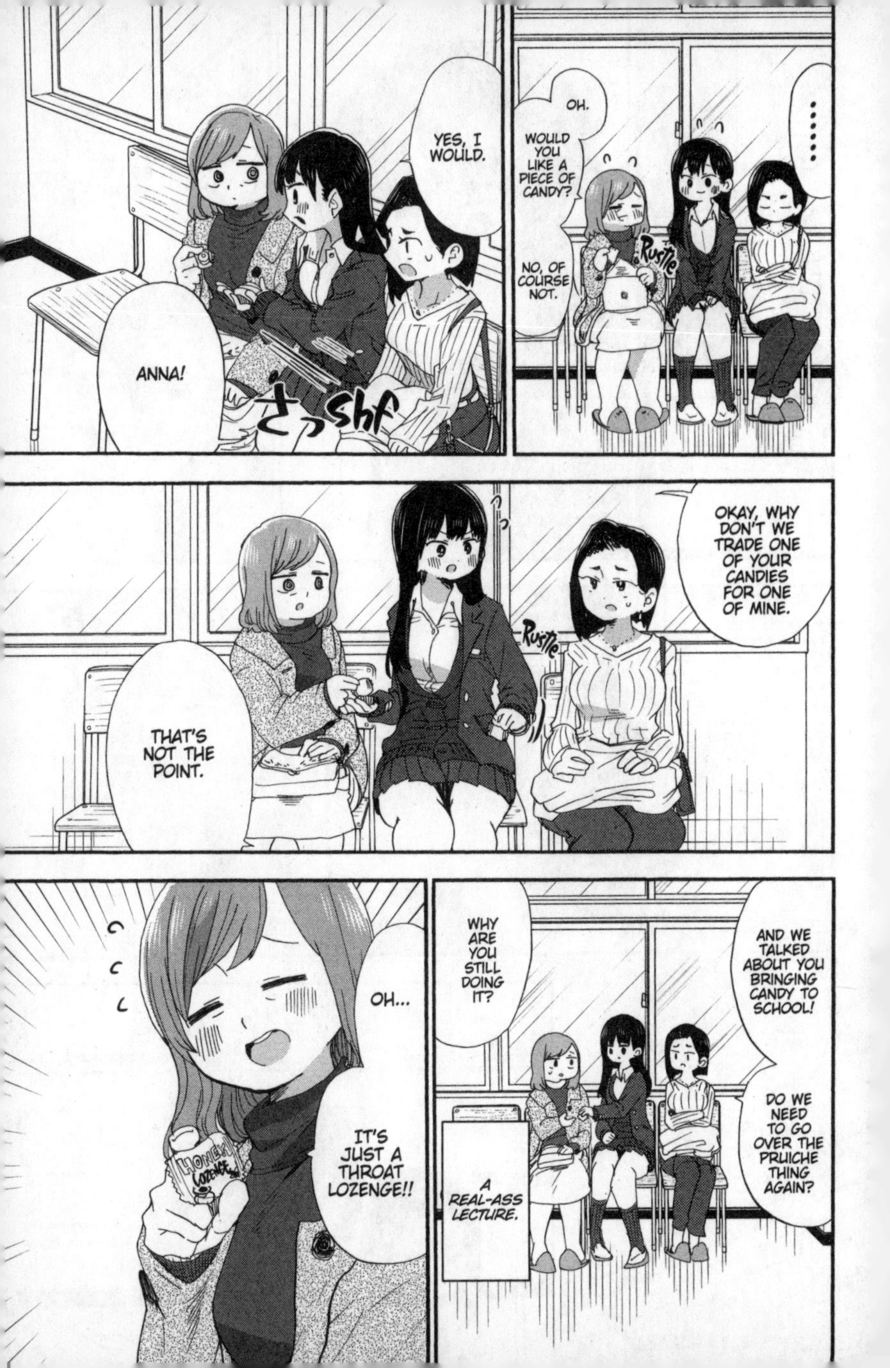
......
OH.
WOULD YOU LIKE A PIECE OF CANDY?
NO, OF COURSE NOT.
Rustle
YES, I WOULD.
ANNA!
さっ shf
OKAY, WHY DON'T WE TRADE ONE OF YOUR CANDIES FOR ONE OF MINE.
Rustle
THAT'S NOT THE POINT.
AND WE TALKED ABOUT YOU BRINGING CANDY TO SCHOOL!
DO WE NEED TO GO OVER THE PRUICHE THING AGAIN?
WHY ARE YOU STILL DOING IT?
A REAL-ASS LECTURE.
OH...
IT'S JUST A THROAT LOZENGE!!
HONEY LOZENGE

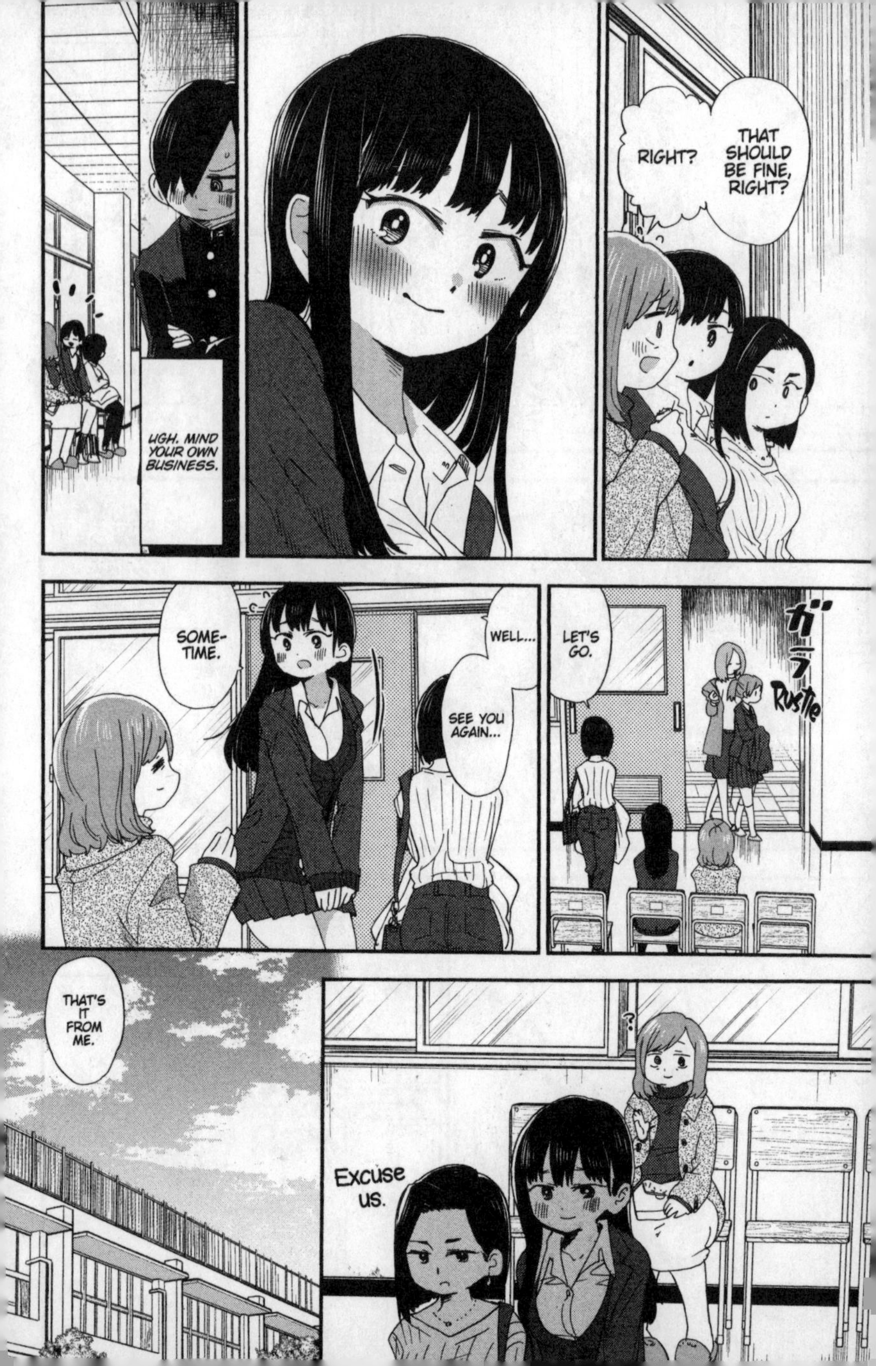
THAT SHOULD BE FINE, RIGHT?
RIGHT?
UGH. MIND YOUR OWN BUSINESS.
ガラ
Rustle
LET'S GO.
WELL...
SEE YOU AGAIN...
SOME-TIME.
Excuse us.
THAT'S IT FROM ME.

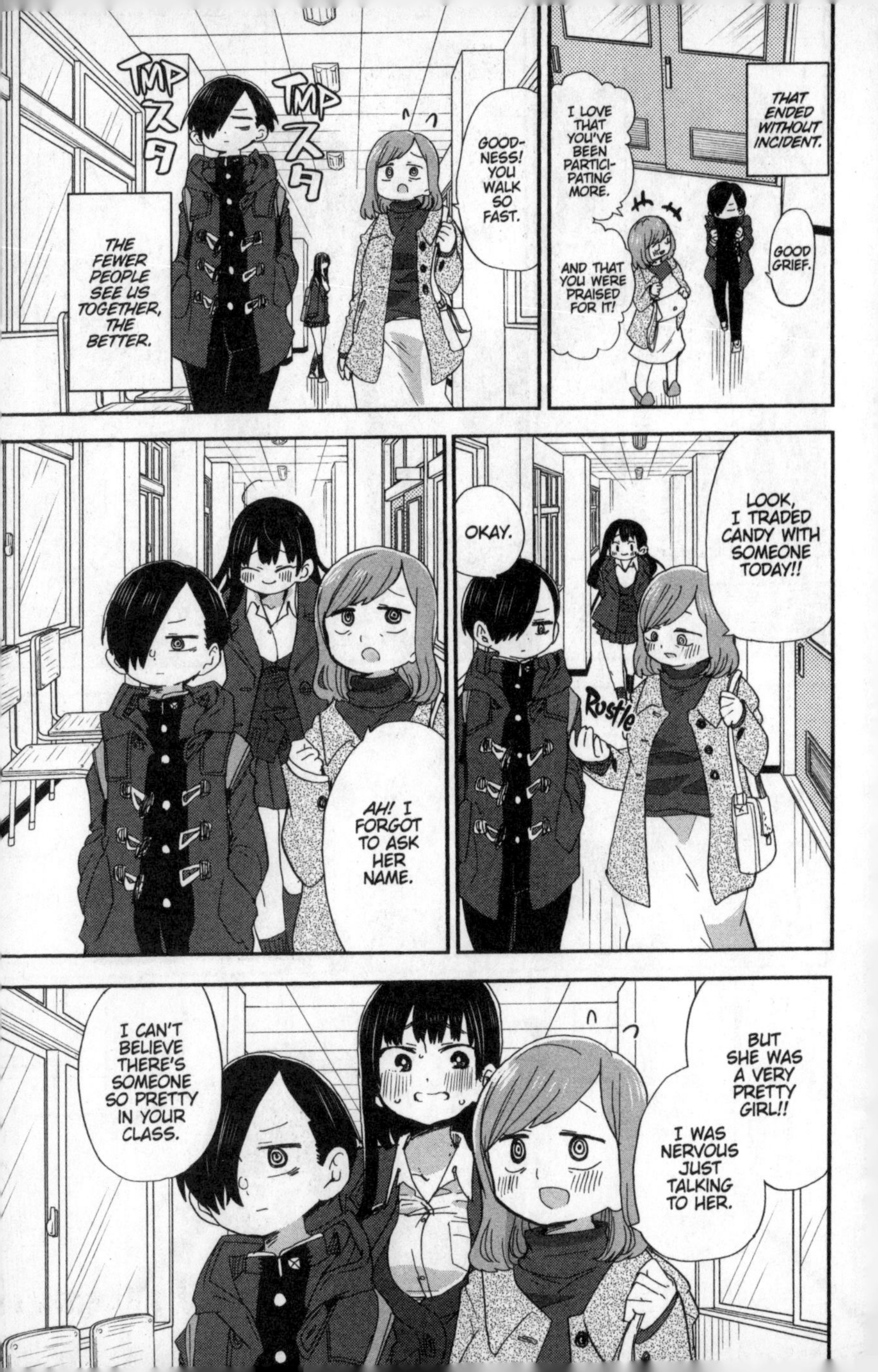
THAT ENDED WITHOUT INCIDENT.
I LOVE THAT YOU'VE BEEN PARTICIPATING MORE.
AND THAT YOU WERE PRAISED FOR IT!
GOOD GRIEF.
GOODNESS! YOU WALK SO FAST.
TMP スタ
TMP スタ
THE FEWER PEOPLE SEE US TOGETHER, THE BETTER.
LOOK, I TRADED CANDY WITH SOMEONE TODAY!!
Rustle
OKAY.
AH! I FORGOT TO ASK HER NAME.
BUT SHE WAS A VERY PRETTY GIRL!!
I WAS NERVOUS JUST TALKING TO HER.
I CAN'T BELIEVE THERE'S SOMEONE SO PRETTY IN YOUR CLASS.

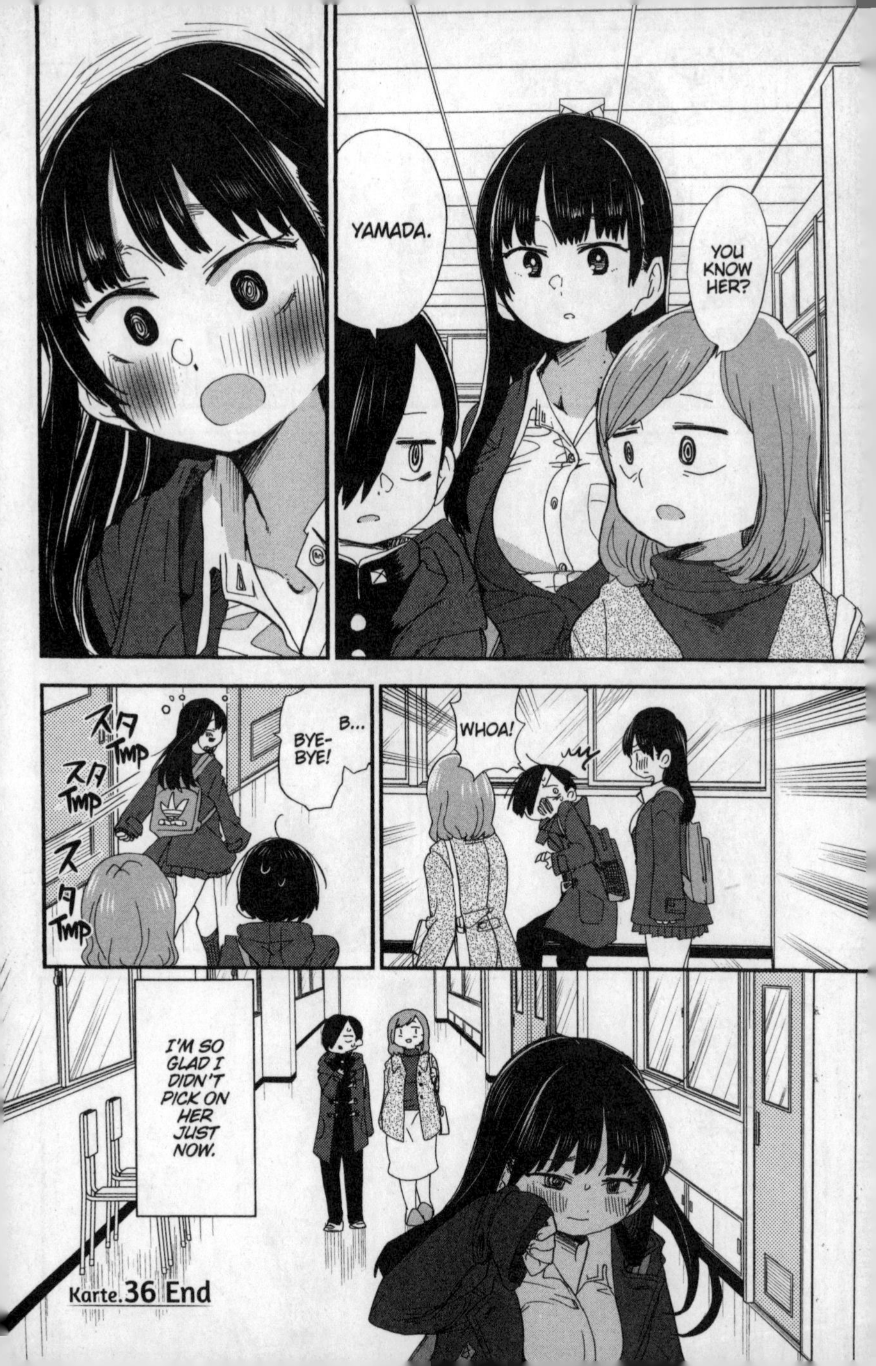
YOU KNOW HER?
YAMADA.
WHOA!
B... BYE-BYE!
スタ TMP
スタ TMP
スタ TMP
I'M SO GLAD I DIDN'T PICK ON HER JUST NOW.
Karte.36 End

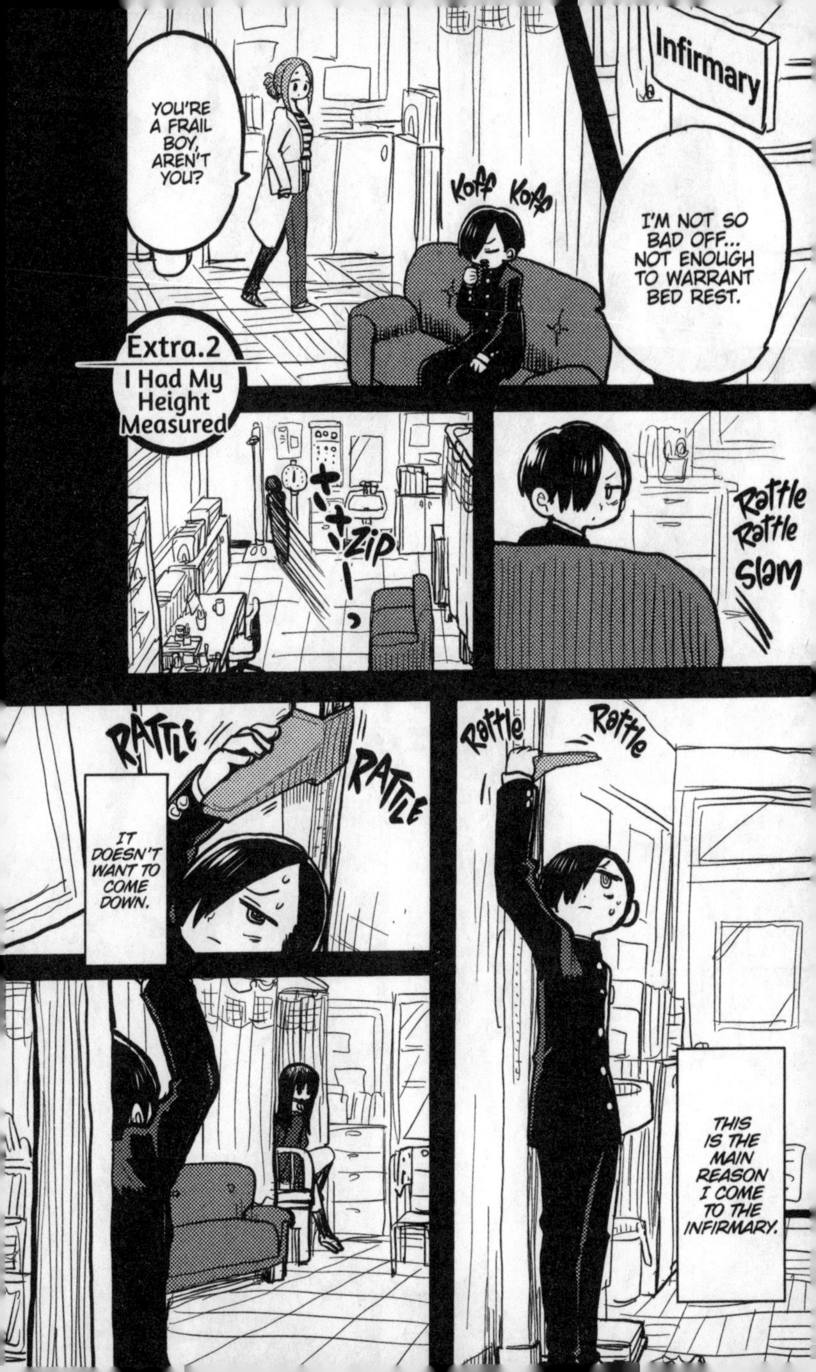
Infirmary
YOU'RE A FRAIL BOY, AREN'T YOU?
Koff Koff
I'M NOT SO BAD OFF... NOT ENOUGH TO WARRANT BED REST.
Extra.2
I Had My Height Measured
Rattle Rattle
Slam
ZIP
Rattle Rattle
THIS IS THE MAIN REASON I COME TO THE INFIRMARY.
RATTLE RATTLE
IT DOESN'T WANT TO COME DOWN.

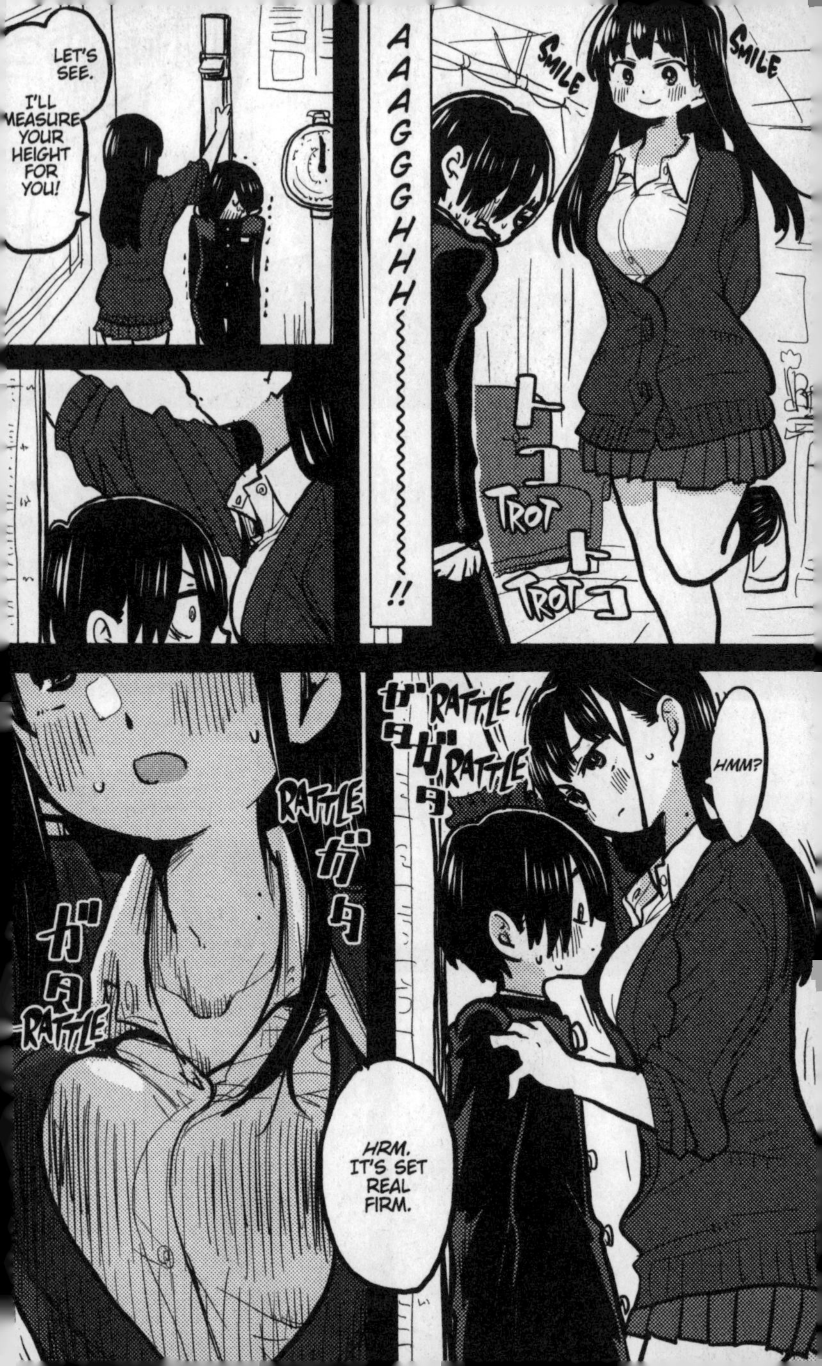
SMILE
SMILE
トコ TROT
トコ TROT
AAAAGGGHHHH~!!
LET'S SEE.
I'LL MEASURE YOUR HEIGHT FOR YOU!
HMM?
ガタ RATTLE
ガタ RATTLE
HRM. IT'S SET REAL FIRM.
RATTLE ガタ
ガタ RATTLE

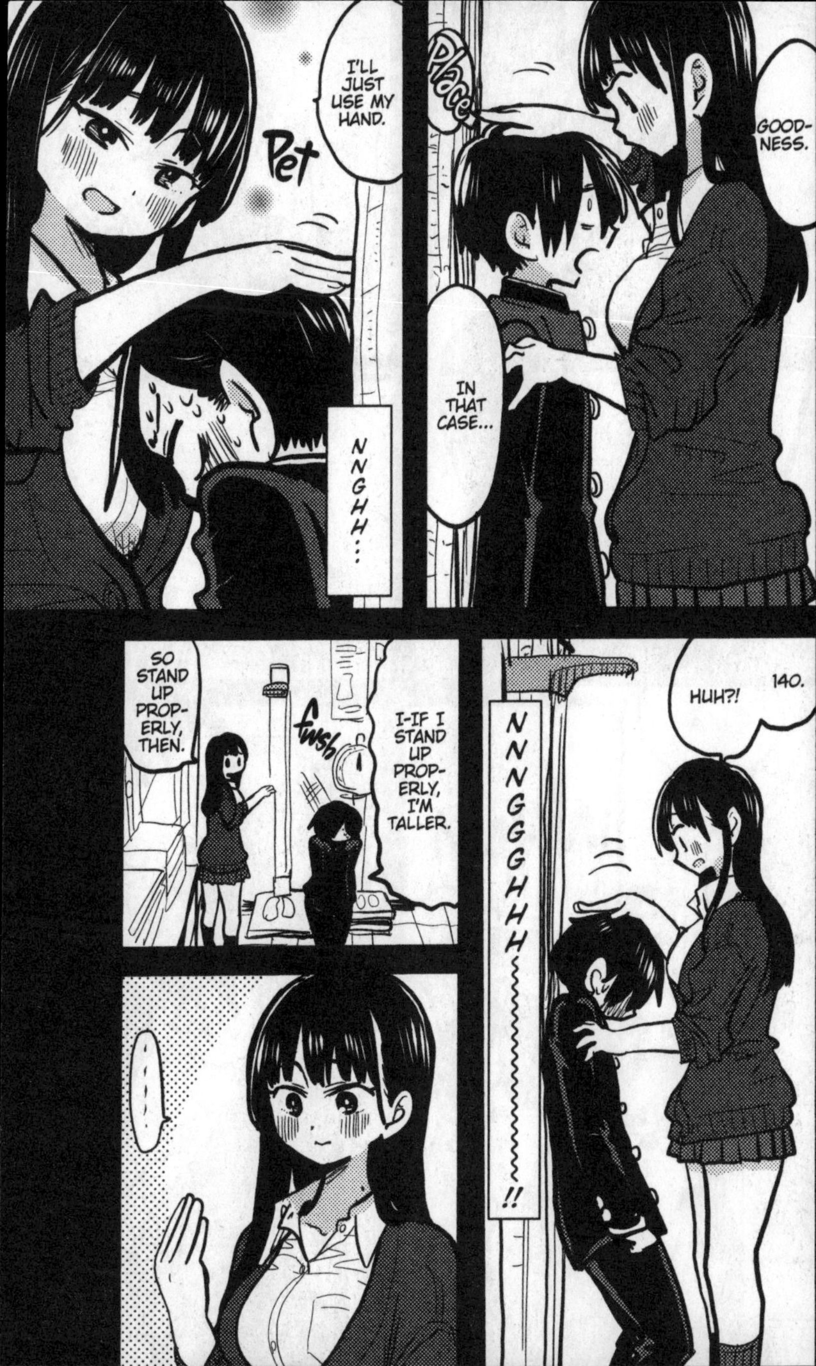
Place
GOODNESS.
IN THAT CASE...
I'LL JUST USE MY HAND.
Pet
NNGHH...
140.
HUH?!
NNNGGGHHH~!!
I-IF I STAND UP PROPERLY, I'M TALLER.
fwsh
SO STAND UP PROPERLY, THEN.
......

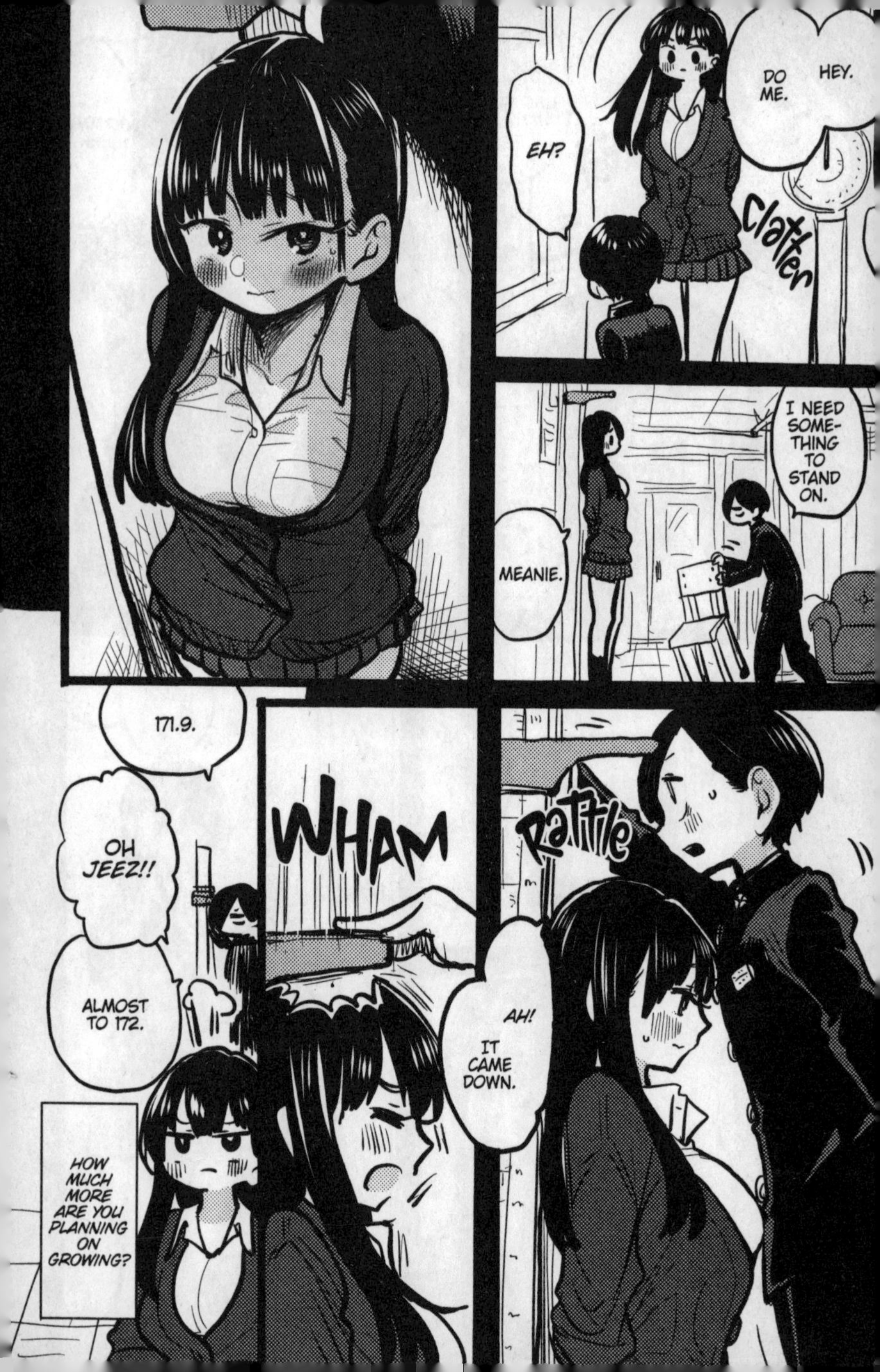
HEY.
DO ME.
EH?
Clatter
I NEED SOMETHING TO STAND ON.
MEANIE.
Rattle
AH!
IT CAME DOWN.
WHAM
171.9.
OH JEEZ!!
ALMOST TO 172.
HOW MUCH MORE ARE YOU PLANNING ON GROWING?

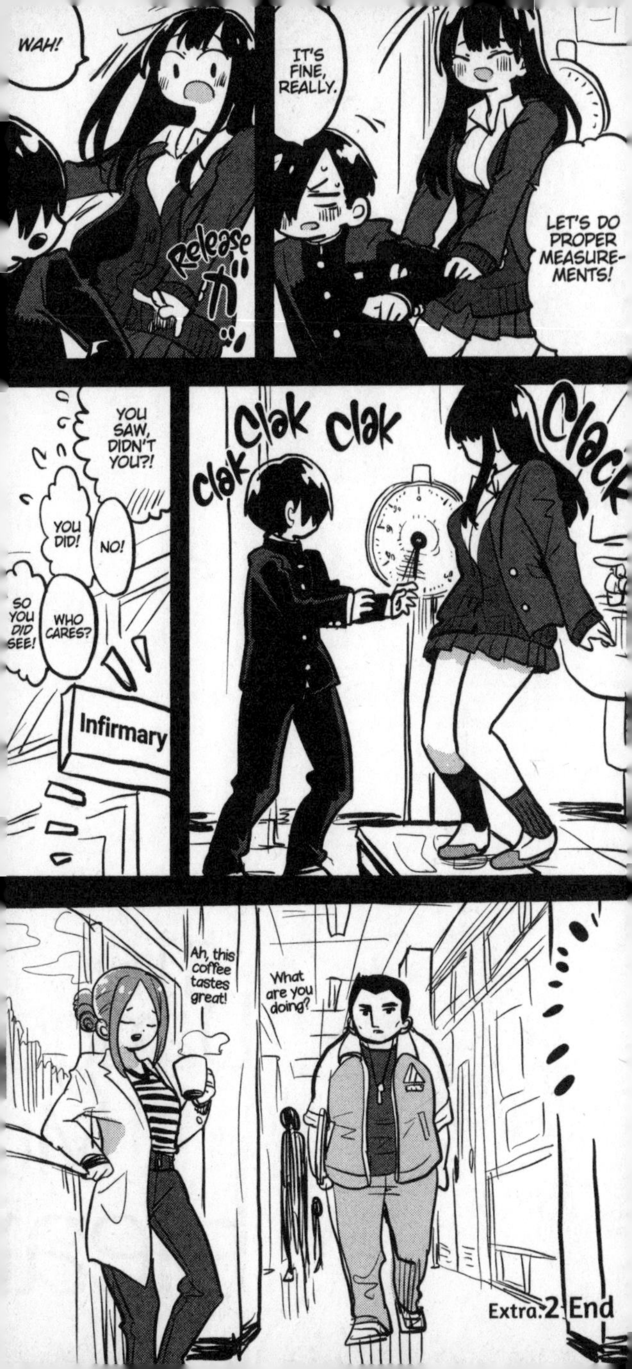
IT'S FINE, REALLY.
LET'S DO PROPER MEASUREMENTS!
WAH!
Release
Clack
clak clak clak
YOU SAW, DIDN'T YOU?!
NO!
YOU DID!
WHO CARES?
SO YOU DID SEE!
Infirmary
What are you doing?
Ah, this coffee tastes great!
Extra.2 End

The
Dangers
in My
Heart

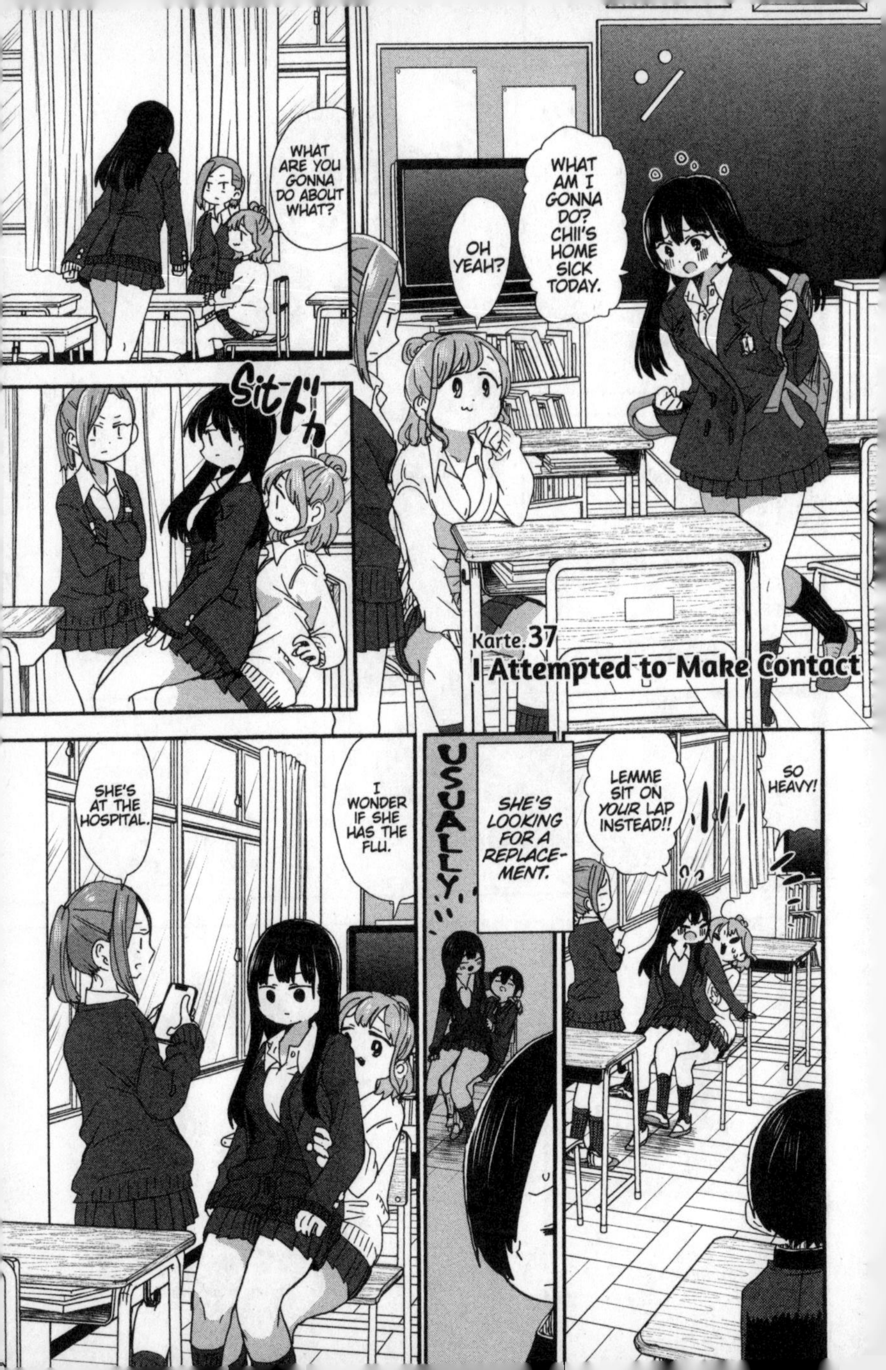
WHAT AM I GONNA DO? CHII'S HOME SICK TODAY.
OH YEAH?
WHAT ARE YOU GONNA DO ABOUT WHAT?
Sit ドカ
Karte. 37
I Attempted to Make Contact
SO HEAVY!
LEMME SIT ON YOUR LAP INSTEAD!!
SHE'S LOOKING FOR A REPLACEMENT.
USUALLY
I WONDER IF SHE HAS THE FLU.
SHE'S AT THE HOSPITAL.

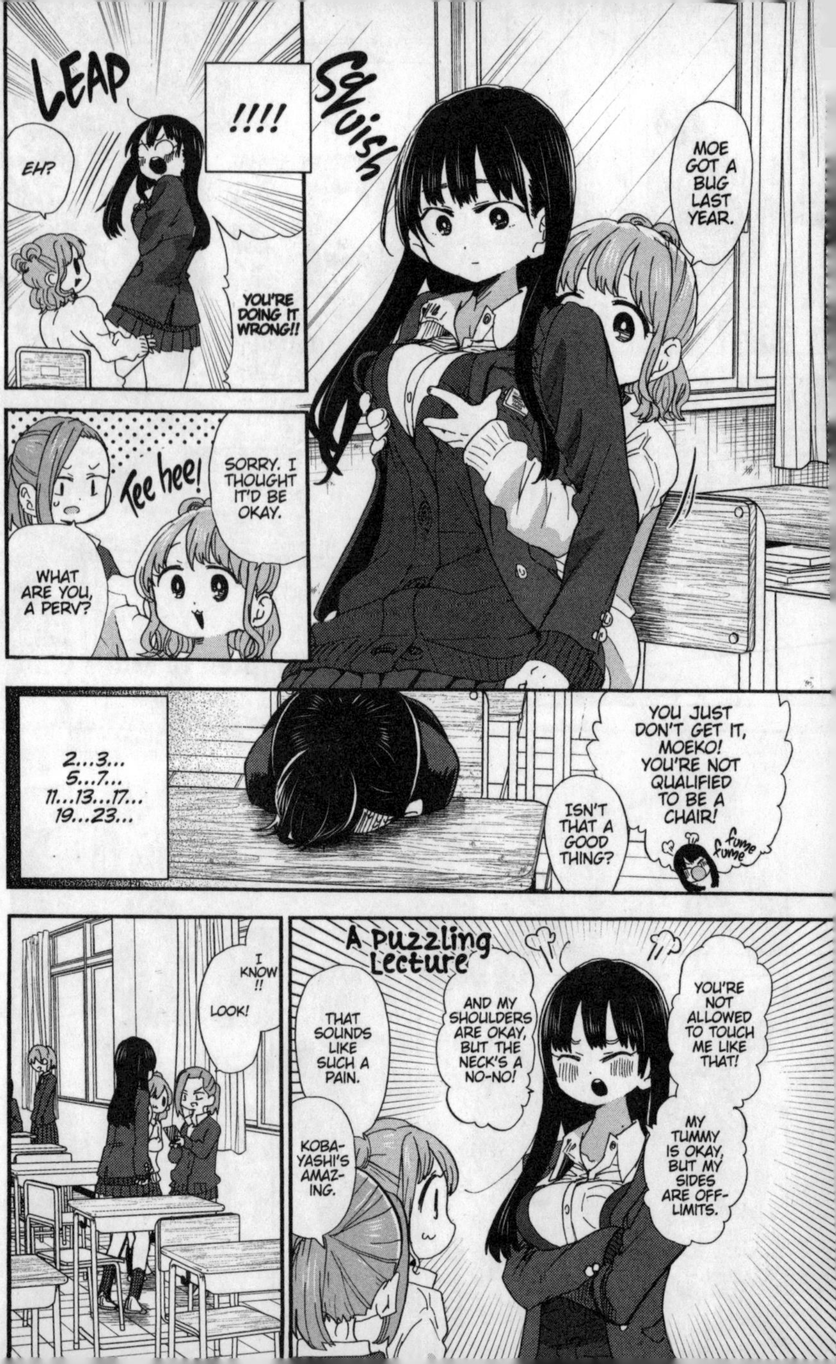
Squish
MOE GOT A BUG LAST YEAR.
!!!!
LEAP
EH?
YOU'RE DOING IT WRONG!!
SORRY. I THOUGHT IT'D BE OKAY.
Tee hee!
WHAT ARE YOU, A PERV?
YOU JUST DON'T GET IT, MOEKO! YOU'RE NOT QUALIFIED TO BE A CHAIR!
fume fume
ISN'T THAT A GOOD THING?
2...3... 5...7... 11...13...17... 19...23...
A Puzzling Lecture
YOU'RE NOT ALLOWED TO TOUCH ME LIKE THAT!
MY TUMMY IS OKAY, BUT MY SIDES ARE OFF-LIMITS.
AND MY SHOULDERS ARE OKAY, BUT THE NECK'S A NO-NO!
THAT SOUNDS LIKE SUCH A PAIN.
KOBA-YASHI'S AMAZ-ING.
I KNOW!!
LOOK!

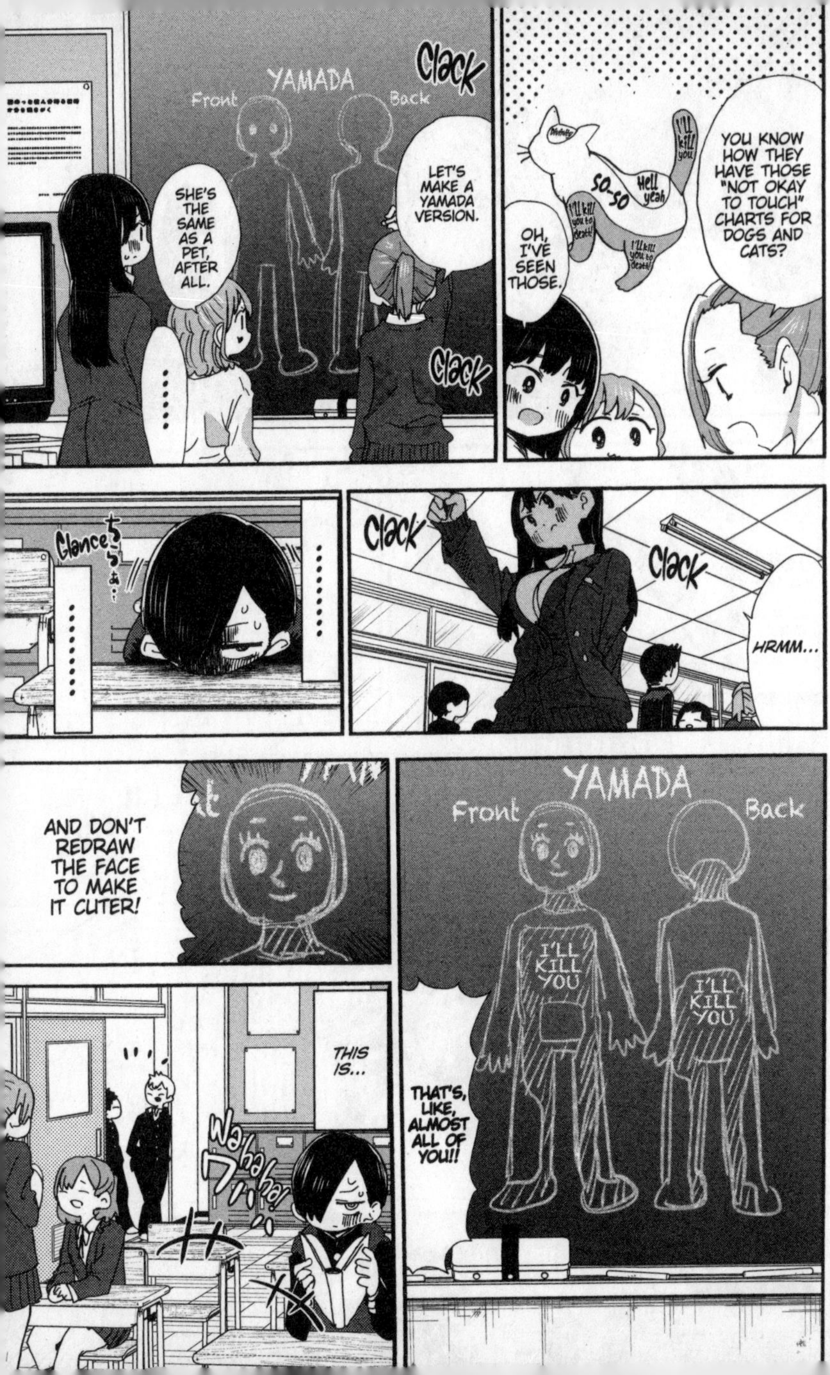
YOU KNOW HOW THEY HAVE THOSE "NOT OKAY TO TOUCH" CHARTS FOR DOGS AND CATS?
I'll kill you
Hell yeah
so-so
I'll kill you to death!
I'll kill you to death!
OH, I'VE SEEN THOSE.
Clack
YAMADA
Front
Back
LET'S MAKE A YAMADA VERSION.
SHE'S THE SAME AS A PET, AFTER ALL.
......
Clack
Clack
Clack
HRMM...
Glance
......
....
YAMADA
Front
Back
I'LL KILL YOU
I'LL KILL YOU
THAT'S, LIKE, ALMOST ALL OF YOU!!
AND DON'T REDRAW THE FACE TO MAKE IT CUTER!
THIS IS...
Wahaha
ワハハ

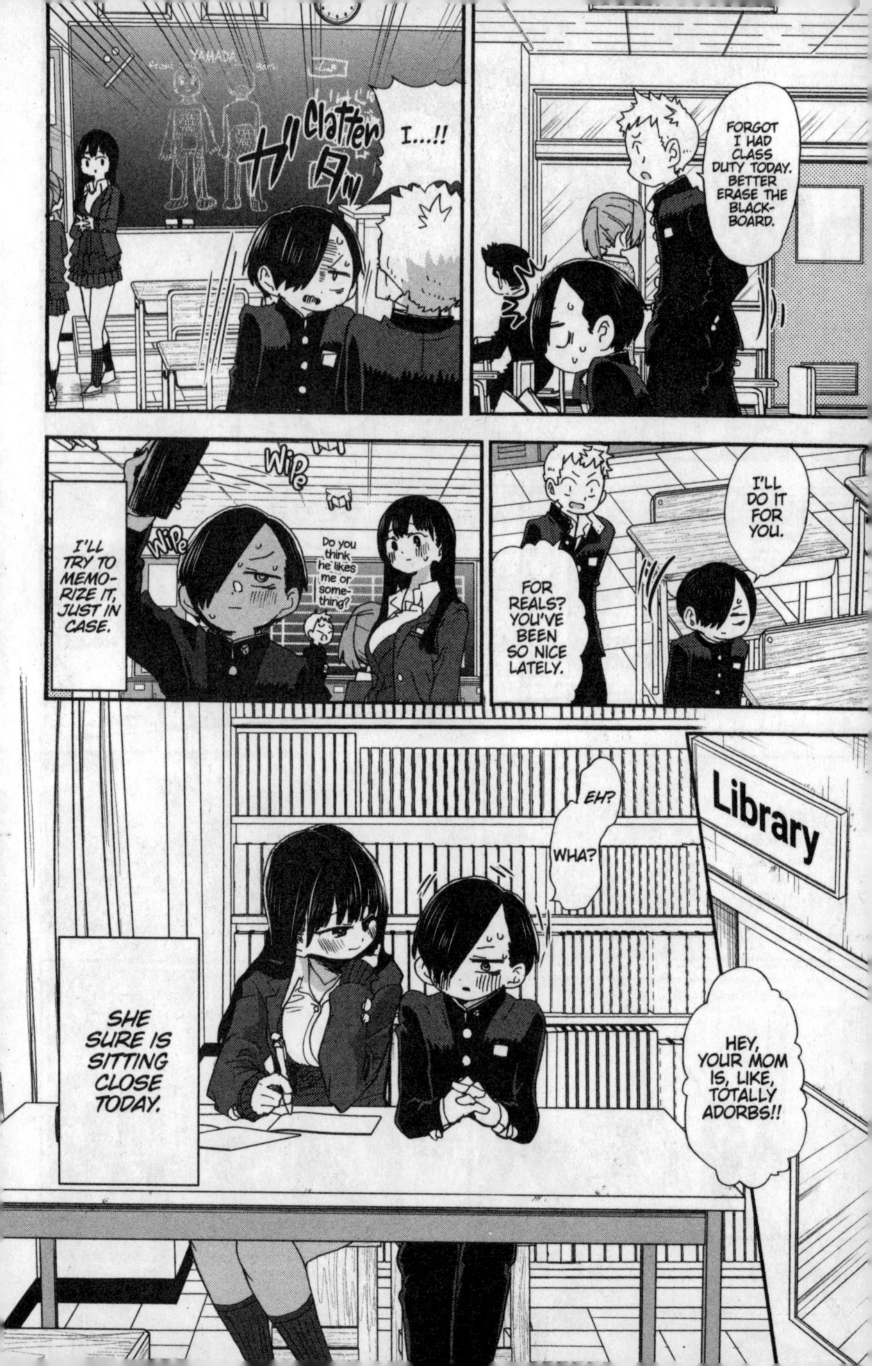
FORGOT I HAD CLASS DUTY TODAY. BETTER ERASE THE BLACK-BOARD.
I...!!
Clatter
ガタッ
YAMADA
I'LL DO IT FOR YOU.
FOR REALS? YOU'VE BEEN SO NICE LATELY.
Wipe
Wipe
Do you think he likes me or some-thing?
I'LL TRY TO MEMO-RIZE IT, JUST IN CASE.
Library
EH?
WHA?
HEY, YOUR MOM IS, LIKE, TOTALLY ADORBS!!
SHE SURE IS SITTING CLOSE TODAY.

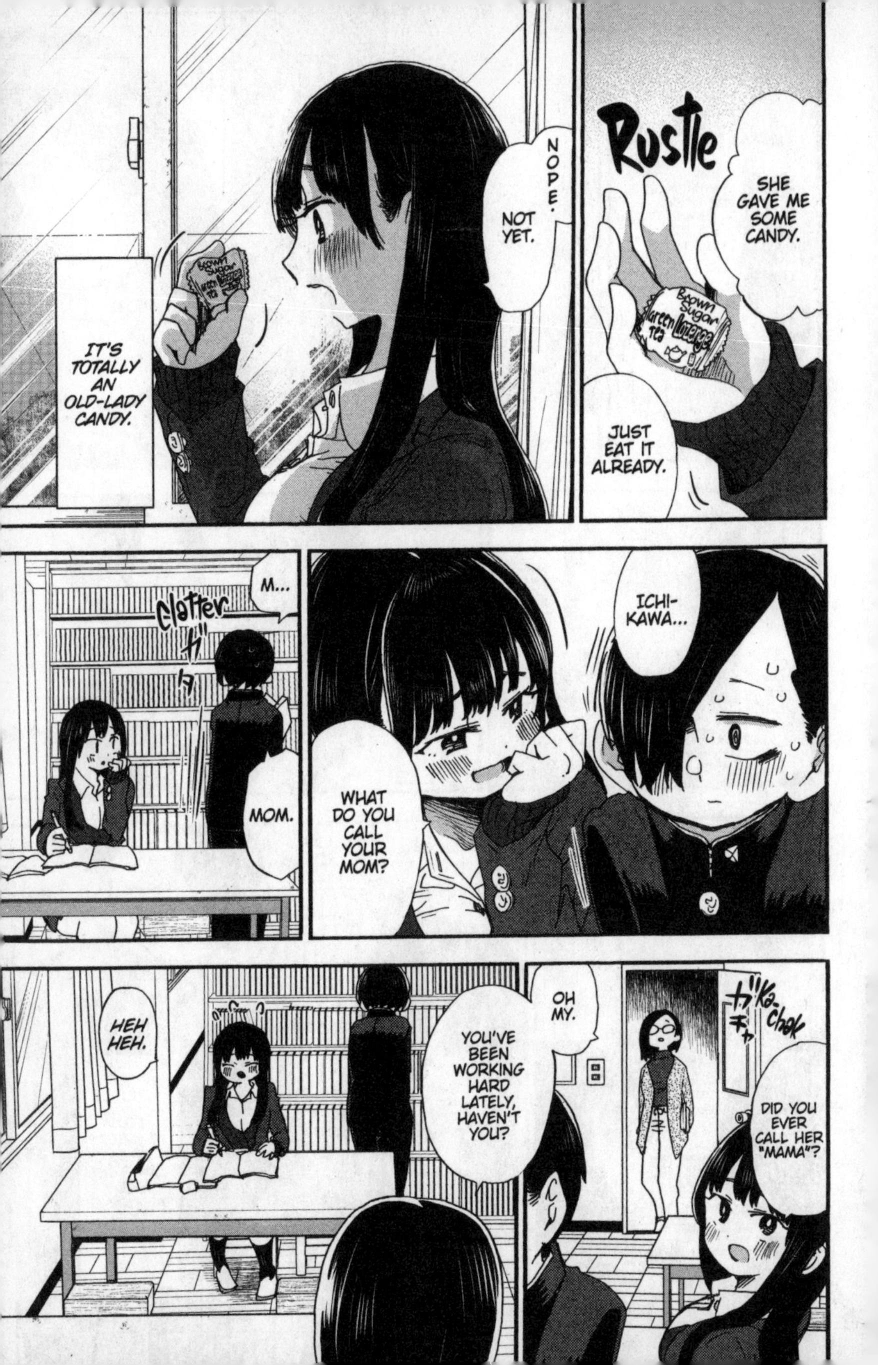
Rustle
SHE GAVE ME SOME CANDY.
Brown Sugar green tea Lozenge
JUST EAT IT ALREADY.
NOPE. NOT YET.
IT'S TOTALLY AN OLD-LADY CANDY.
ICHI-KAWA...
WHAT DO YOU CALL YOUR MOM?
M...
Clatter
MOM.
Ka-chak
DID YOU EVER CALL HER "MAMA"?
OH MY.
YOU'VE BEEN WORKING HARD LATELY, HAVEN'T YOU?
HEH HEH.

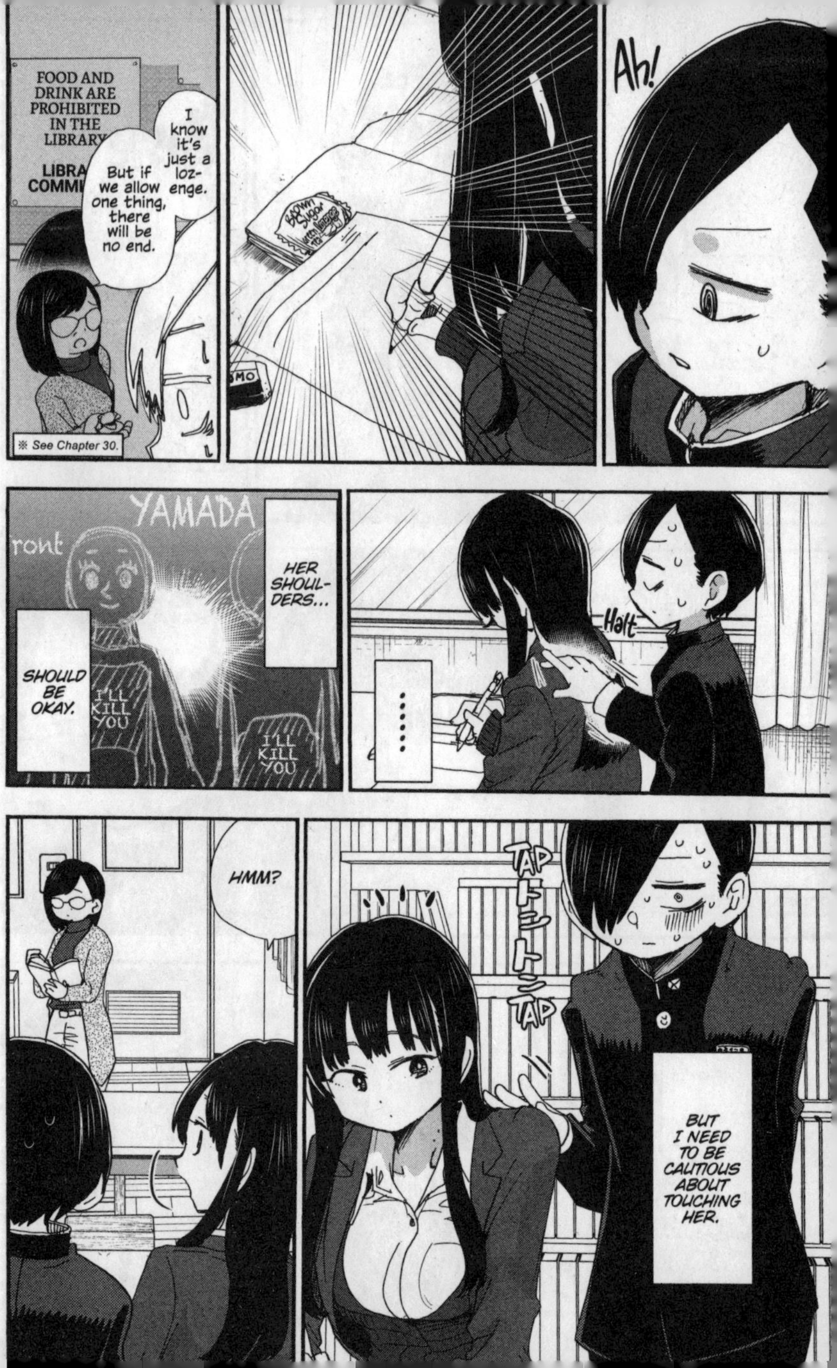
Ah!
FOOD AND DRINK ARE PROHIBITED IN THE LIBRARY
I know it's just a lozenge.
But if we allow one thing, there will be no end.
※ See Chapter 30.
Halt
......
HER SHOULDERS...
YAMADA
Front
SHOULD BE OKAY.
I'LL KILL YOU
I'LL KILL YOU
TAP TAP
BUT I NEED TO BE CAUTIOUS ABOUT TOUCHING HER.
HMM?

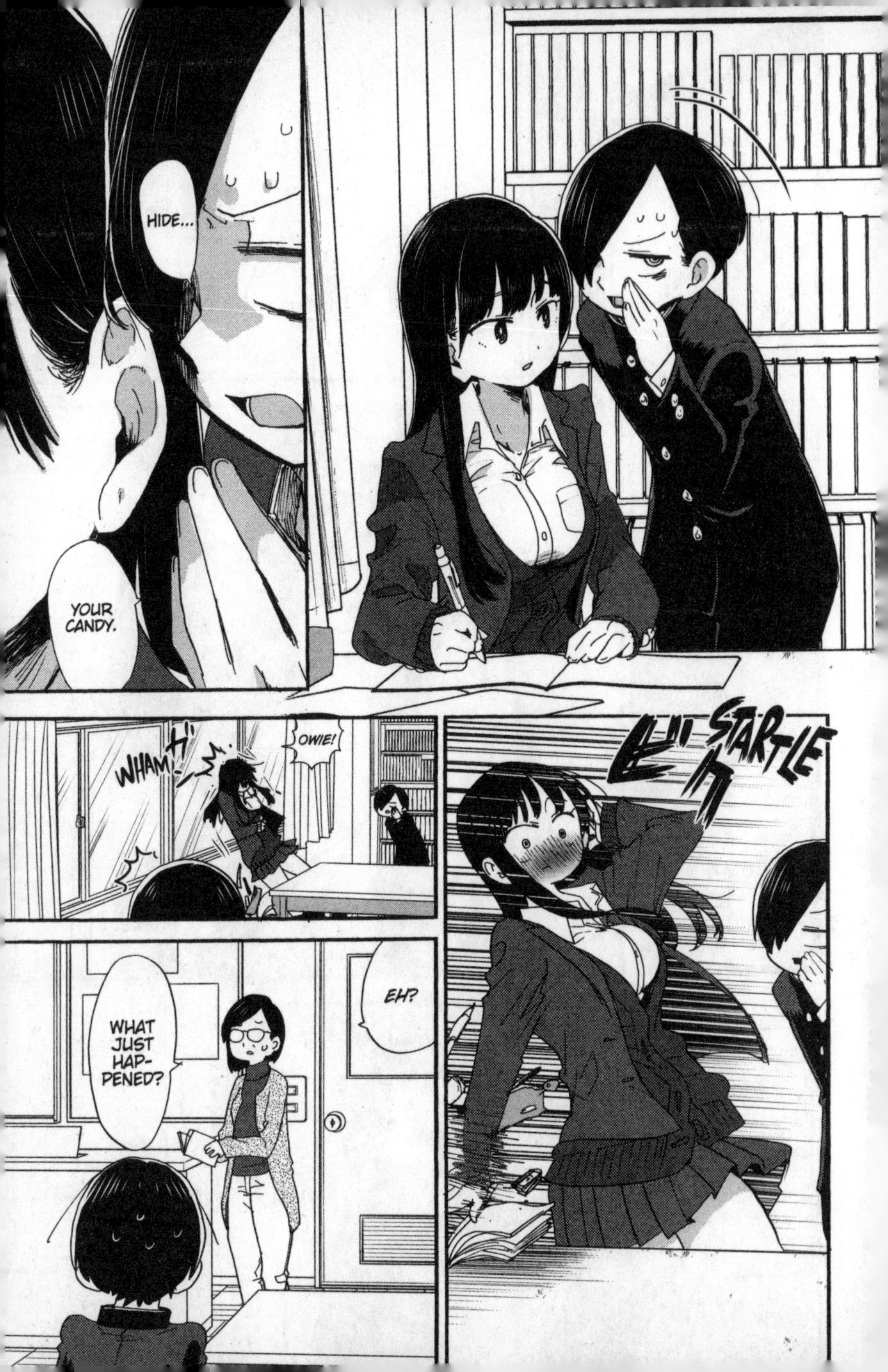

HIDE...
YOUR CANDY.
STARTLE
OWIE!
WHAM
EH?
WHAT JUST HAP-PENED?

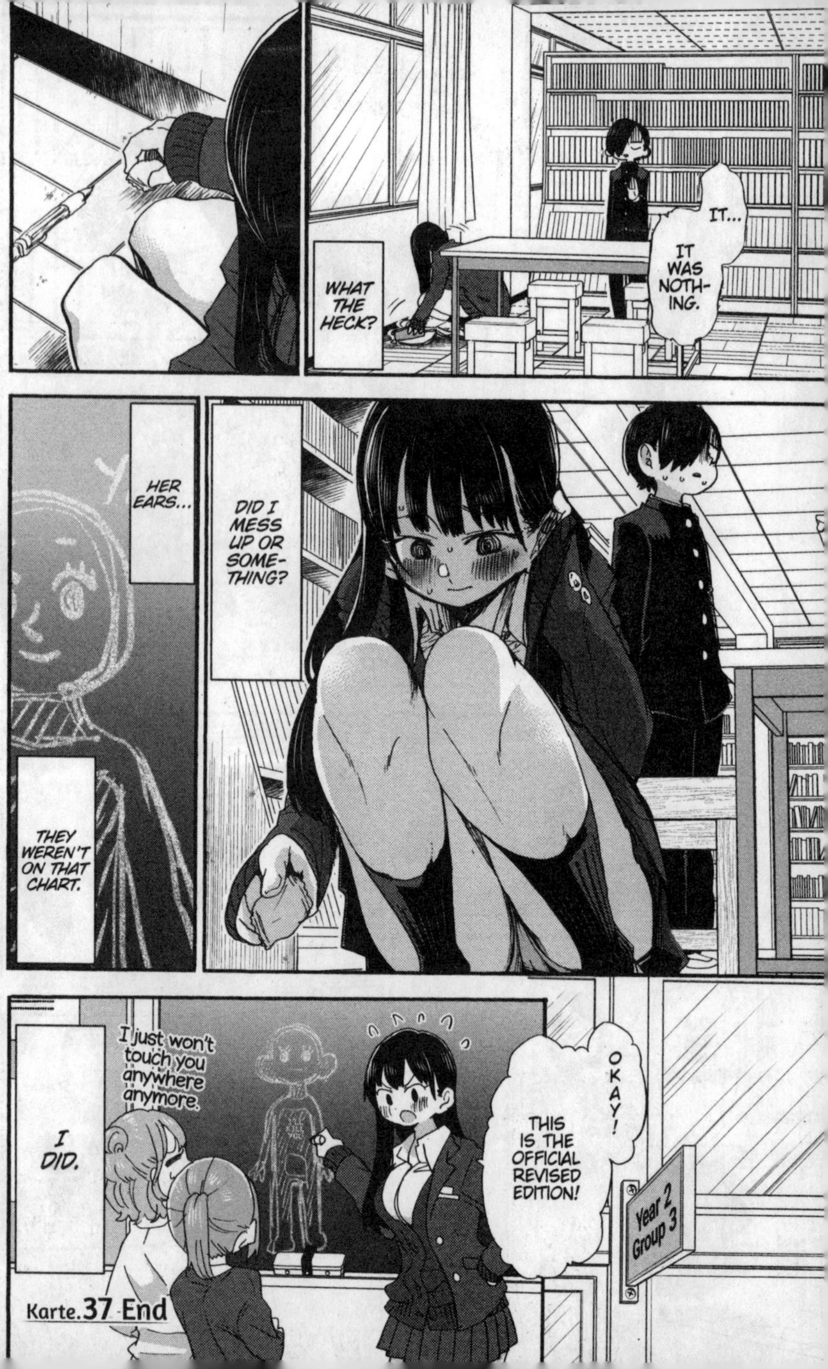
IT...
IT WAS NOTHING.
WHAT THE HECK?
DID I MESS UP OR SOMETHING?
HER EARS...
THEY WEREN'T ON THAT CHART.
Year 2 Group 3
OKAY!
THIS IS THE OFFICIAL REVISED EDITION!
I just won't touch you anywhere anymore.
I DID.
Karte.37 End

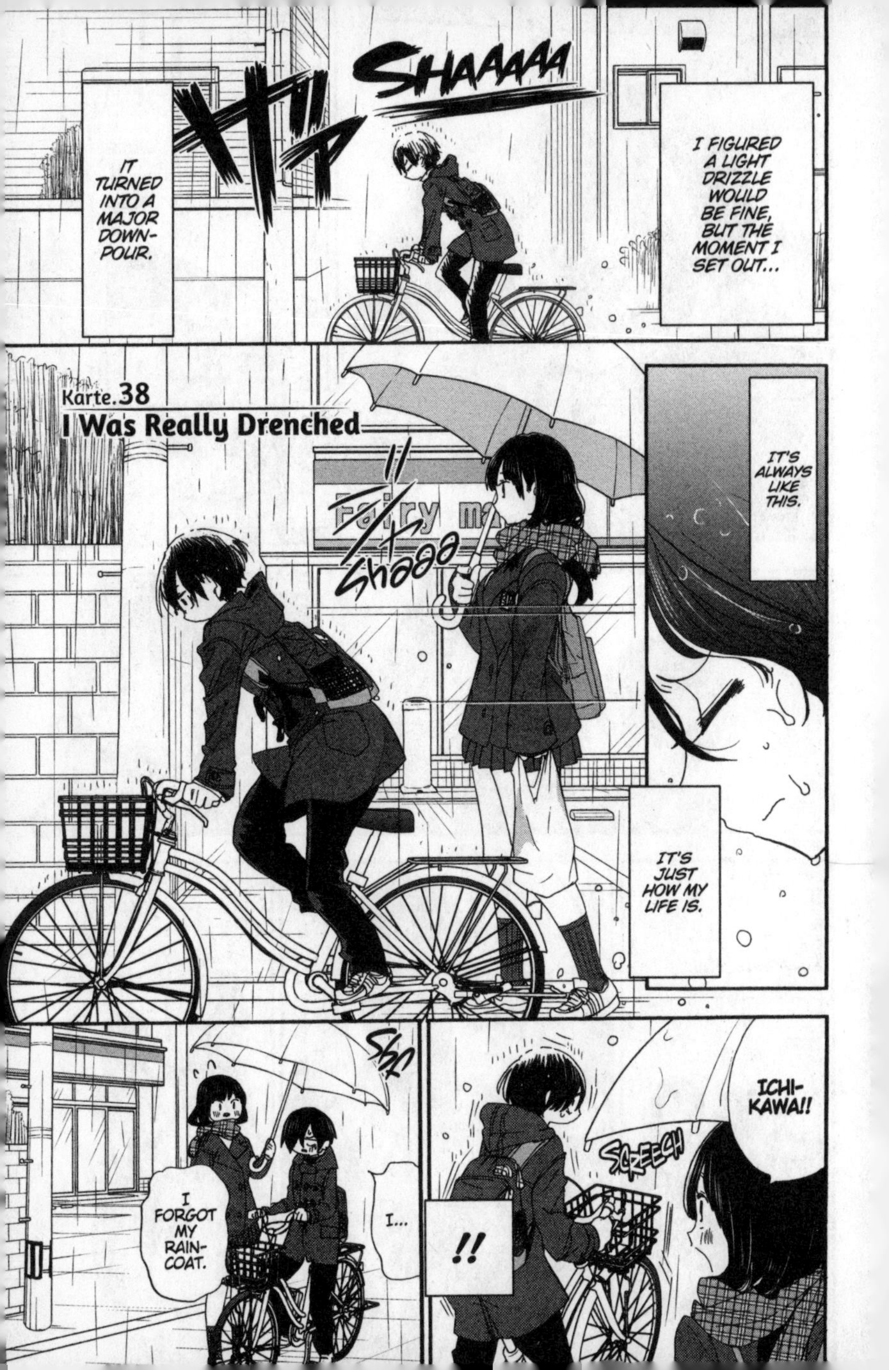
I FIGURED A LIGHT DRIZZLE WOULD BE FINE, BUT THE MOMENT I SET OUT...
SHAAAAA
IT TURNED INTO A MAJOR DOWN-POUR.
IT'S ALWAYS LIKE THIS.
IT'S JUST HOW MY LIFE IS.
Karte.38
I Was Really Drenched
!!
Shaaa
ICHI-KAWA!!
SCREECH
!!
I...
I FORGOT MY RAIN-COAT.

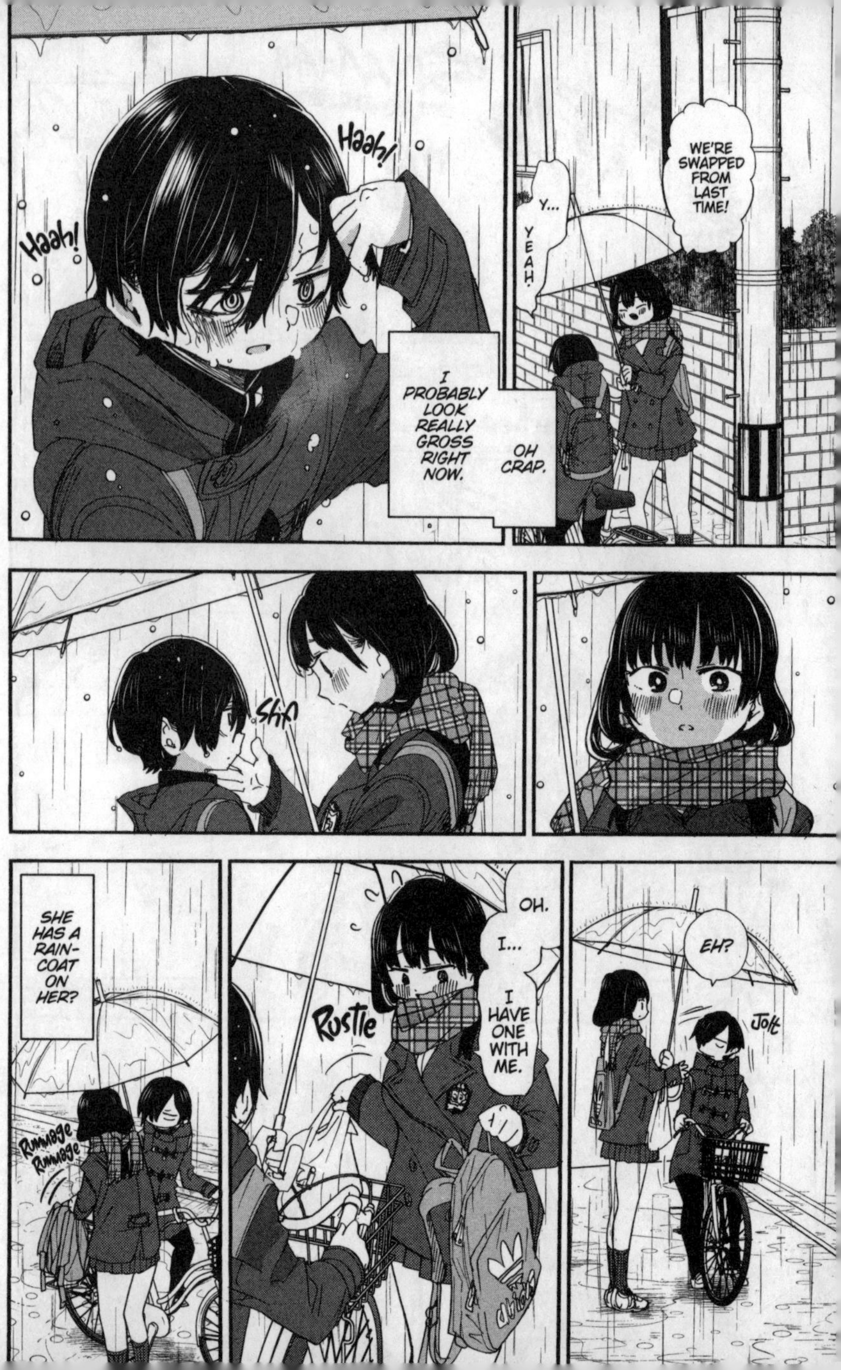
WE'RE SWAPPED FROM LAST TIME!
Y... YEAH.
OH CRAP.
I PROBABLY LOOK REALLY GROSS RIGHT NOW.
Haah!
Haah!
Shif
EH?
Jolt
OH.
I...
I HAVE ONE WITH ME.
Rustle
SHE HAS A RAIN-COAT ON HER?
Rummage Rummage

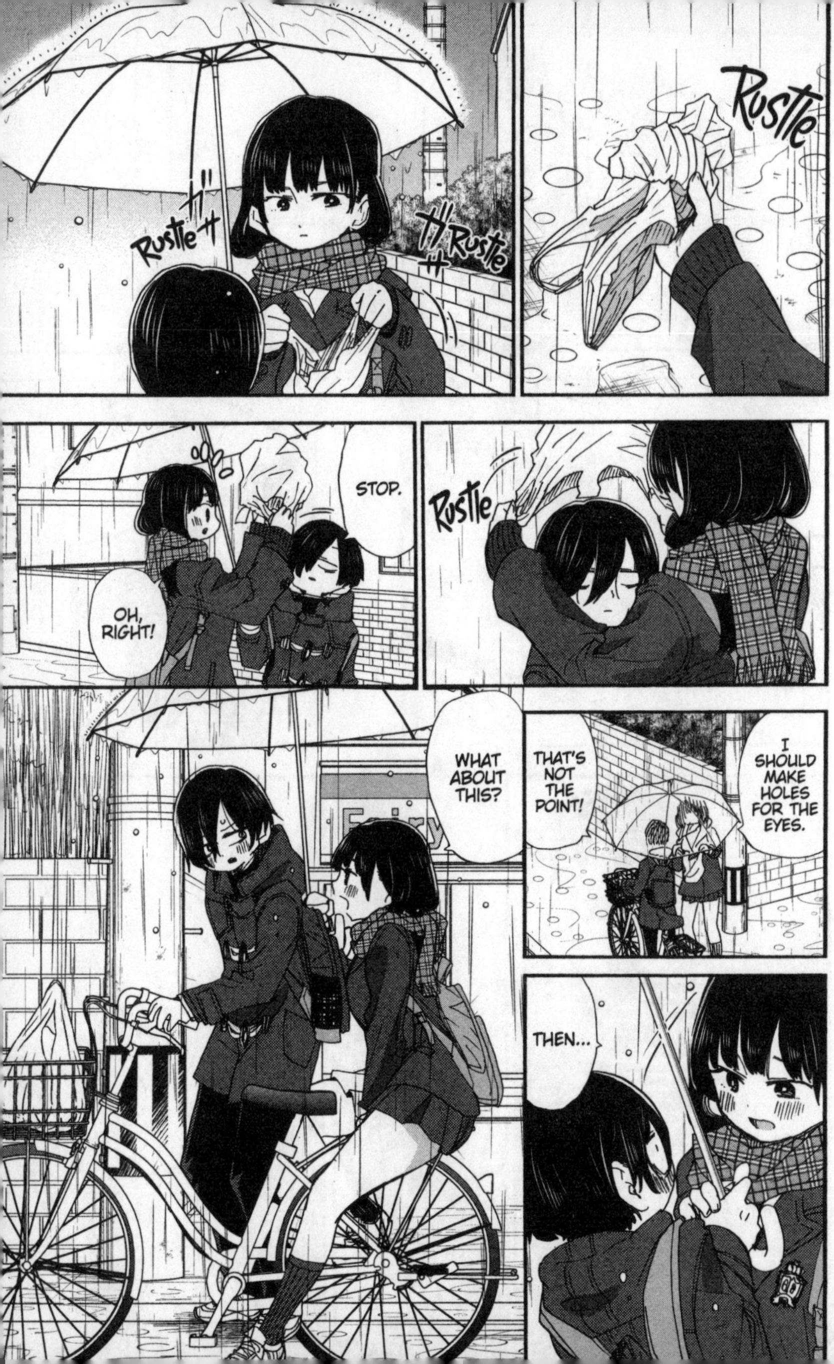
Rustle
Rustle
Rustle
Rustle
STOP.
OH, RIGHT!
I SHOULD MAKE HOLES FOR THE EYES.
THAT'S NOT THE POINT!
THEN...
WHAT ABOUT THIS?

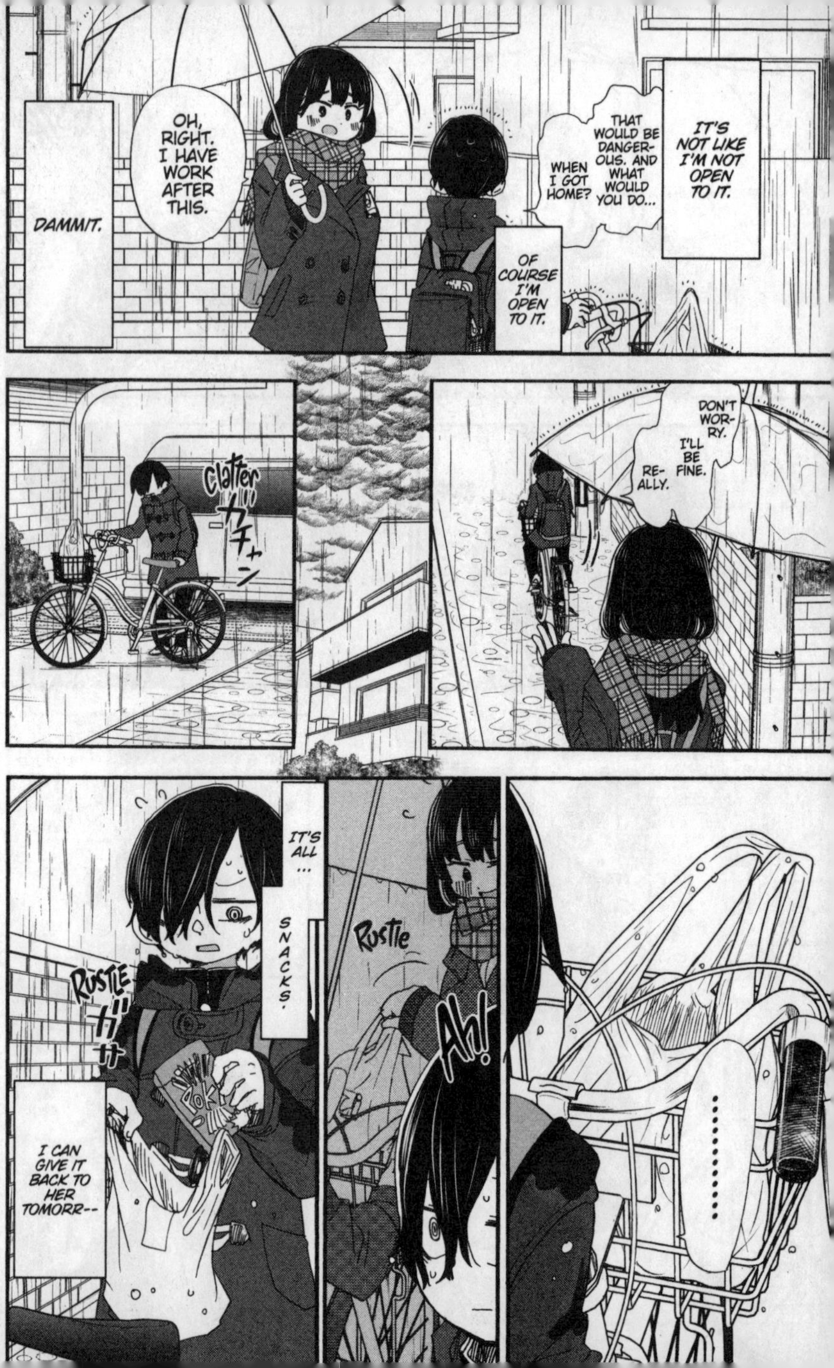
IT'S NOT LIKE I'M NOT OPEN TO IT.
THAT WOULD BE DANGER-OUS. AND WHAT WOULD YOU DO...
WHEN I GOT HOME?
OF COURSE I'M OPEN TO IT.
OH, RIGHT. I HAVE WORK AFTER THIS.
DAMMIT.
DON'T WORRY.
I'LL BE FINE.
RE-ALLY.
Clatter
ガチャン
......
Rustle
Ah!
IT'S ALL...
SNACKS.
RUSTLE
ガサ
I CAN GIVE IT BACK TO HER TOMORR--

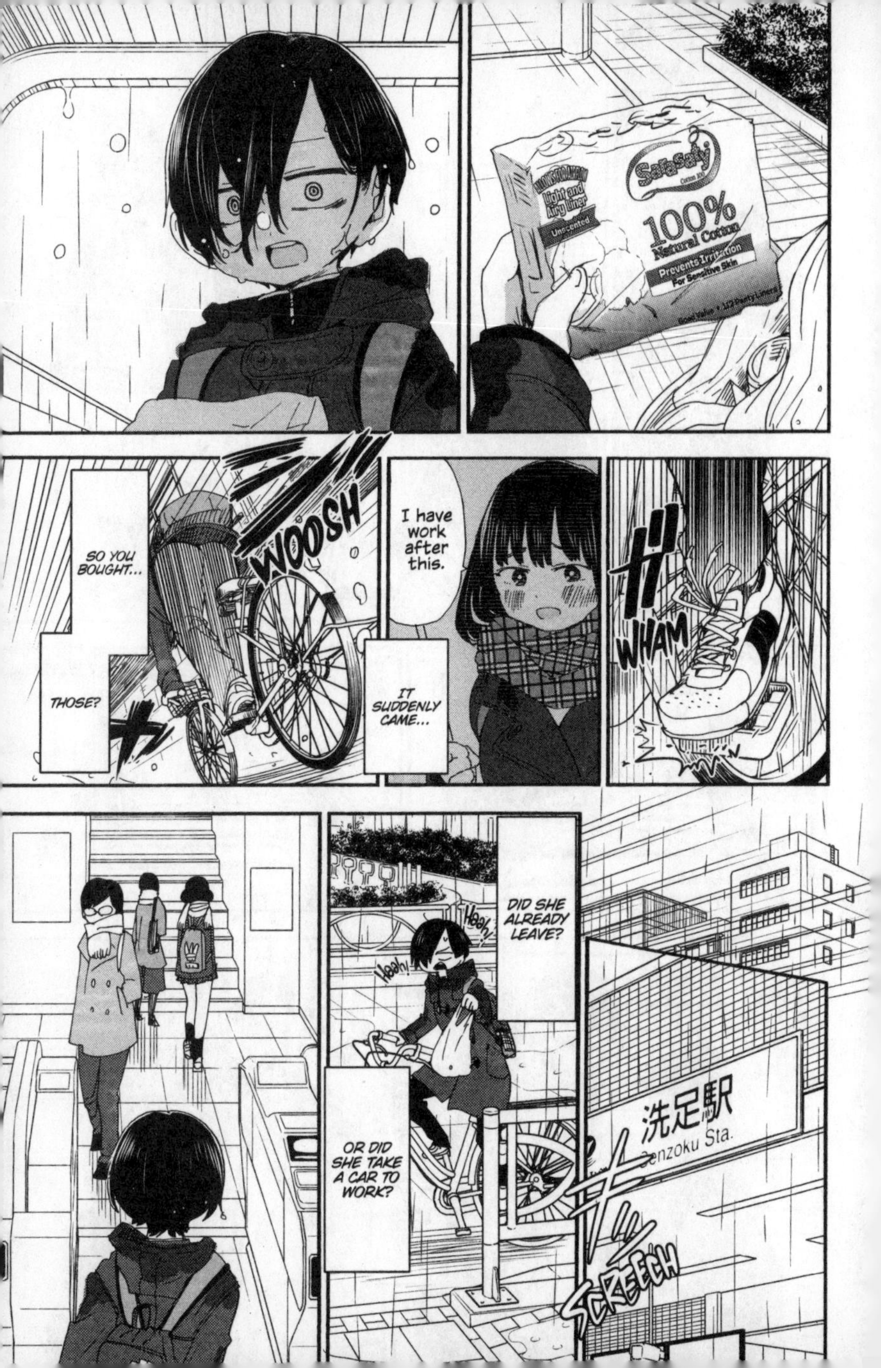
Safe-Safy
Cotton 100
100%
Natural Cotton
Prevents Irritation
For Sensitive Skin
Light and Airy Liner
Unscented
WHAM
I have work after this.
IT SUDDENLY CAME...
WOOSH
SO YOU BOUGHT...
THOSE?
DID SHE ALREADY LEAVE?
Haah!
Haah!
OR DID SHE TAKE A CAR TO WORK?
洗足駅
Senzoku Sta.
SCREECH

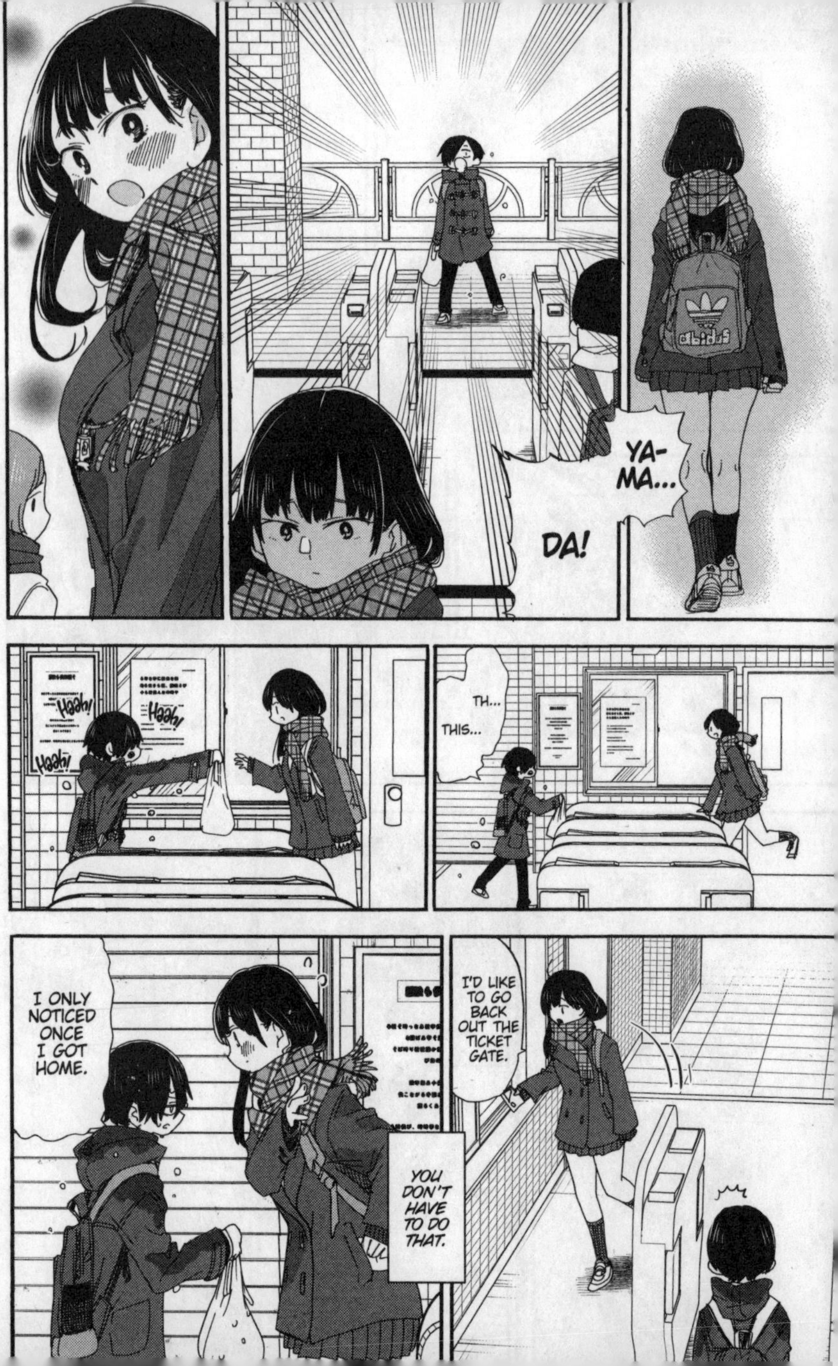

YA-MA...
DA!
TH...
THIS...
Haah!
Haah!
Haah!
I'D LIKE TO GO BACK OUT THE TICKET GATE.
YOU DON'T HAVE TO DO THAT.
I ONLY NOTICED ONCE I GOT HOME.

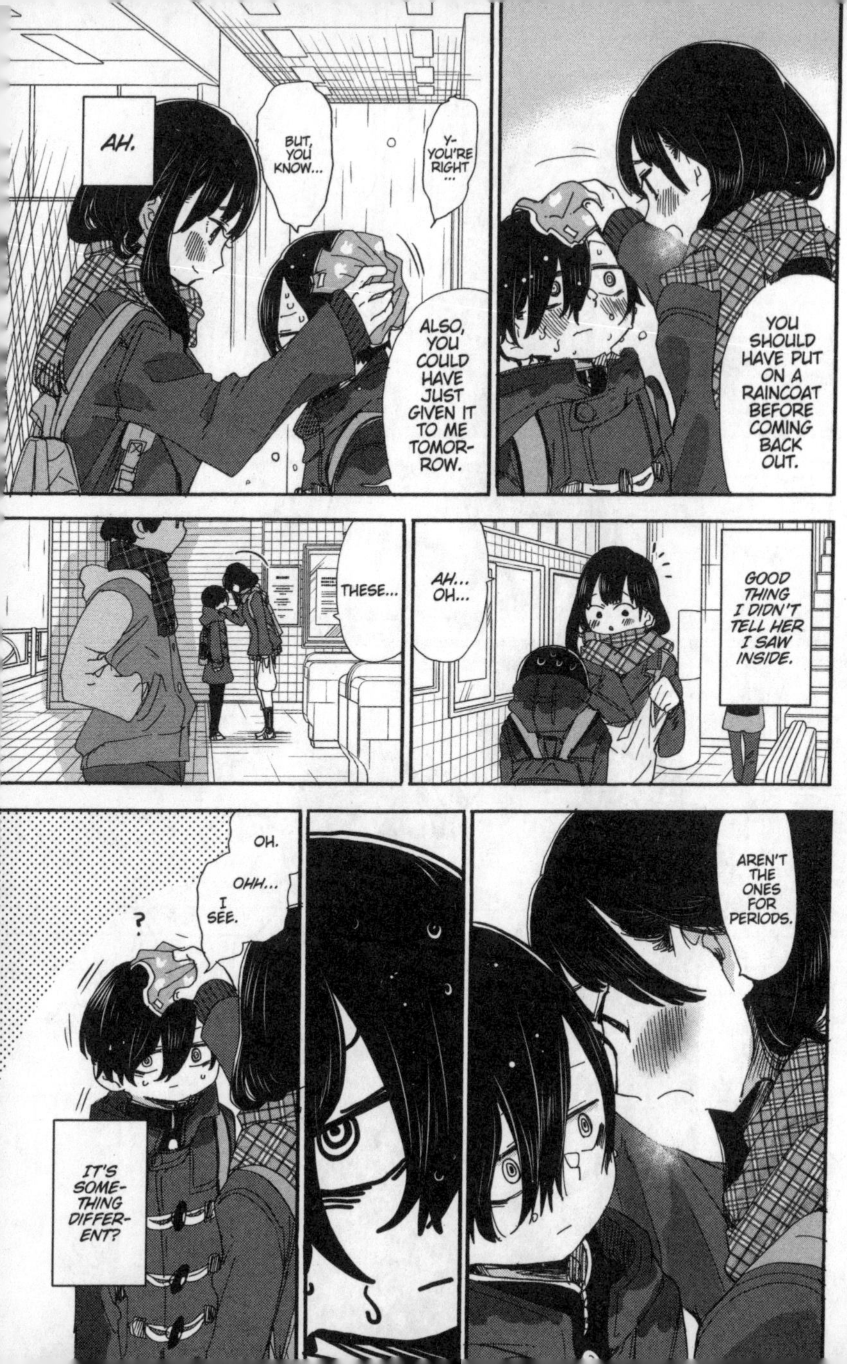
YOU SHOULD HAVE PUT ON A RAINCOAT BEFORE COMING BACK OUT.
Y- YOU'RE RIGHT ...
BUT, YOU KNOW...
AH.
ALSO, YOU COULD HAVE JUST GIVEN IT TO ME TOMORROW.
GOOD THING I DIDN'T TELL HER I SAW INSIDE.
AH... OH...
THESE...
AREN'T THE ONES FOR PERIODS.
OH.
OHH...
I SEE.
?
IT'S SOMETHING DIFFERENT?

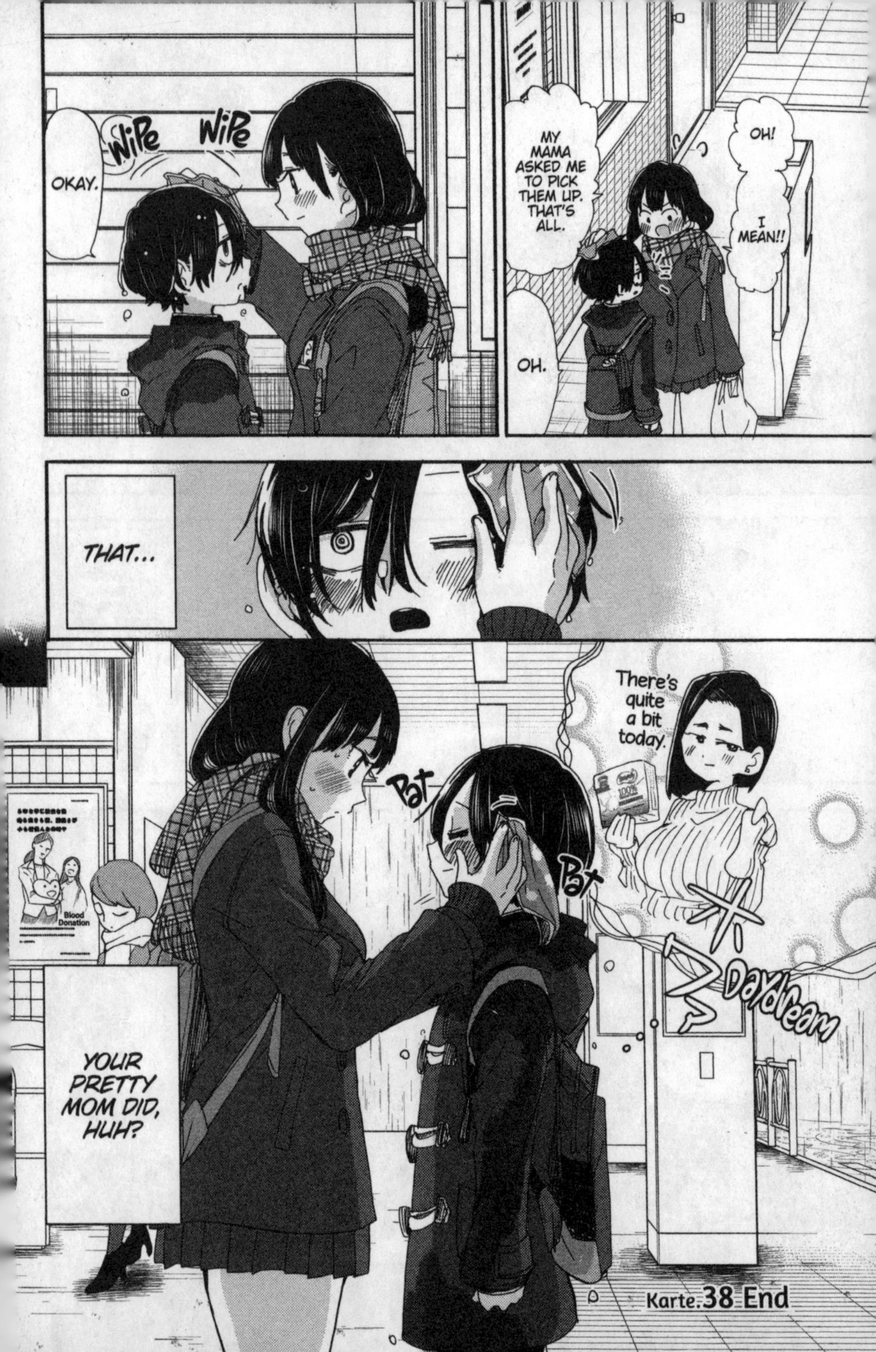
OH!
I MEAN!!
MY MAMA ASKED ME TO PICK THEM UP. THAT'S ALL.
OH.
WiPe
WiPe
OKAY.
THAT...
There's quite a bit today.
Pat
Pat
100%
Blood Donation
Daydream
YOUR PRETTY MOM DID, HUH?
Karte.38 End

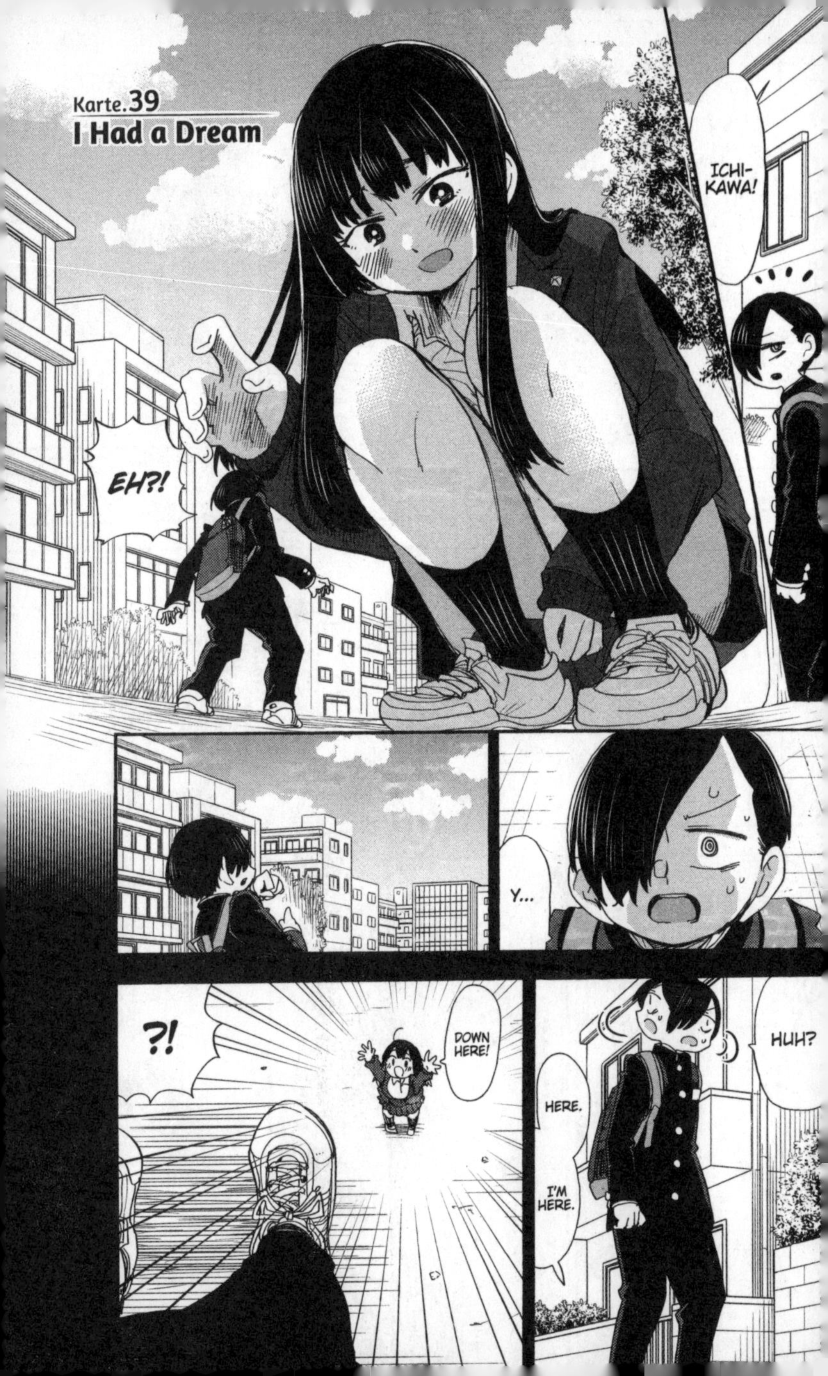
Karte.39
I Had a Dream
ICHI-KAWA!
EH?!
Y...
HUH?
HERE.
I'M HERE.
DOWN HERE!
?!

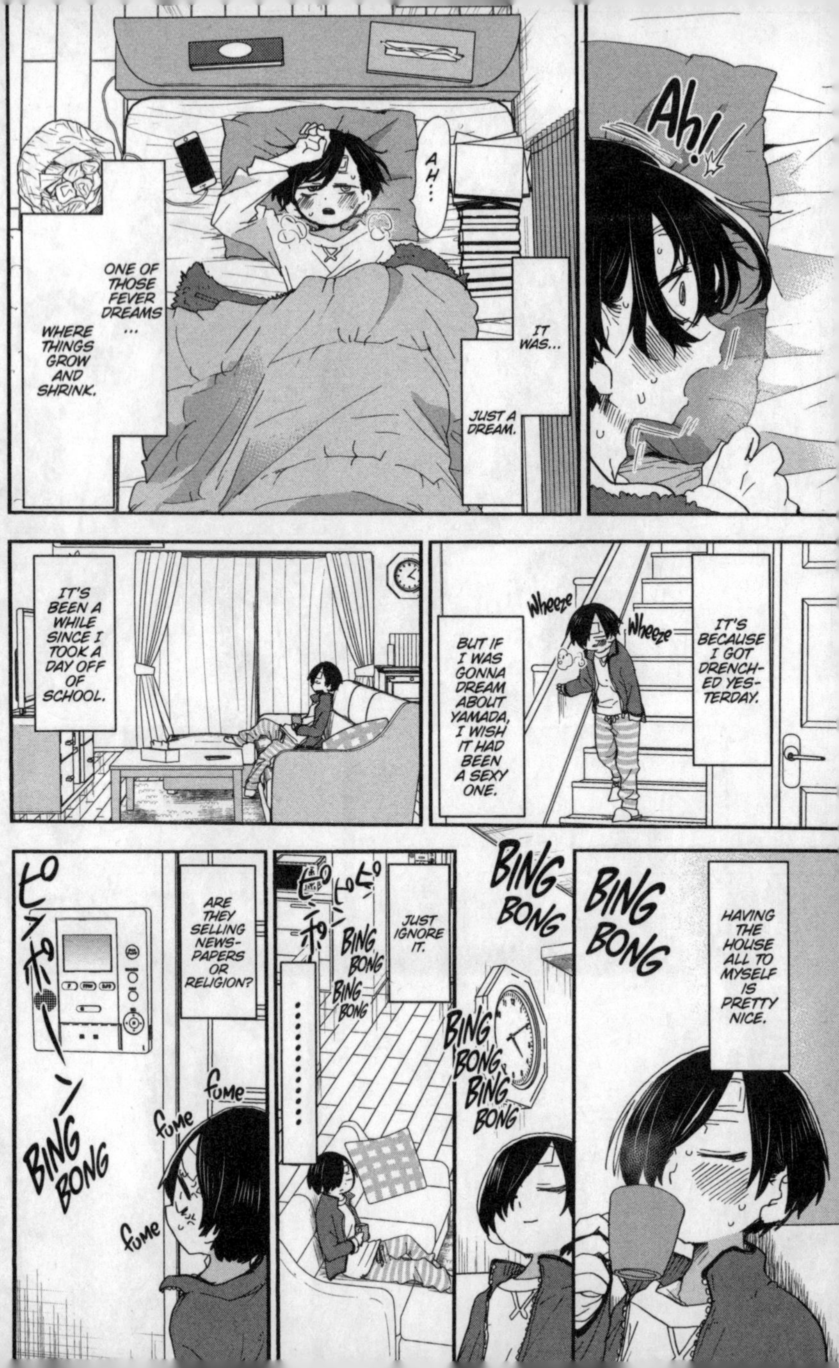
Ah!
AH...
IT WAS...
JUST A DREAM.
ONE OF THOSE FEVER DREAMS...
WHERE THINGS GROW AND SHRINK.
IT'S BECAUSE I GOT DRENCHED YESTERDAY.
Wheeze
Wheeze
BUT IF I WAS GONNA DREAM ABOUT YAMADA, I WISH IT HAD BEEN A SEXY ONE.
IT'S BEEN A WHILE SINCE I TOOK A DAY OFF OF SCHOOL.
BING BONG
HAVING THE HOUSE ALL TO MYSELF IS PRETTY NICE.
BING BONG
BING BONG BING BONG
JUST IGNORE IT.
BING BONG BING BONG
....
ARE THEY SELLING NEWSPAPERS OR RELIGION?
ピンポーン
BING BONG
fume
fume
fume

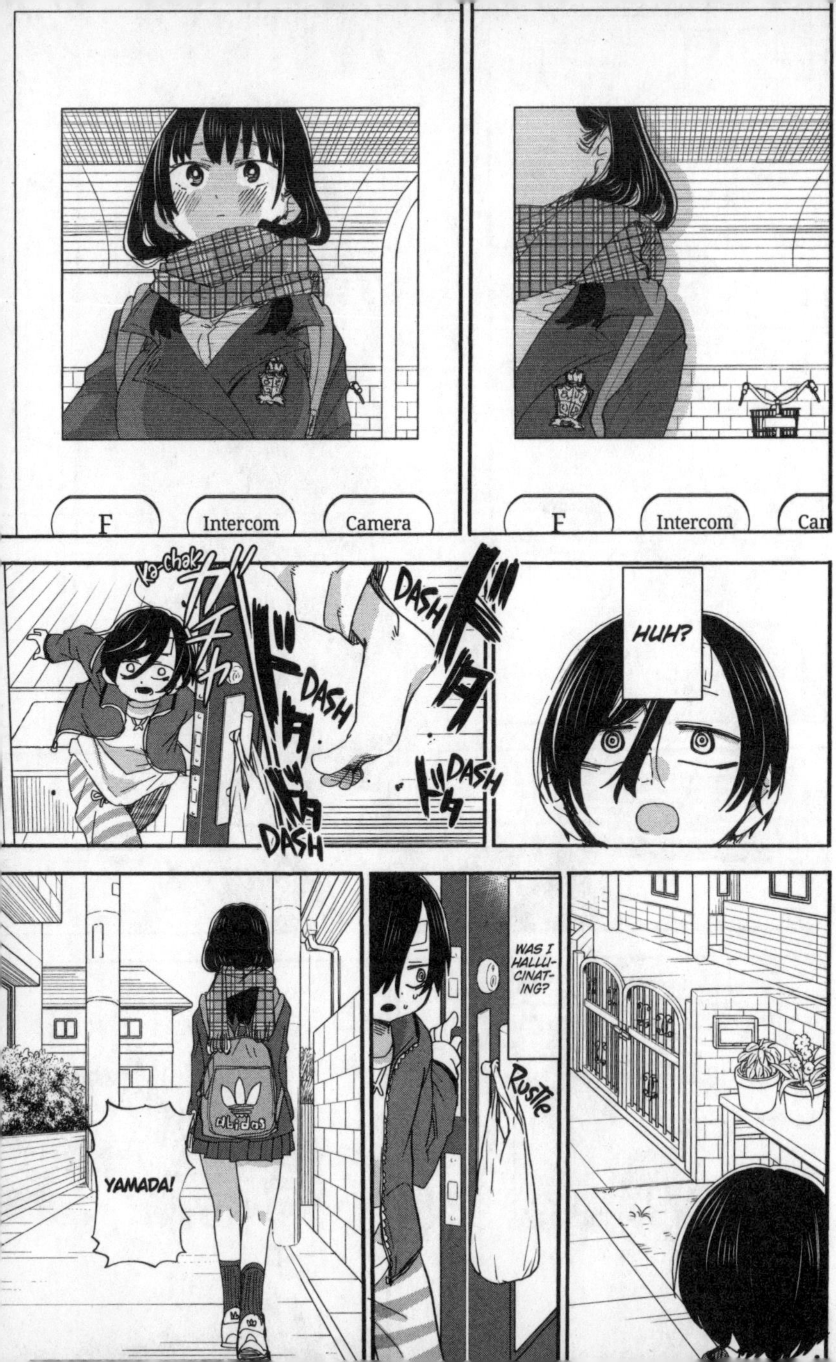
F
Intercom
Can
F
Intercom
Camera
HUH?
DASH
DASH
DASH
DASH
ka-chak
WAS I HALLUCINATING?
Rustle
YAMADA!

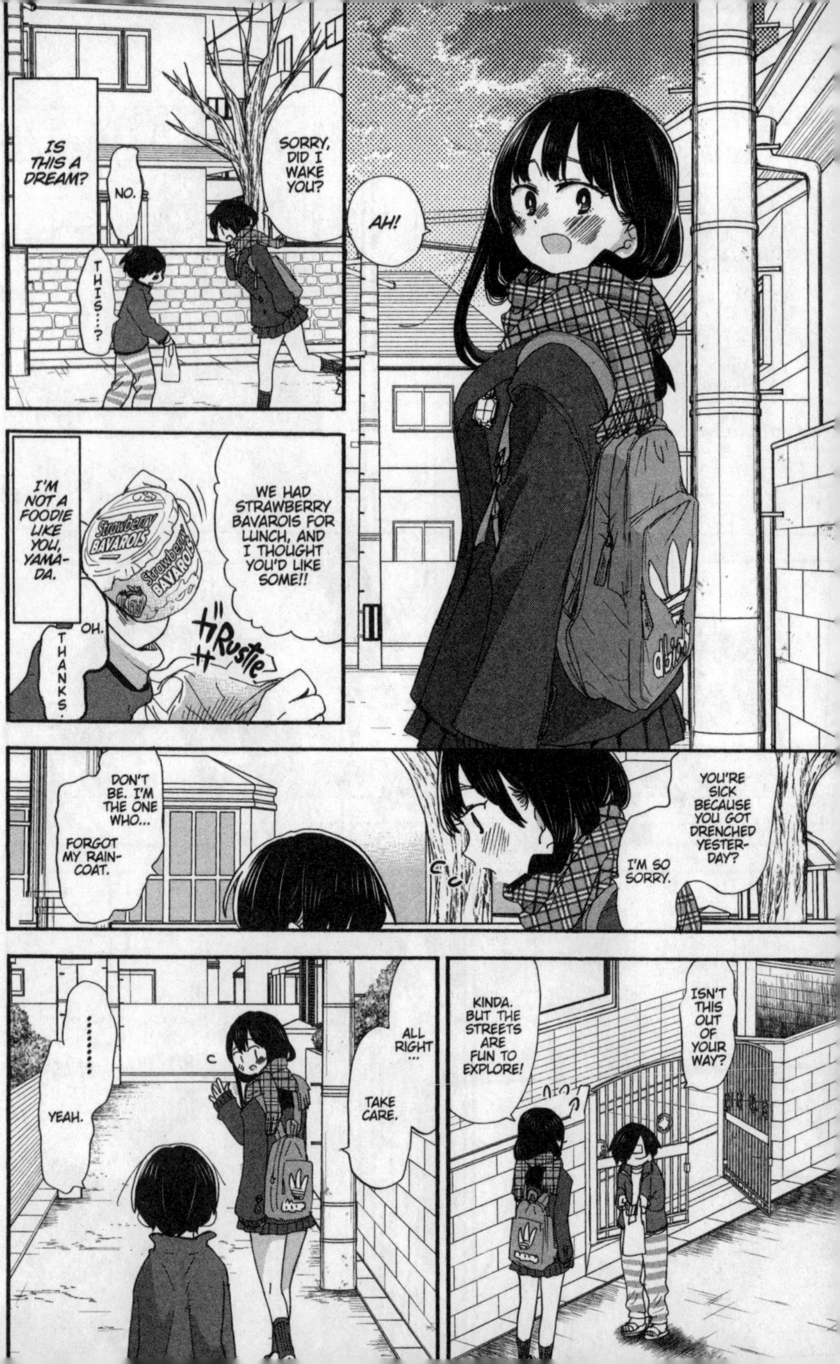
AH!
SORRY, DID I WAKE YOU?
IS THIS A DREAM?
NO.
THIS...?
WE HAD STRAWBERRY BAVAROIS FOR LUNCH, AND I THOUGHT YOU'D LIKE SOME!!
I'M NOT A FOODIE LIKE YOU, YAMADA.
Strawberry BAVAROIS
Strawberry BAVAROIS
RUSTLE
OH.
THANKS.
YOU'RE SICK BECAUSE YOU GOT DRENCHED YESTERDAY?
I'M SO SORRY.
DON'T BE. I'M THE ONE WHO...
FORGOT MY RAIN-COAT.
ISN'T THIS OUT OF YOUR WAY?
KINDA. BUT THE STREETS ARE FUN TO EXPLORE!
ALL RIGHT...
TAKE CARE.
....
YEAH.

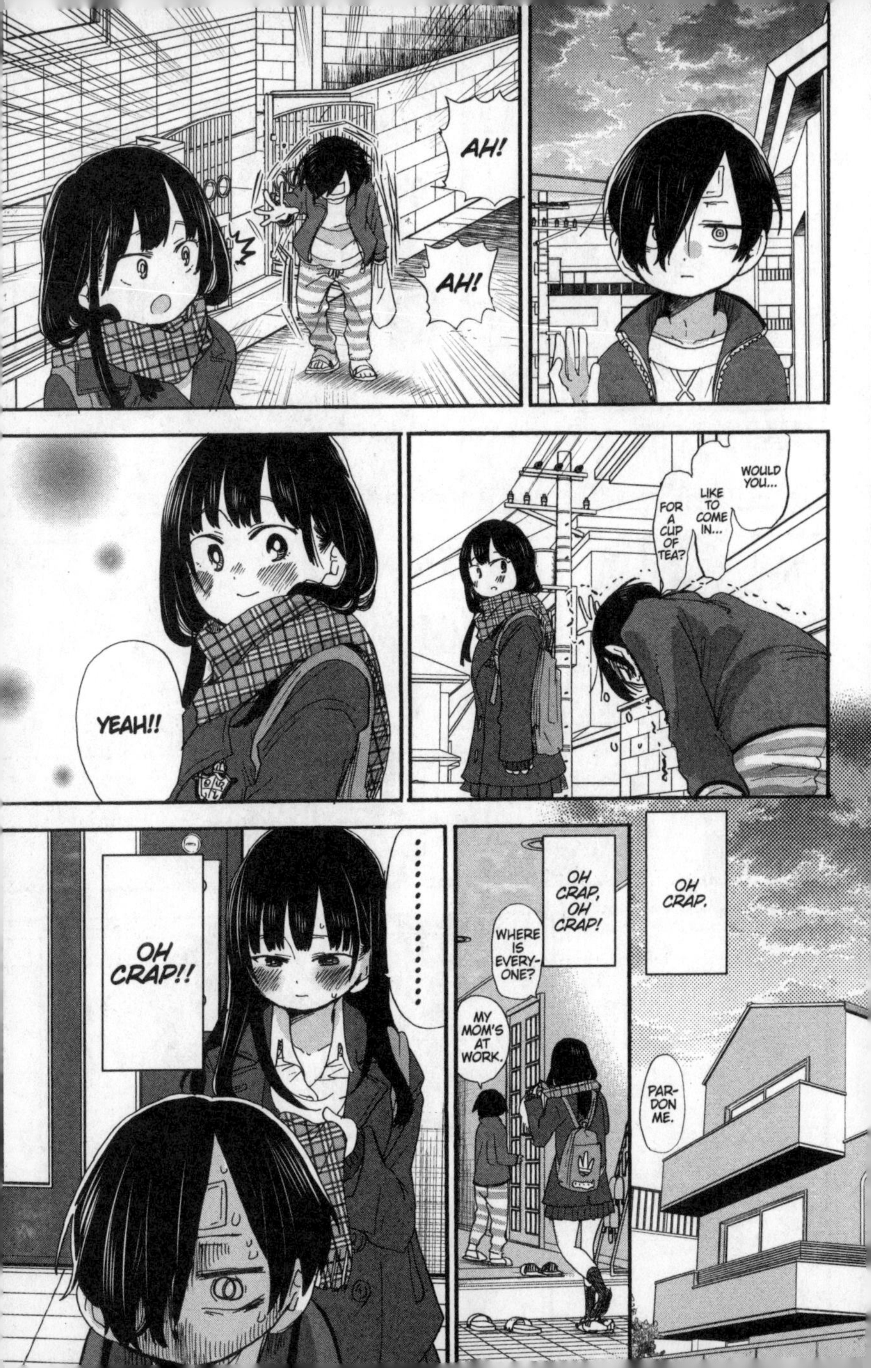
AH!
AH!
WOULD YOU...
LIKE TO COME IN...
FOR A CUP OF TEA?
YEAH!!
OH CRAP.
PARDON ME.
OH CRAP, OH CRAP!
WHERE IS EVERYONE?
MY MOM'S AT WORK.
......
OH CRAP!!

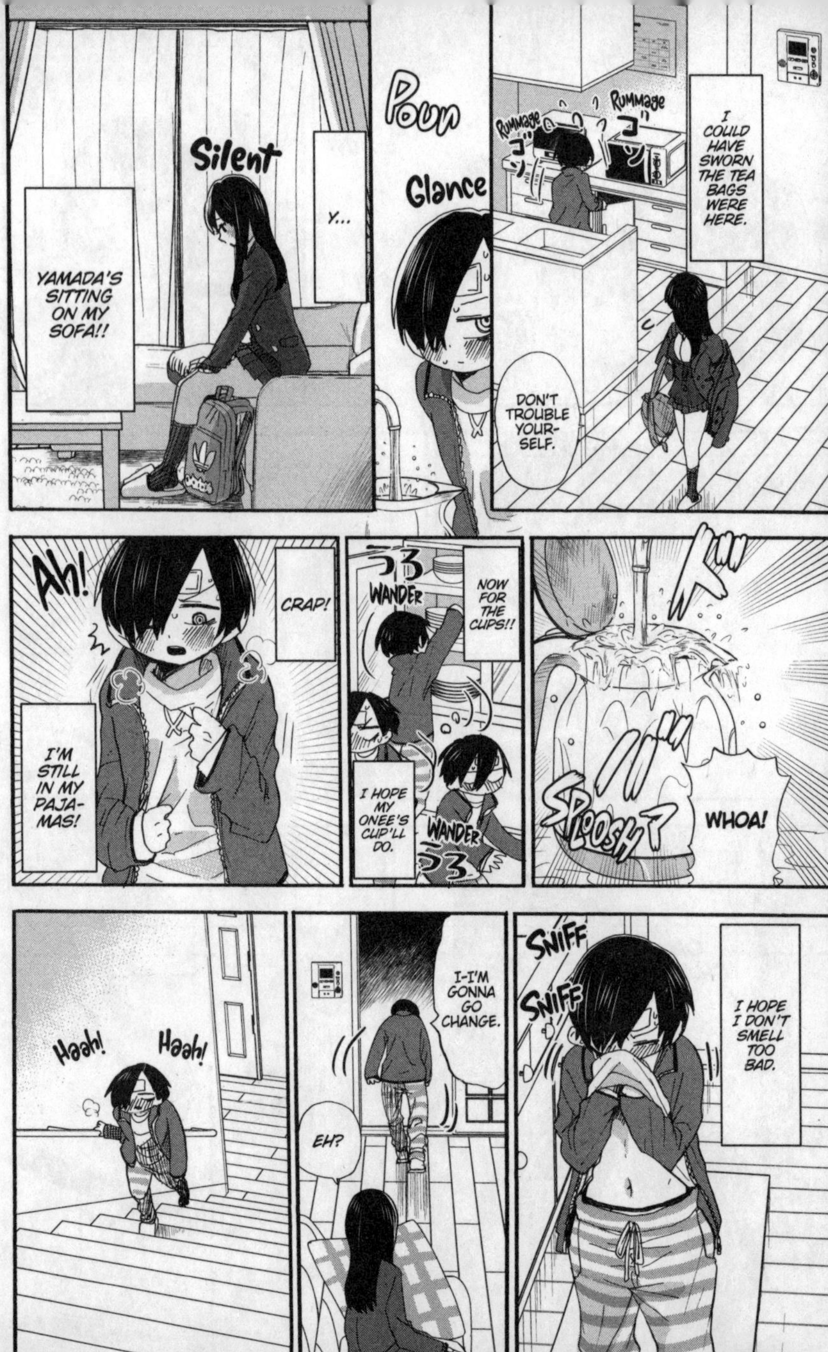

I COULD HAVE SWORN THE TEA BAGS WERE HERE.
Rummage
Rummage
DON'T TROUBLE YOURSELF.
Poun
Glance
Y...
Silent
YAMADA'S SITTING ON MY SOFA!!
WHOA!
SPLOOSH
NOW FOR THE CUPS!!
WANDER
I HOPE MY ONEE'S CUP'LL DO.
WANDER
Ah!
CRAP!
I'M STILL IN MY PAJAMAS!
SNIFF
SNIFF
I HOPE I DON'T SMELL TOO BAD.
I-I'M GONNA GO CHANGE.
EH?
Haah!
Haah!

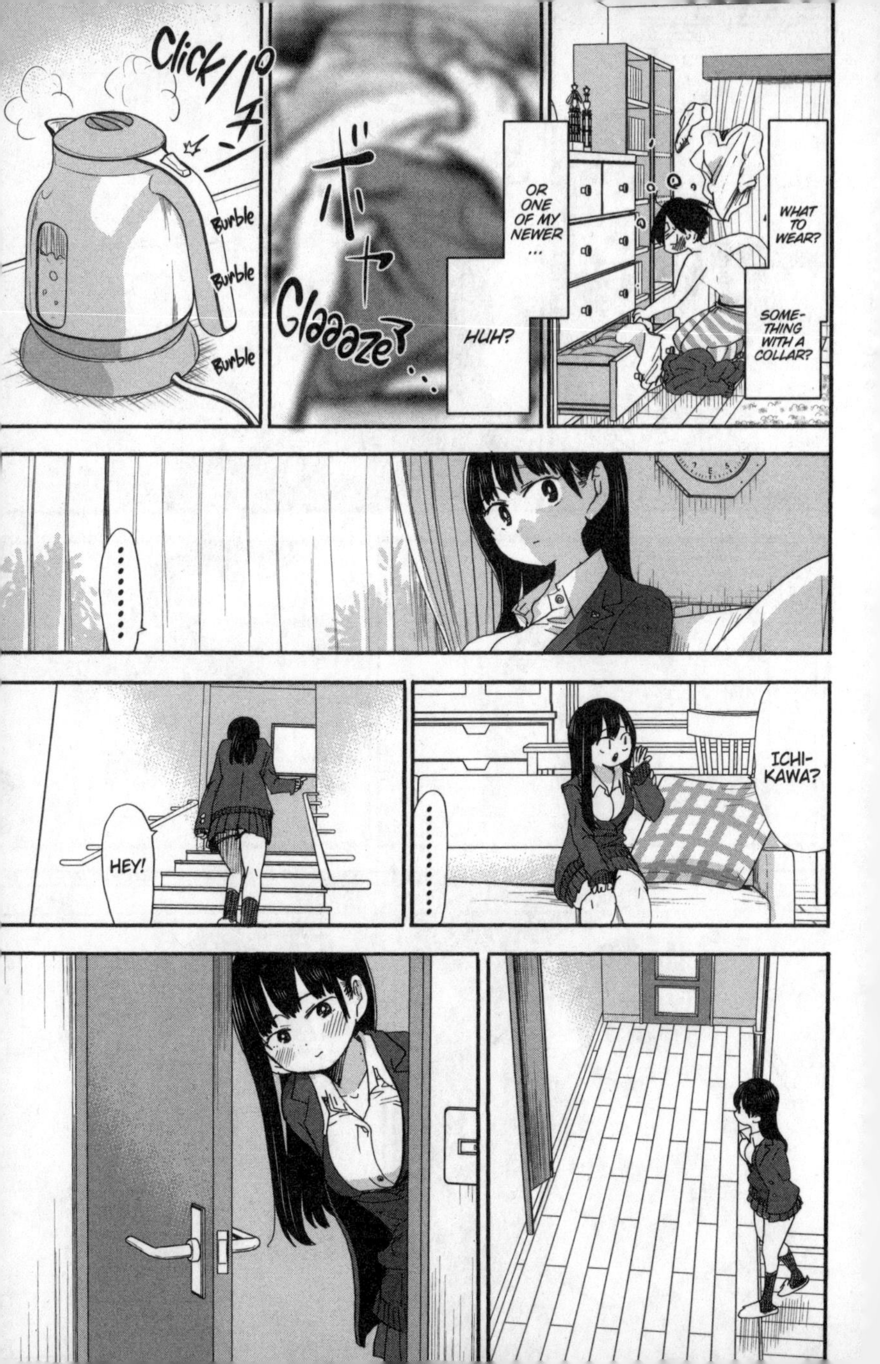
WHAT TO WEAR?
SOME-THING WITH A COLLAR?
OR ONE OF MY NEWER ...
HUH?
ボヤ
Glaaaze...
Click パチッ
Burble
Burble
Burble
......
ICHI-KAWA?
......
HEY!

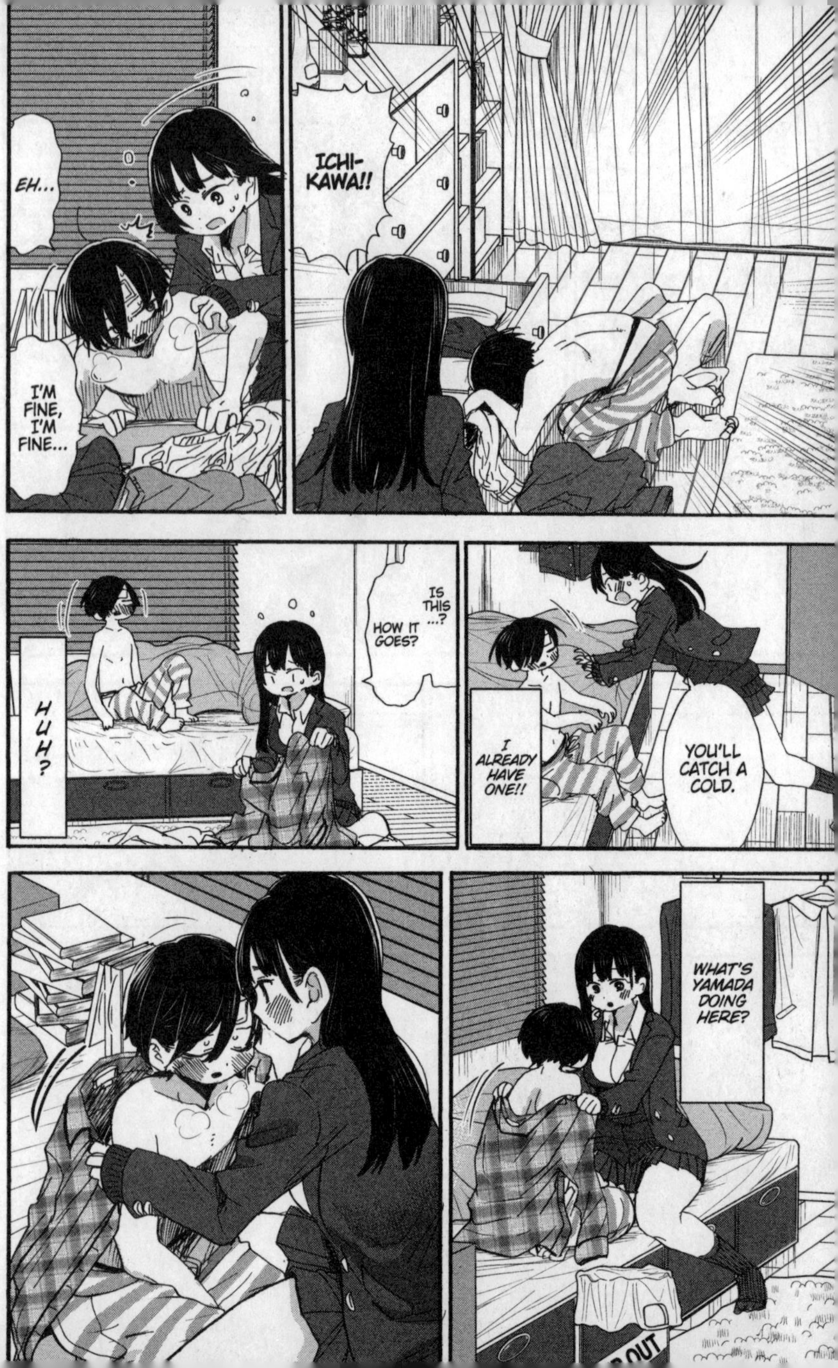
ICHI-KAWA!!
EH...
I'M FINE, I'M FINE...
YOU'LL CATCH A COLD.
I ALREADY HAVE ONE!!
IS THIS ...? HOW IT GOES?
HUH?
WHAT'S YAMADA DOING HERE?

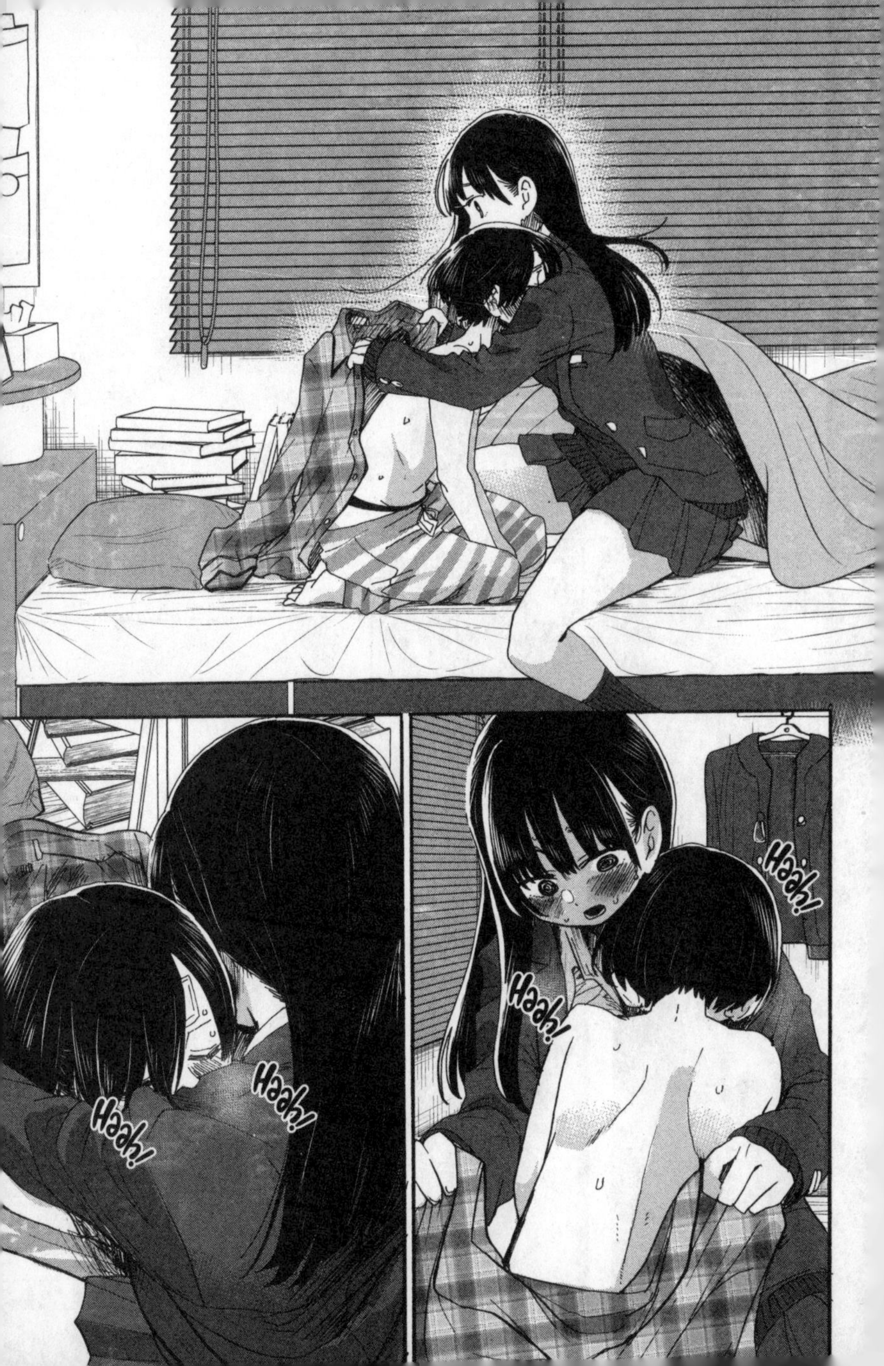
Haah!
Haah!
Haah!
Haah!

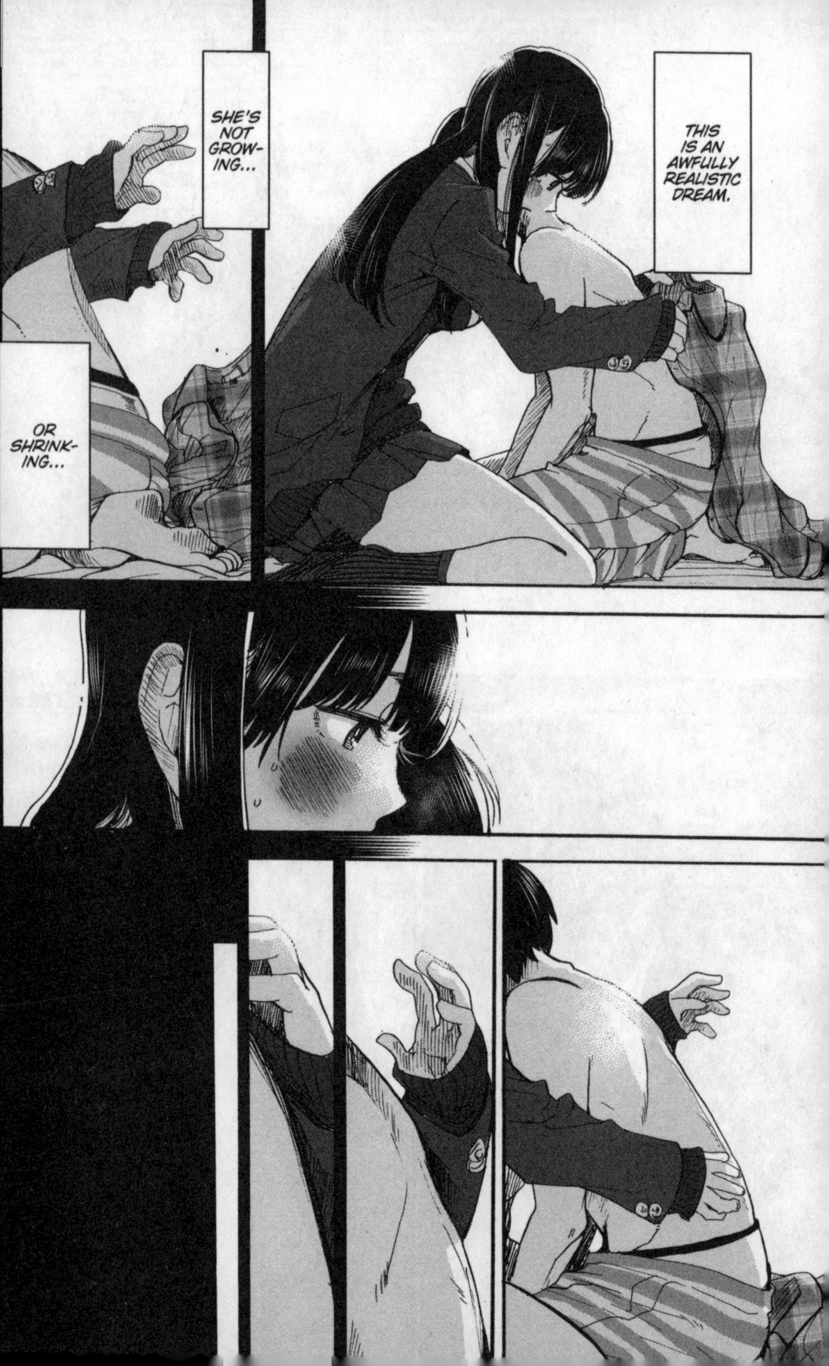
THIS IS AN AWFULLY REALISTIC DREAM.
SHE'S NOT GROWING...
OR SHRINKING...

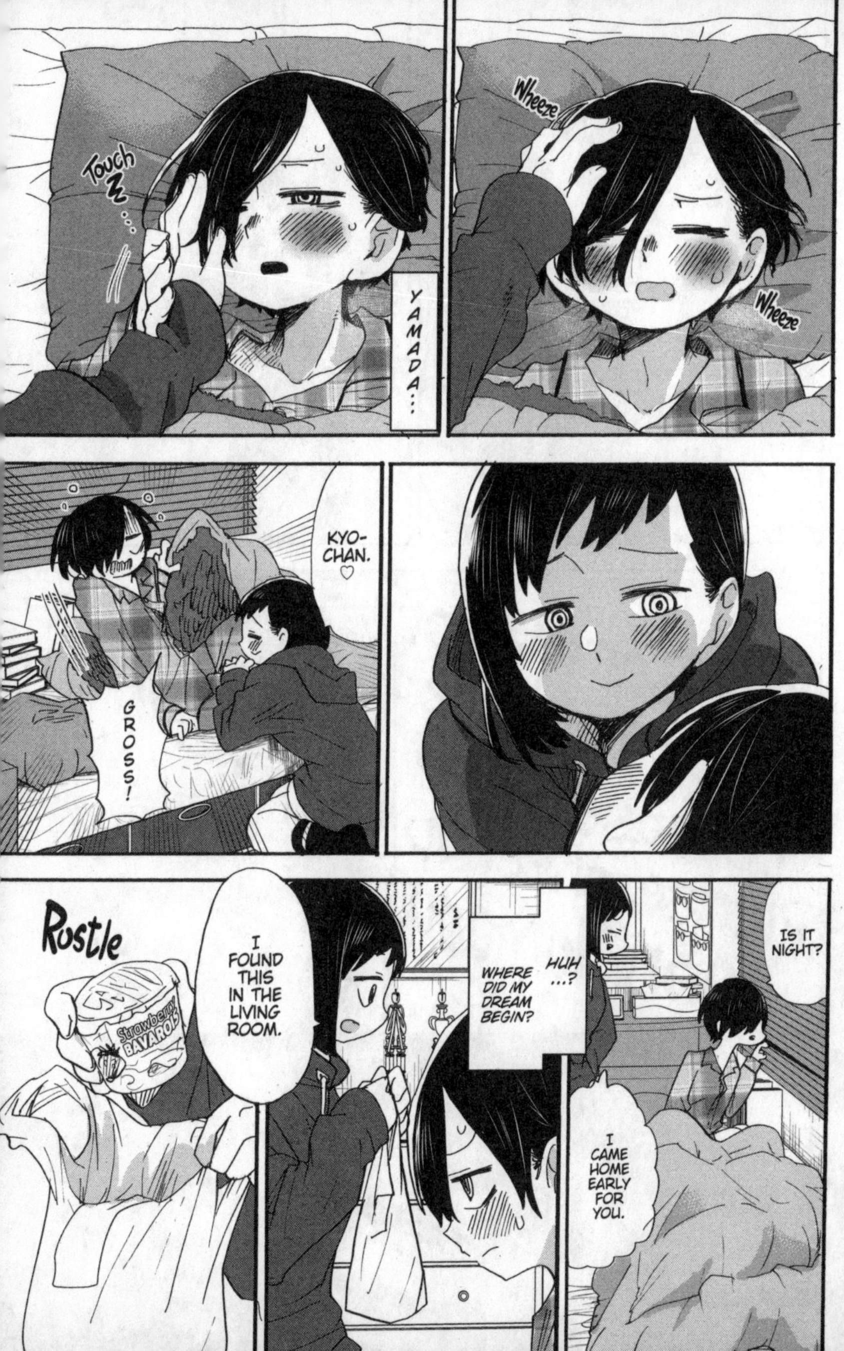
Wheeze
Wheeze
YAMADA...
Touch
KYO-CHAN. ♡
GROSS!
IS IT NIGHT?
HUH ...?
WHERE DID MY DREAM BEGIN?
I CAME HOME EARLY FOR YOU.
Rustle
I FOUND THIS IN THE LIVING ROOM.
Strawberry BAVAROIS

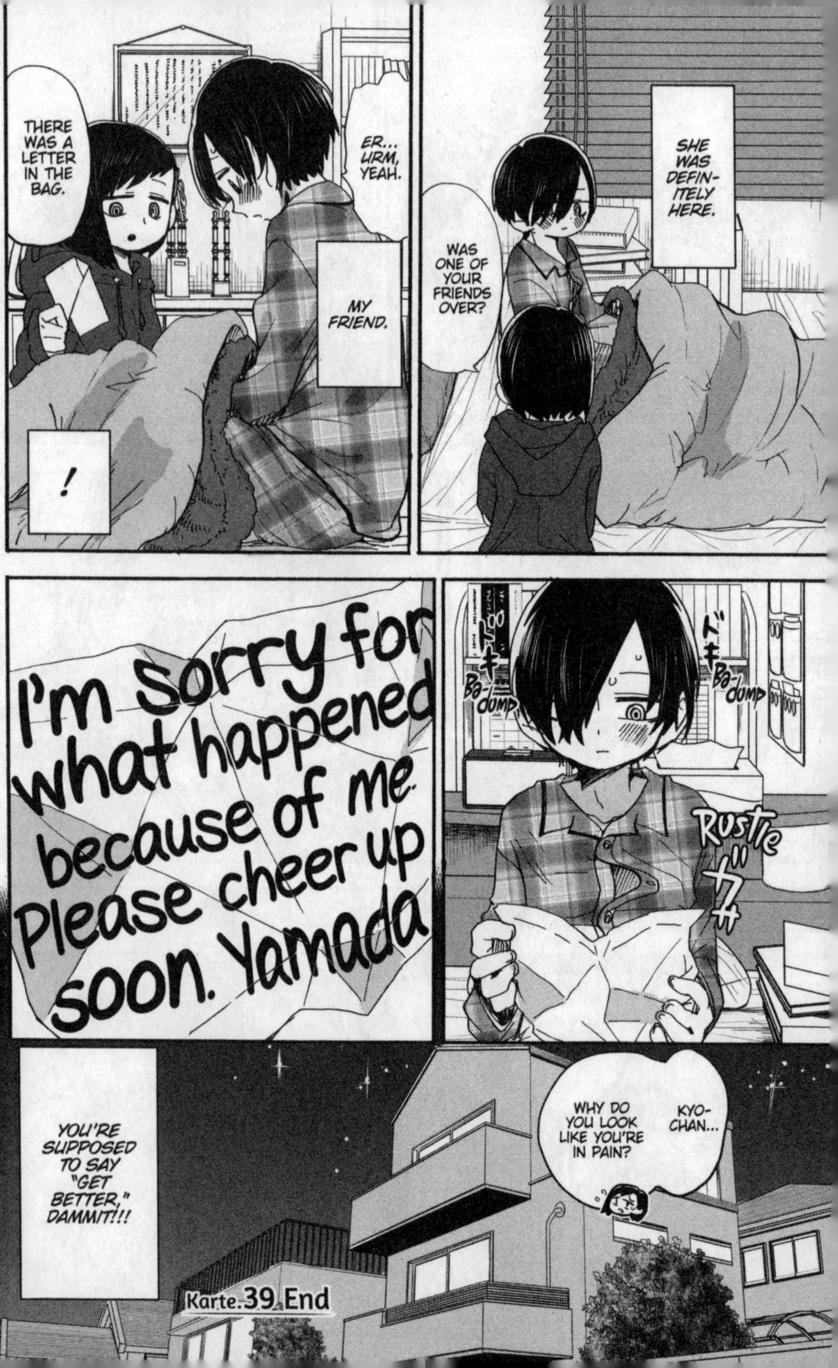
SHE WAS DEFINITELY HERE.
WAS ONE OF YOUR FRIENDS OVER?
ER... URM, YEAH.
MY FRIEND.
THERE WAS A LETTER IN THE BAG.
!
ドキ Ba-dump
ドキ Ba-dump
Rustle ガサ
I'm sorry for what happened because of me. Please cheer up soon. Yamada
KYO-CHAN...
WHY DO YOU LOOK LIKE YOU'RE IN PAIN?
YOU'RE SUPPOSED TO SAY "GET BETTER," DAMMIT!!!
Karte.39 End

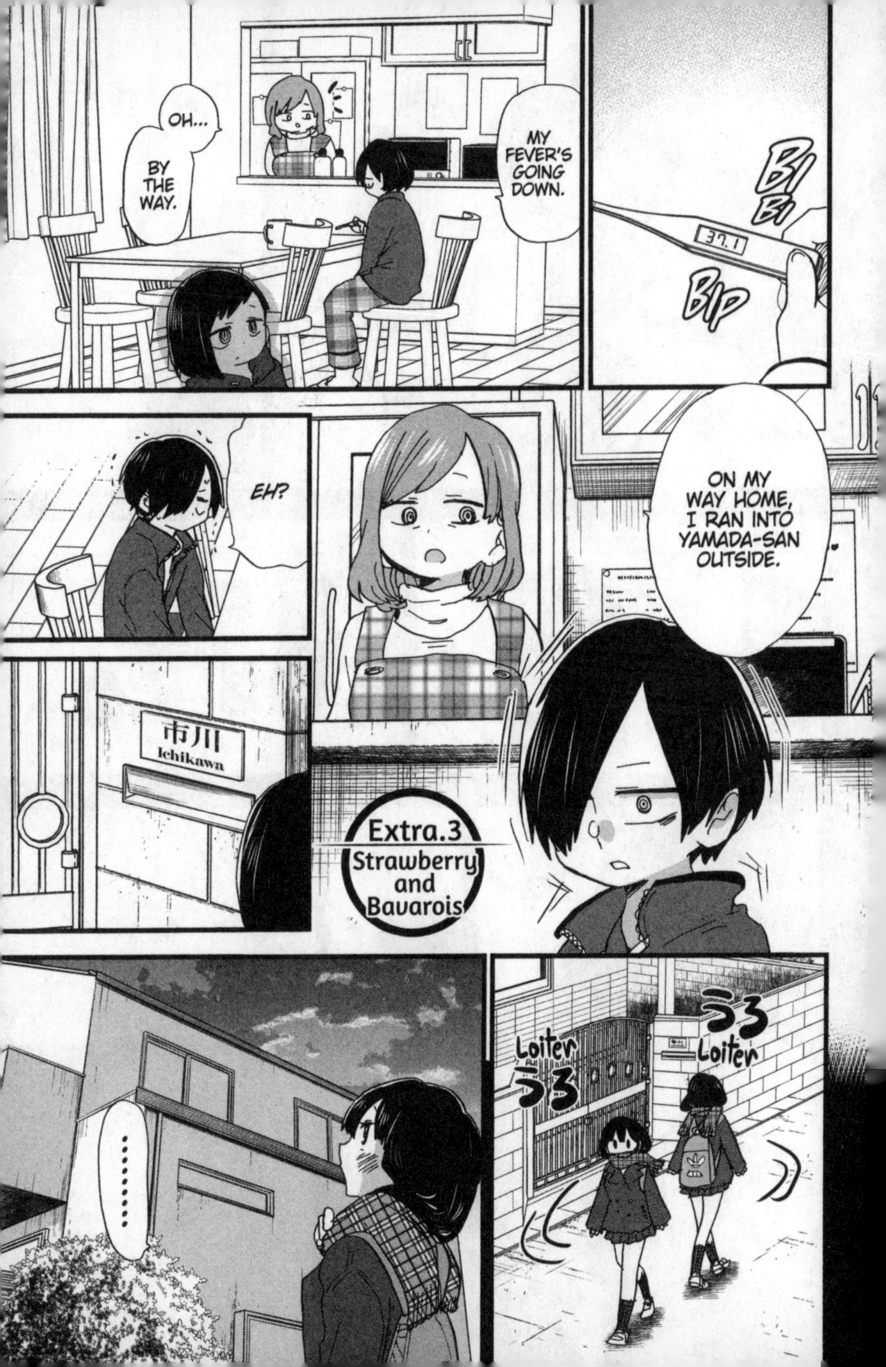
BI BI
37.1
BIP
MY FEVER'S GOING DOWN.
OH...
BY THE WAY.
ON MY WAY HOME, I RAN INTO YAMADA-SAN OUTSIDE.
EH?
市川
Ichikawa
Extra.3
Strawberry and Bavarois
うろ
Loiter
うろ
Loiter
....

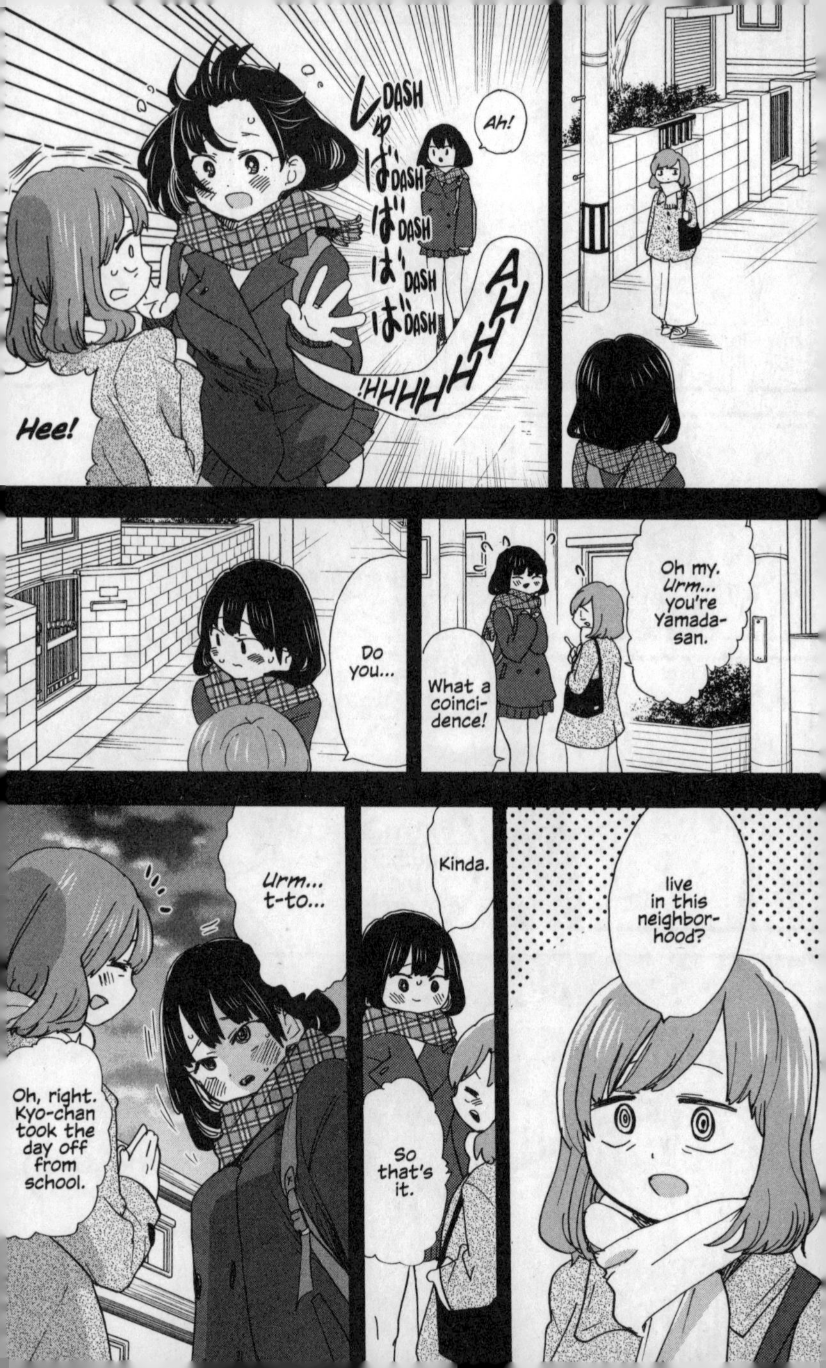
Ah!
しゅばばばば
DASH DASH DASH DASH DASH
AHHHHHHH!!
Hee!
Oh my. Urm... you're Yamada-san.
What a coincidence!
Do you...
live in this neighborhood?
Kinda.
So that's it.
Urm... t-to...
Oh, right. Kyo-chan took the day off from school.

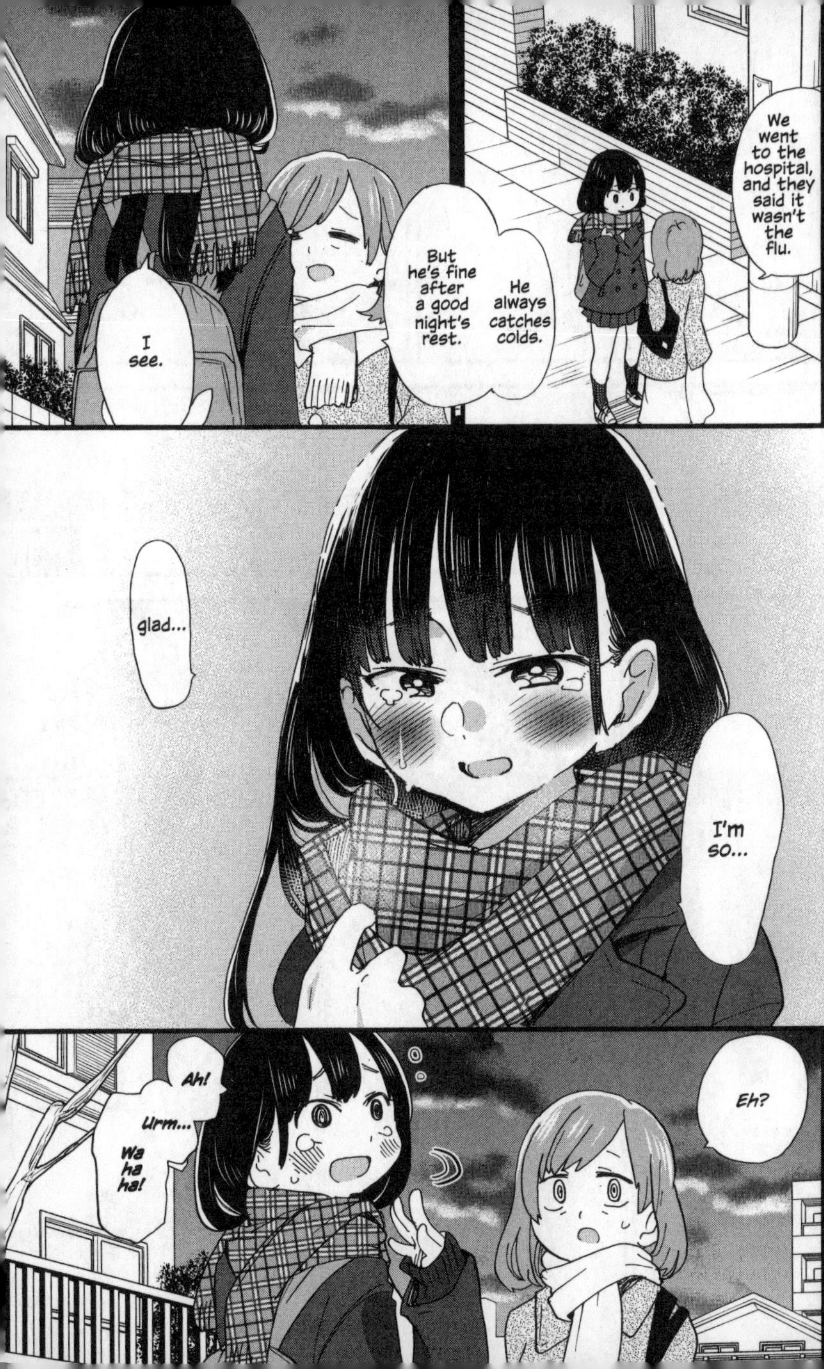
We went to the hospital, and they said it wasn't the flu.
He always catches colds.
But he's fine after a good night's rest.
I see.
I'm so...
glad...
Eh?
Ah!
Urm...
Wa ha ha!

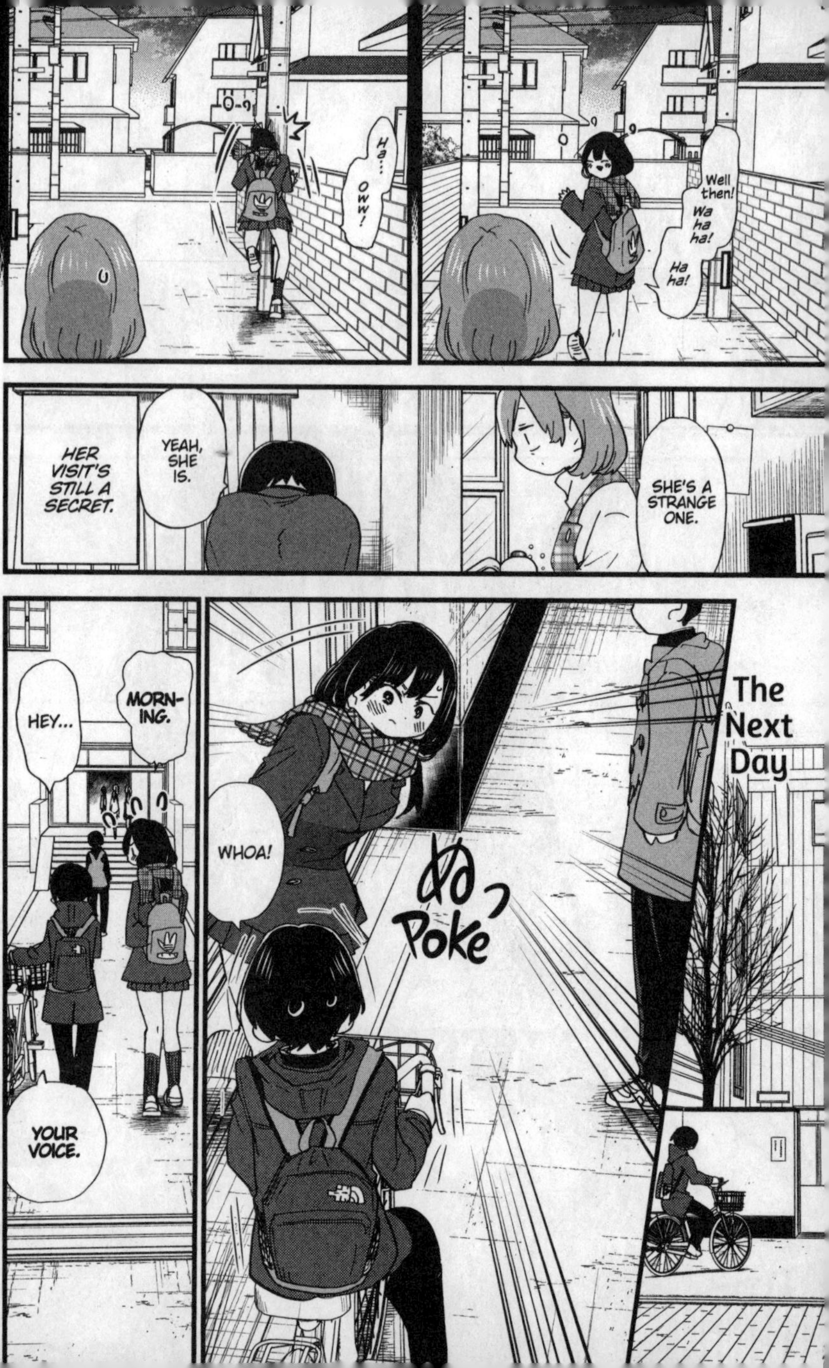
Well then!
Wa ha ha!
Ha ha!
Ha... Oww!
SHE'S A STRANGE ONE.
YEAH, SHE IS.
HER VISIT'S STILL A SECRET.
The Next Day
ぬっ
Poke
WHOA!
MORNING.
HEY...
YOUR VOICE.

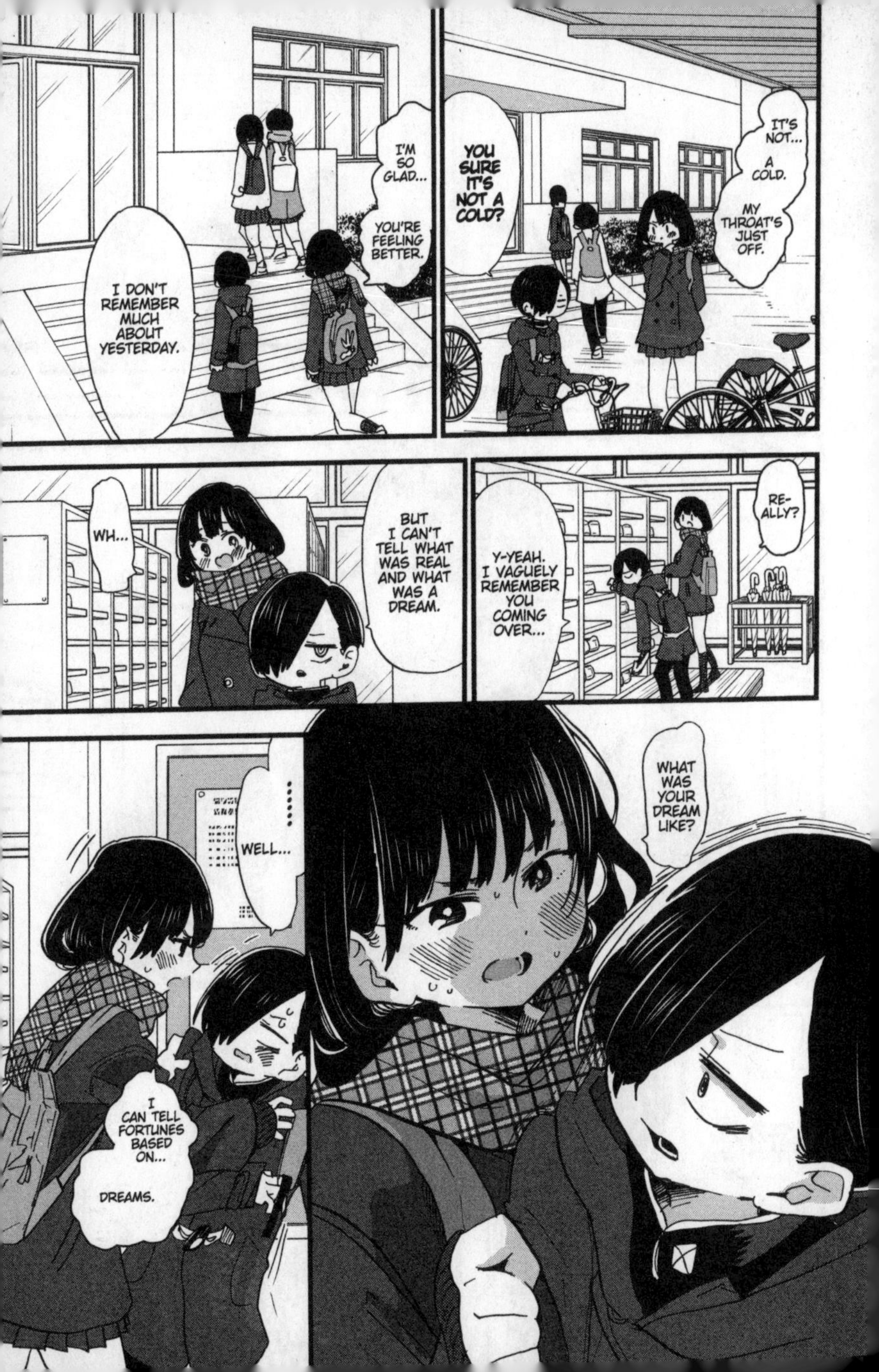
IT'S NOT... A COLD. MY THROAT'S JUST OFF.
YOU SURE IT'S NOT A COLD?
I'M SO GLAD... YOU'RE FEELING BETTER.
I DON'T REMEMBER MUCH ABOUT YESTERDAY.
RE-ALLY?
Y-YEAH. I VAGUELY REMEMBER YOU COMING OVER...
BUT I CAN'T TELL WHAT WAS REAL AND WHAT WAS A DREAM.
WH...
WHAT WAS YOUR DREAM LIKE?
WELL...
I CAN TELL FORTUNES BASED ON... DREAMS.

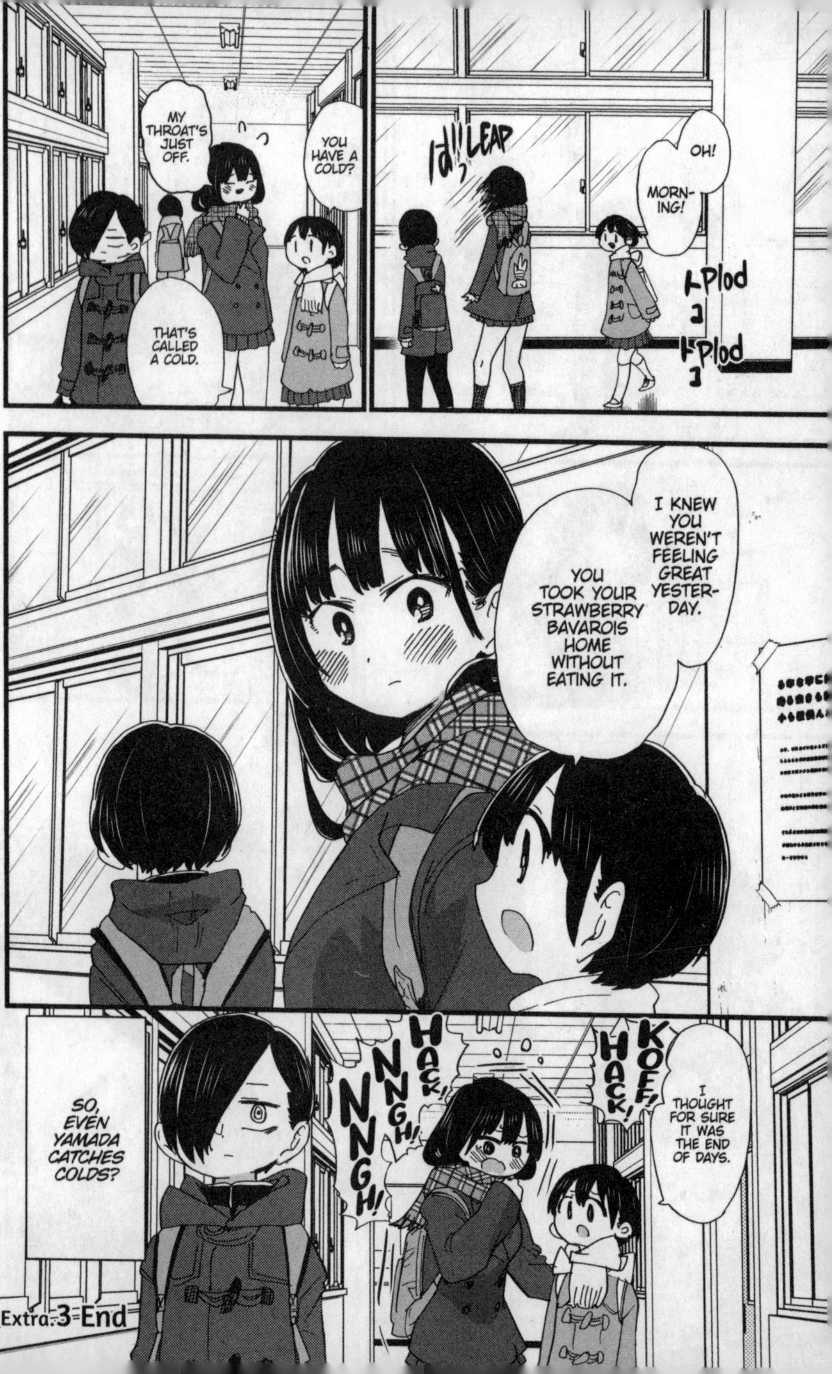
OH!
MORNING!
LEAP
Plod
Plod
YOU HAVE A COLD?
MY THROAT'S JUST OFF.
THAT'S CALLED A COLD.
I KNEW YOU WEREN'T FEELING GREAT YESTER-DAY.
YOU TOOK YOUR STRAWBERRY BAVAROIS HOME WITHOUT EATING IT.
I THOUGHT FOR SURE IT WAS THE END OF DAYS.
KOFF!
HACK!
HACK!
NNGH!
NNNGH!
SO, EVEN YAMADA CATCHES COLDS?
Extra.3 End

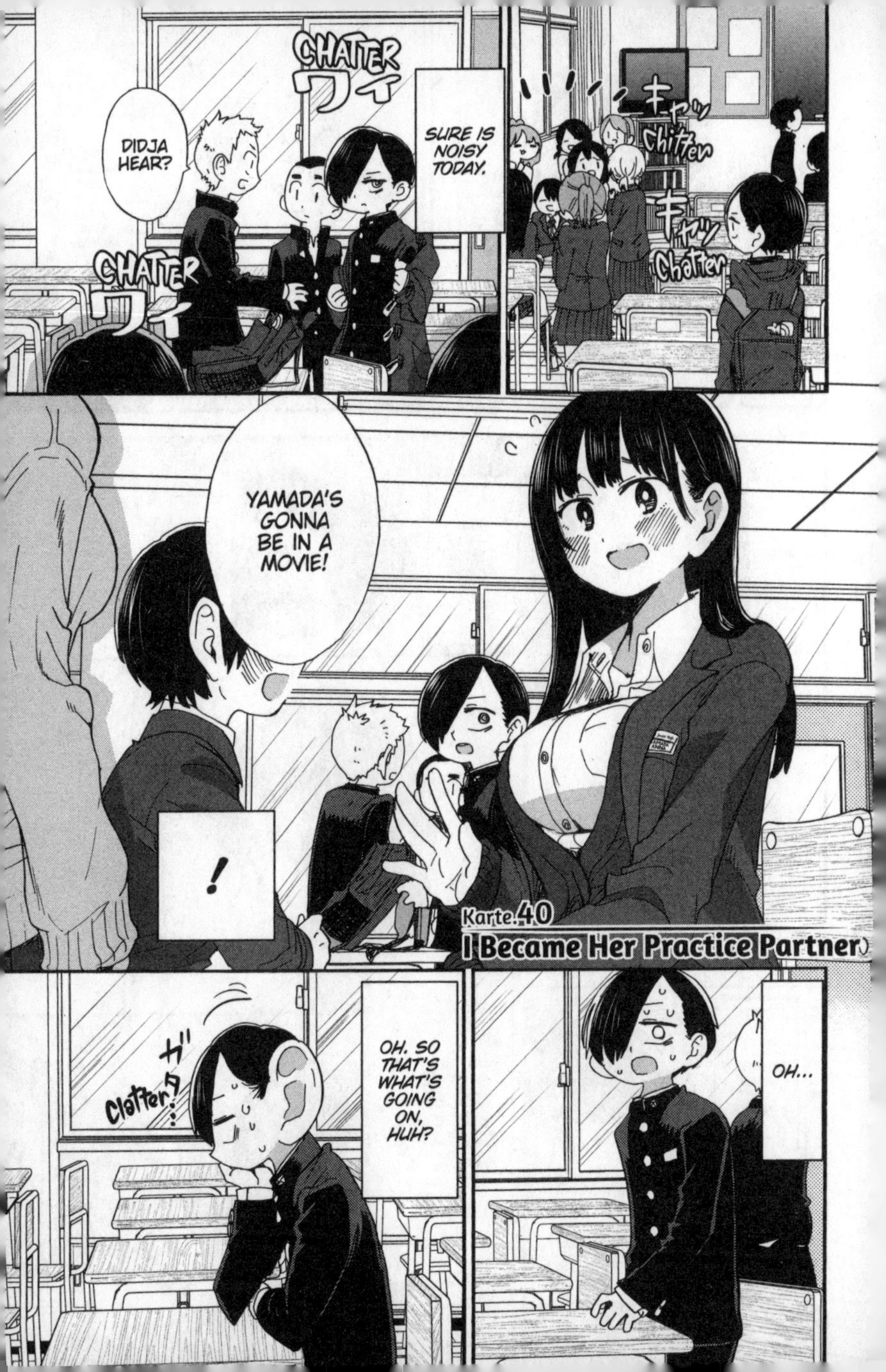
キャッ Chitter
キャッ Chatter
SURE IS NOISY TODAY.
CHATTER ワイ
DIDJA HEAR?
CHATTER ワイ
YAMADA'S GONNA BE IN A MOVIE!
!
Karte.40
I Became Her Practice Partner
OH...
OH. SO THAT'S WHAT'S GOING ON, HUH?
ガタ Clatter...

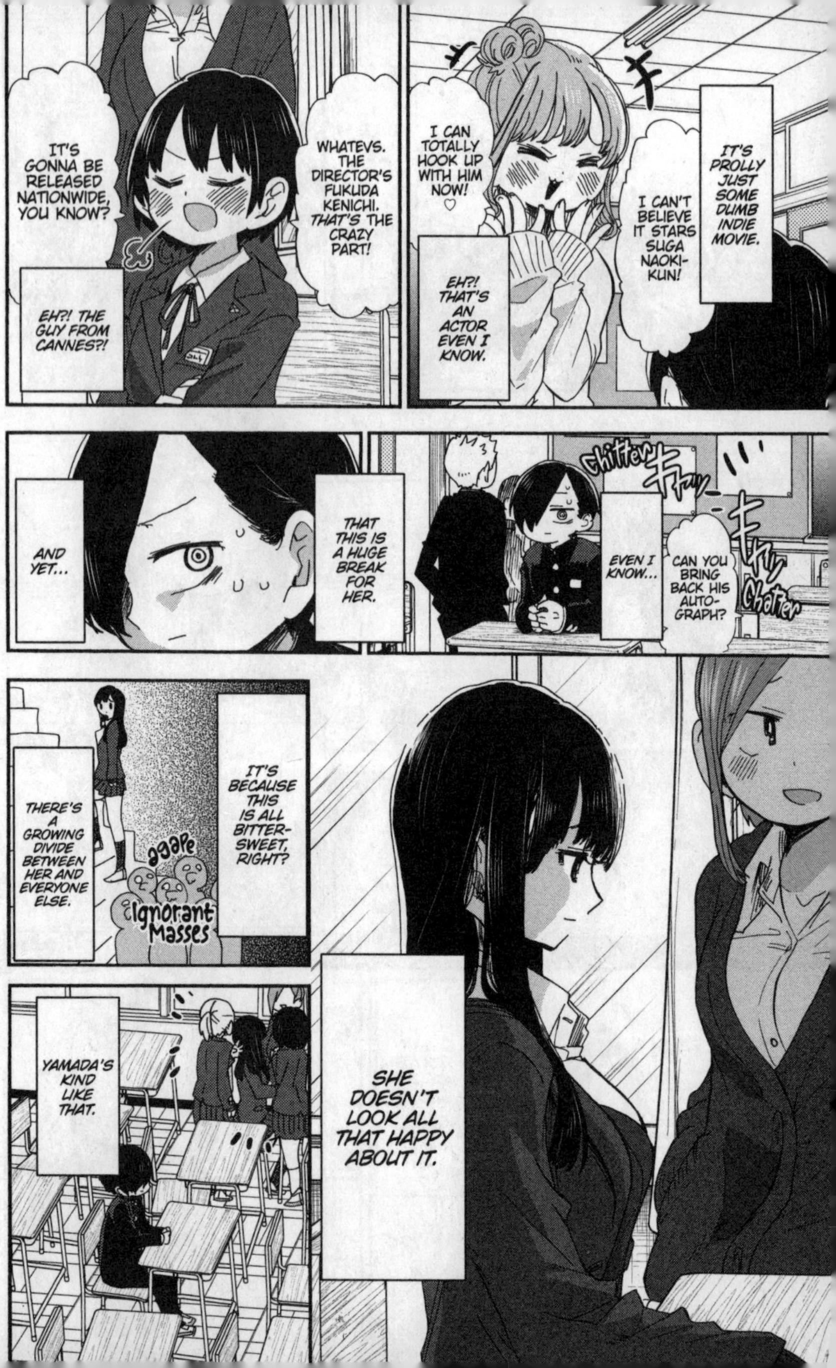
IT'S PROLLY JUST SOME DUMB INDIE MOVIE.
I CAN'T BELIEVE IT STARS SUGA NAOKI-KUN!
I CAN TOTALLY HOOK UP WITH HIM NOW! ♡
EH?! THAT'S AN ACTOR EVEN I KNOW.
WHATEVS. THE DIRECTOR'S FUKUDA KENICHI. THAT'S THE CRAZY PART!
IT'S GONNA BE RELEASED NATIONWIDE, YOU KNOW?
EH?! THE GUY FROM CANNES?!
Chitter
CAN YOU BRING BACK HIS AUTO-GRAPH?
EVEN I KNOW...
Chatter
THAT THIS IS A HUGE BREAK FOR HER.
AND YET...
SHE DOESN'T LOOK ALL THAT HAPPY ABOUT IT.
IT'S BECAUSE THIS IS ALL BITTER-SWEET, RIGHT?
THERE'S A GROWING DIVIDE BETWEEN HER AND EVERYONE ELSE.
agape
Ignorant Masses
YAMADA'S KIND LIKE THAT.

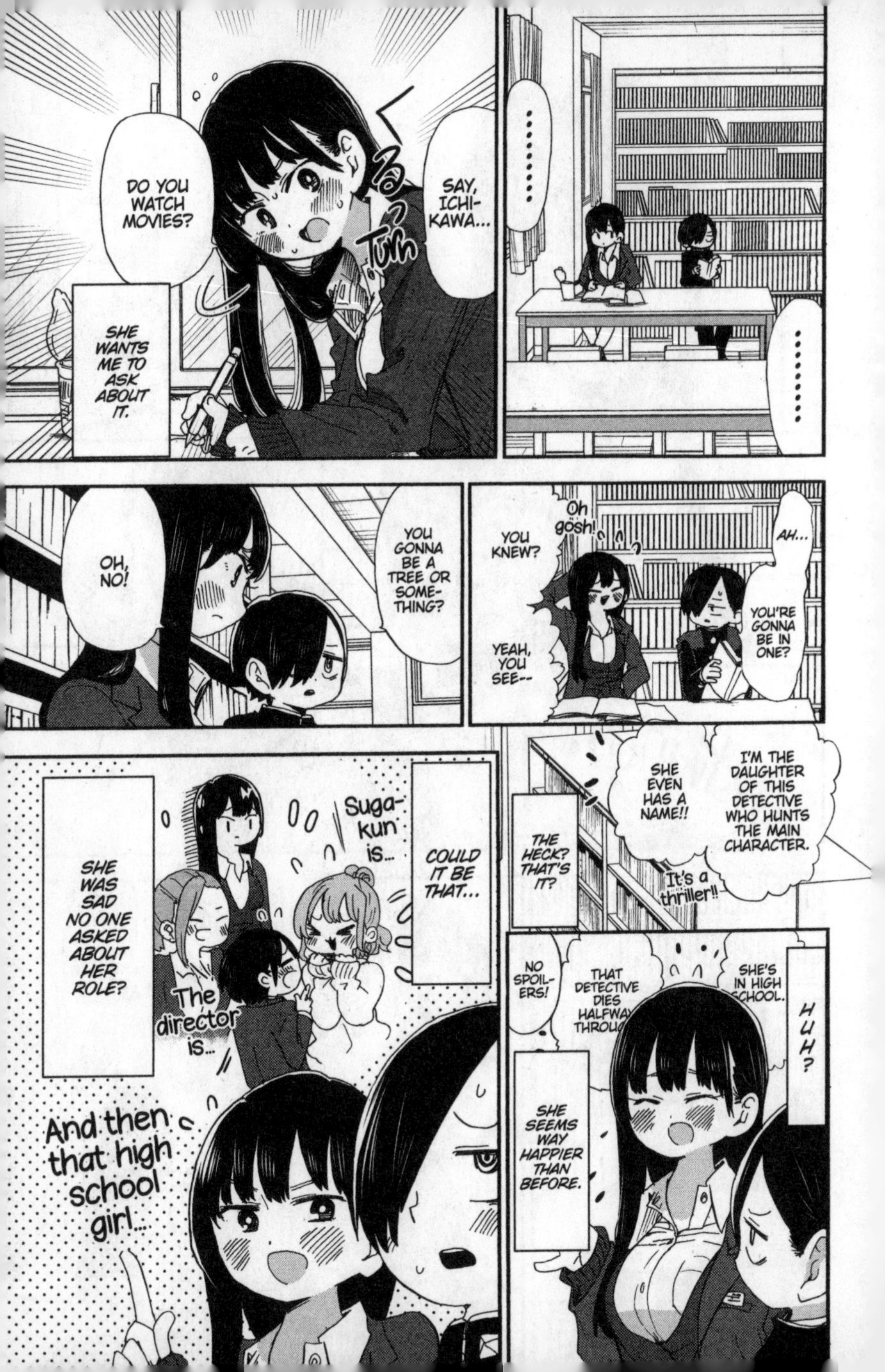
......
......
SAY, ICHI-KAWA...
Turn
DO YOU WATCH MOVIES?
SHE WANTS ME TO ASK ABOUT IT.
AH... YOU'RE GONNA BE IN ONE?
YOU KNEW?
Oh gosh!
YEAH, YOU SEE--
YOU GONNA BE A TREE OR SOME-THING?
OH, NO!
I'M THE DAUGHTER OF THIS DETECTIVE WHO HUNTS THE MAIN CHARACTER.
It's a thriller!!
SHE EVEN HAS A NAME!!
THE HECK? THAT'S IT?
HUH?
SHE'S IN HIGH SCHOOL.
THAT DETECTIVE DIES HALFWAY THROUG
NO SPOIL-ERS!
SHE SEEMS WAY HAPPIER THAN BEFORE.
COULD IT BE THAT...
Suga-kun is...
The director is...
SHE WAS SAD NO ONE ASKED ABOUT HER ROLE?
And then that high school girl...

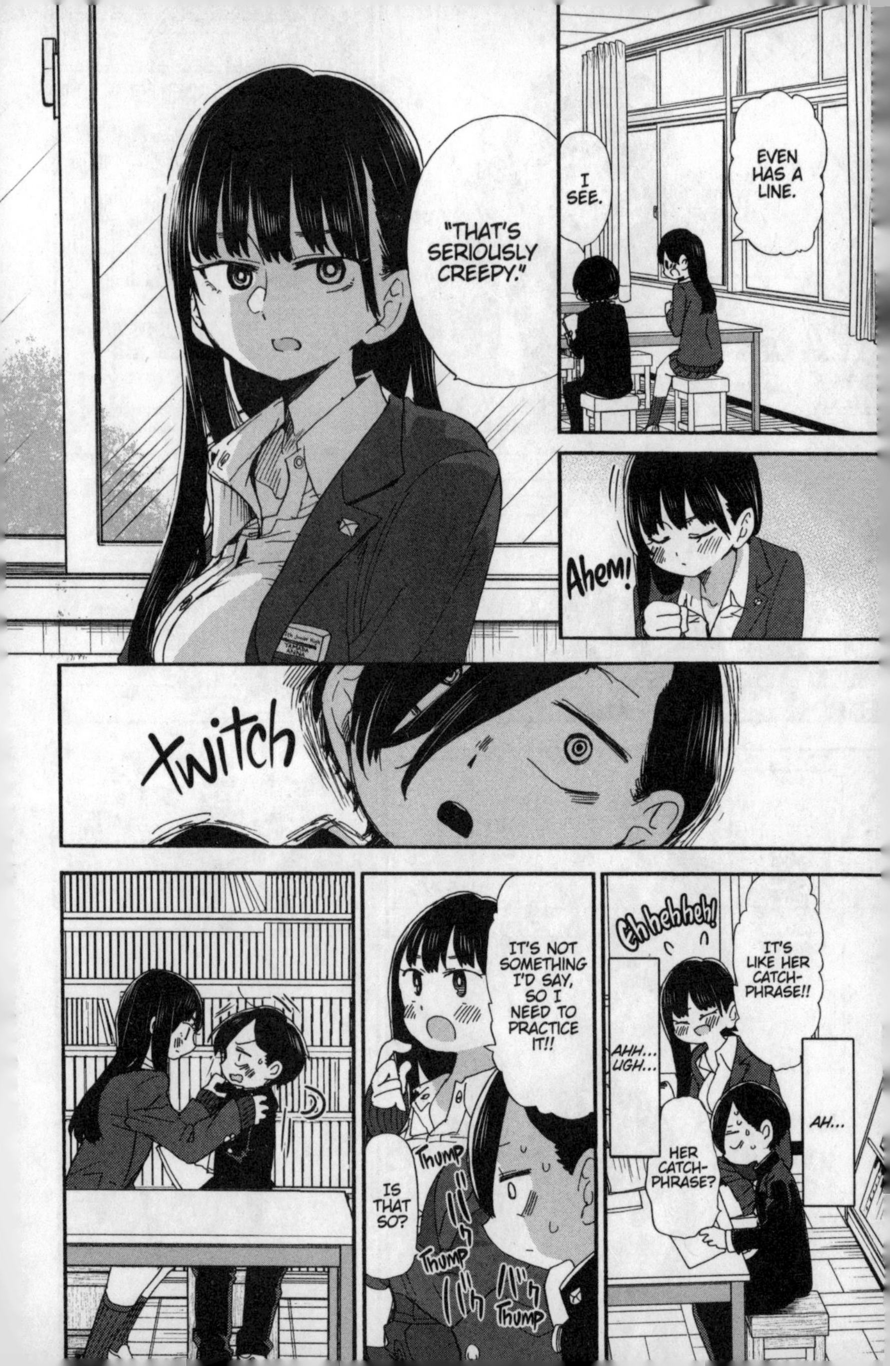
EVEN HAS A LINE.
I SEE.
Ahem!
"THAT'S SERIOUSLY CREEPY."
twitch
Ehhehheh!
IT'S LIKE HER CATCH-PHRASE!!
AHH... UGH...
AH...
HER CATCH-PHRASE?
IT'S NOT SOMETHING I'D SAY, SO I NEED TO PRACTICE IT!!
Thump
IS THAT SO?
Thump
Thump

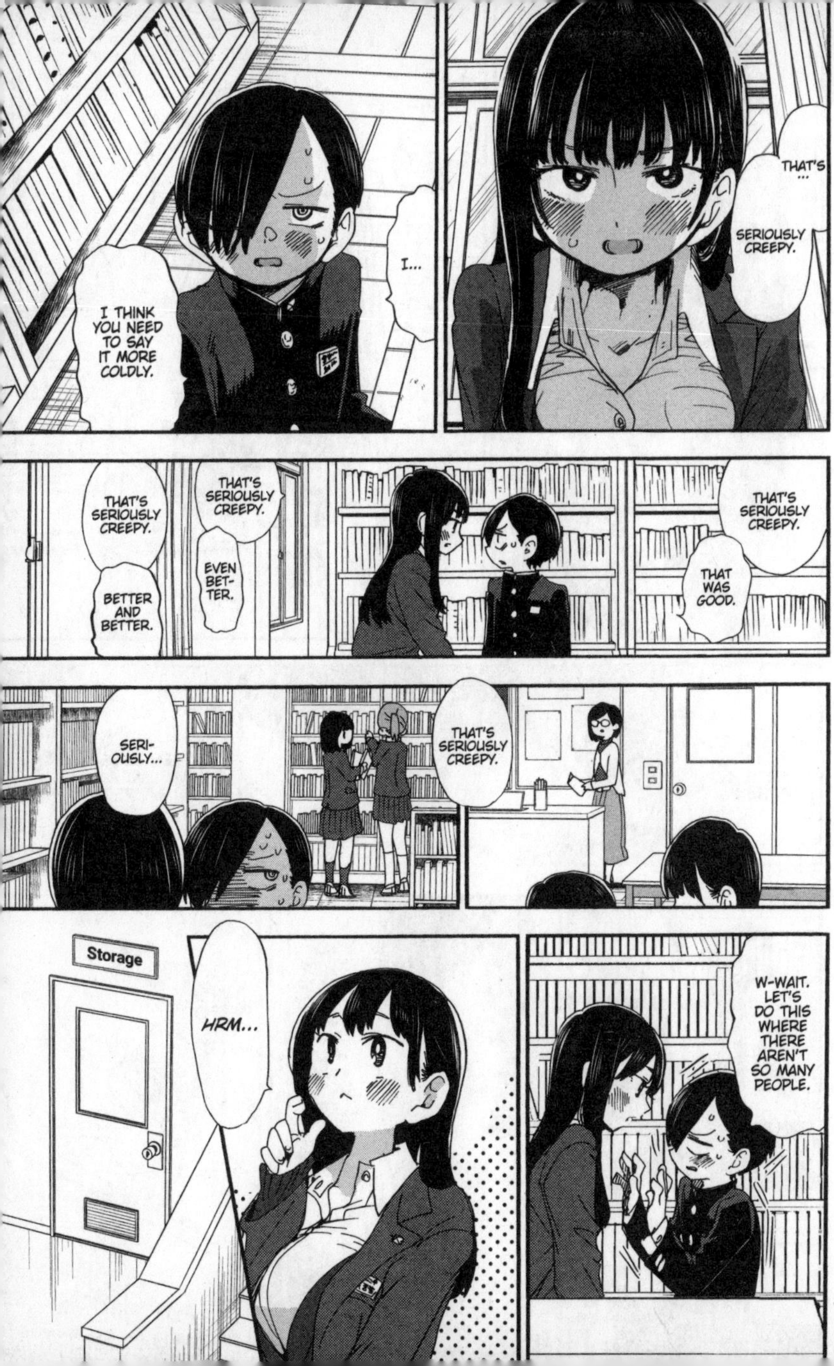
THAT'S ...
SERIOUSLY CREEPY.
I...
I THINK YOU NEED TO SAY IT MORE COLDLY.
THAT'S SERIOUSLY CREEPY.
THAT WAS GOOD.
THAT'S SERIOUSLY CREEPY.
EVEN BET-TER.
THAT'S SERIOUSLY CREEPY.
BETTER AND BETTER.
THAT'S SERIOUSLY CREEPY.
SERI-OUSLY...
W-WAIT. LET'S DO THIS WHERE THERE AREN'T SO MANY PEOPLE.
HRM...
Storage

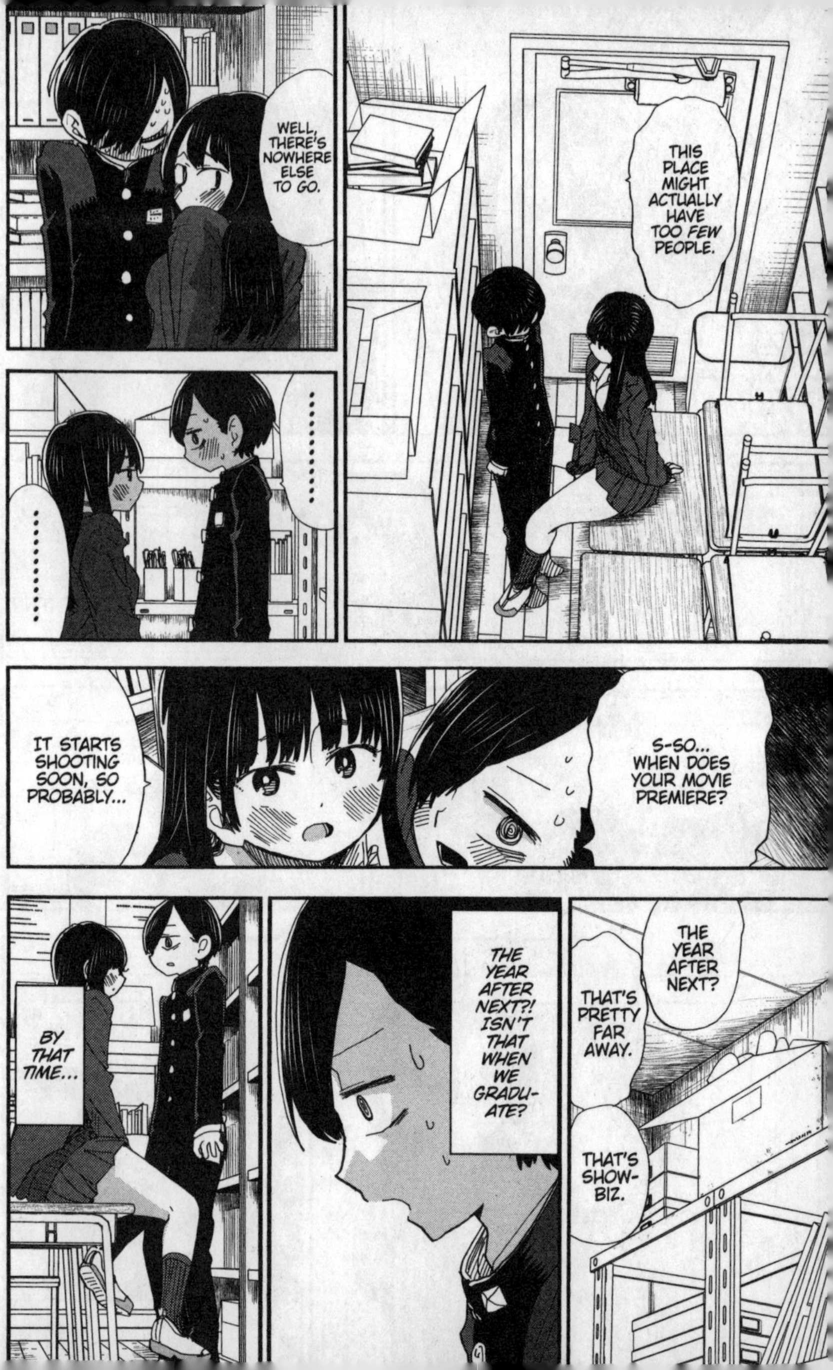
THIS PLACE MIGHT ACTUALLY HAVE TOO FEW PEOPLE.
WELL, THERE'S NOWHERE ELSE TO GO.
......
......
S-SO... WHEN DOES YOUR MOVIE PREMIERE?
IT STARTS SHOOTING SOON, SO PROBABLY...
THE YEAR AFTER NEXT?
THAT'S PRETTY FAR AWAY.
THAT'S SHOW-BIZ.
THE YEAR AFTER NEXT?! ISN'T THAT WHEN WE GRADUATE?
BY THAT TIME...

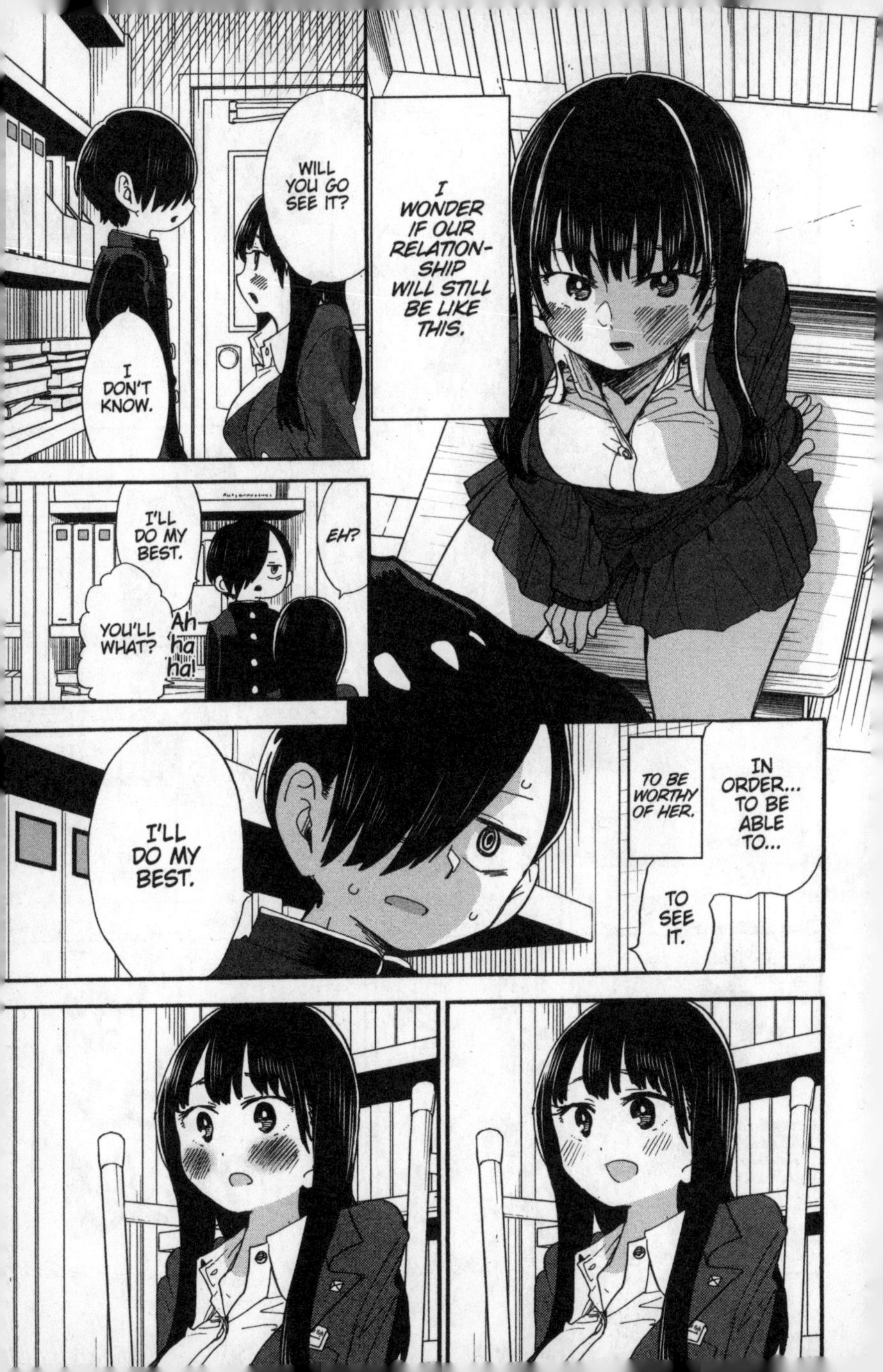
I WONDER IF OUR RELATIONSHIP WILL STILL BE LIKE THIS.
WILL YOU GO SEE IT?
I DON'T KNOW.
EH?
I'LL DO MY BEST.
Ah ha ha!
YOU'LL WHAT?
IN ORDER... TO BE ABLE TO...
TO BE WORTHY OF HER.
TO SEE IT.
I'LL DO MY BEST.

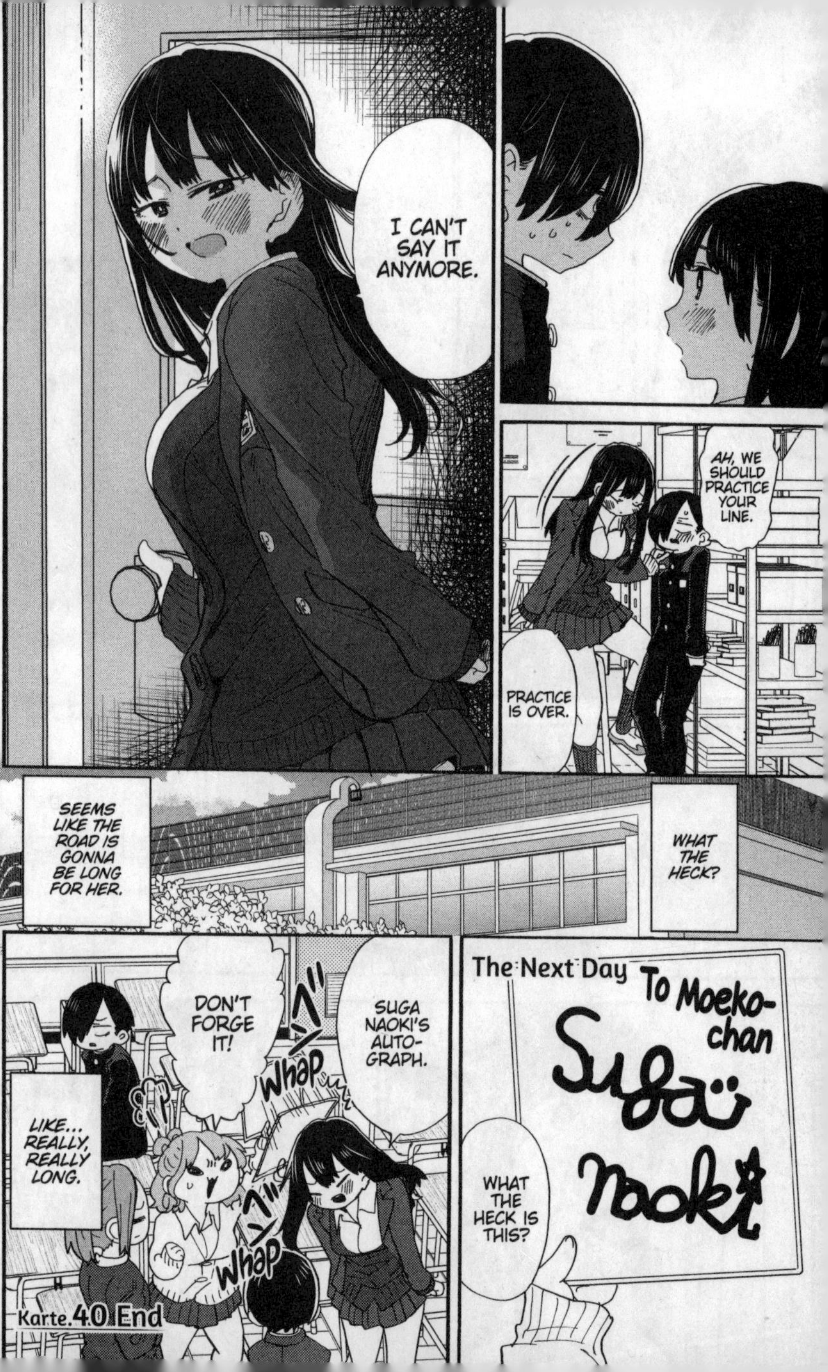
AH, WE SHOULD PRACTICE YOUR LINE.
PRACTICE IS OVER.
I CAN'T SAY IT ANYMORE.
WHAT THE HECK?
SEEMS LIKE THE ROAD IS GONNA BE LONG FOR HER.
The Next Day
To Moeko-chan
Suga naoki
WHAT THE HECK IS THIS?
SUGA NAOKI'S AUTO-GRAPH.
DON'T FORGE IT!
Whap
Whap
LIKE... REALLY, REALLY LONG.
Karte.40 End

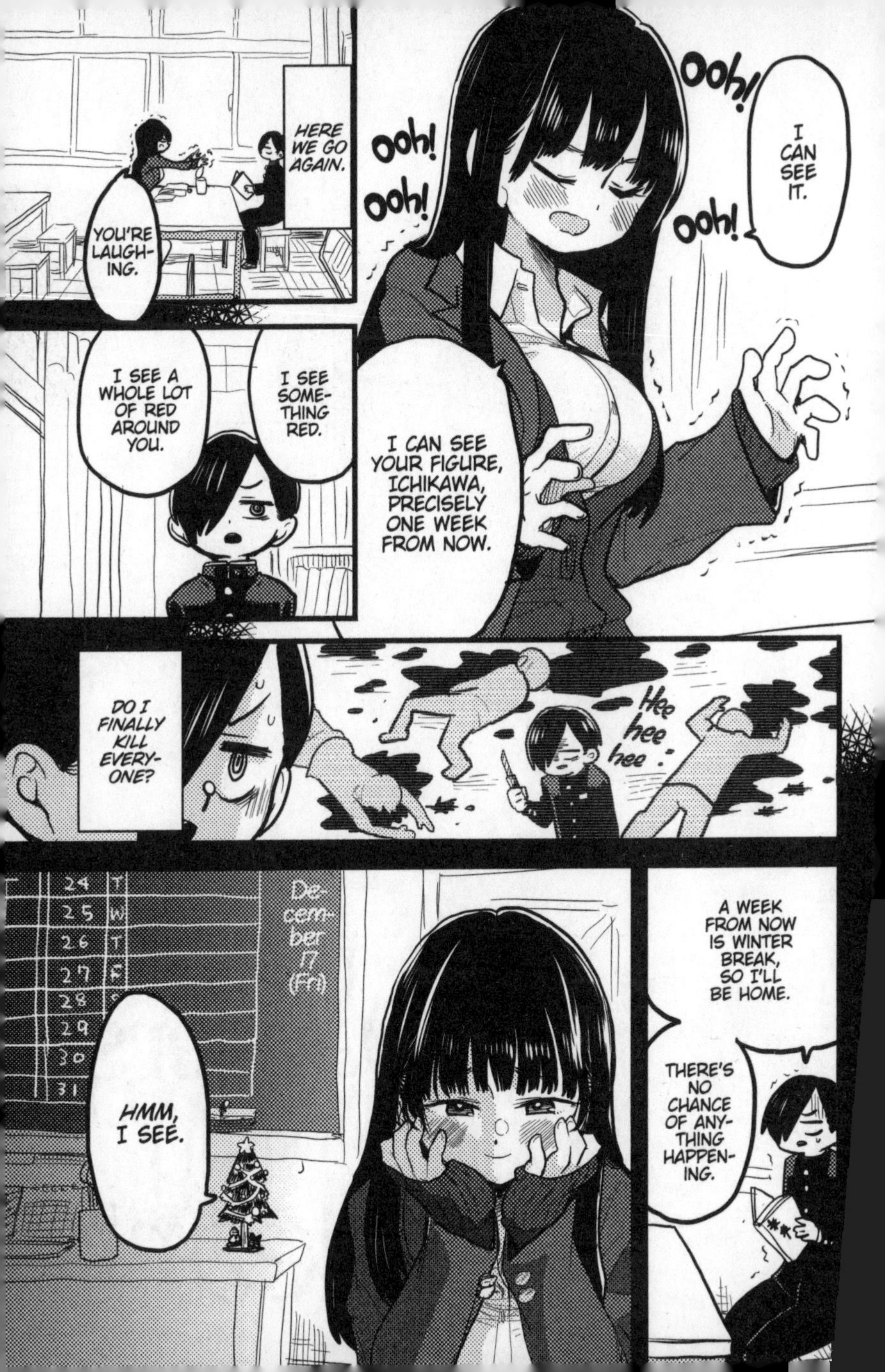
Ooh!
I CAN SEE IT.
Ooh!
Ooh!
Ooh!
I CAN SEE YOUR FIGURE, ICHIKAWA, PRECISELY ONE WEEK FROM NOW.
HERE WE GO AGAIN.
YOU'RE LAUGHING.
I SEE SOMETHING RED.
I SEE A WHOLE LOT OF RED AROUND YOU.
Hee hee hee
DO I FINALLY KILL EVERYONE?
A WEEK FROM NOW IS WINTER BREAK, SO I'LL BE HOME.
THERE'S NO CHANCE OF ANYTHING HAPPENING.
December 17 (Fri)
24 T
25 W
26 T
27 F
28
29
30
31
HMM, I SEE.

The
Dangers
in My
Heart

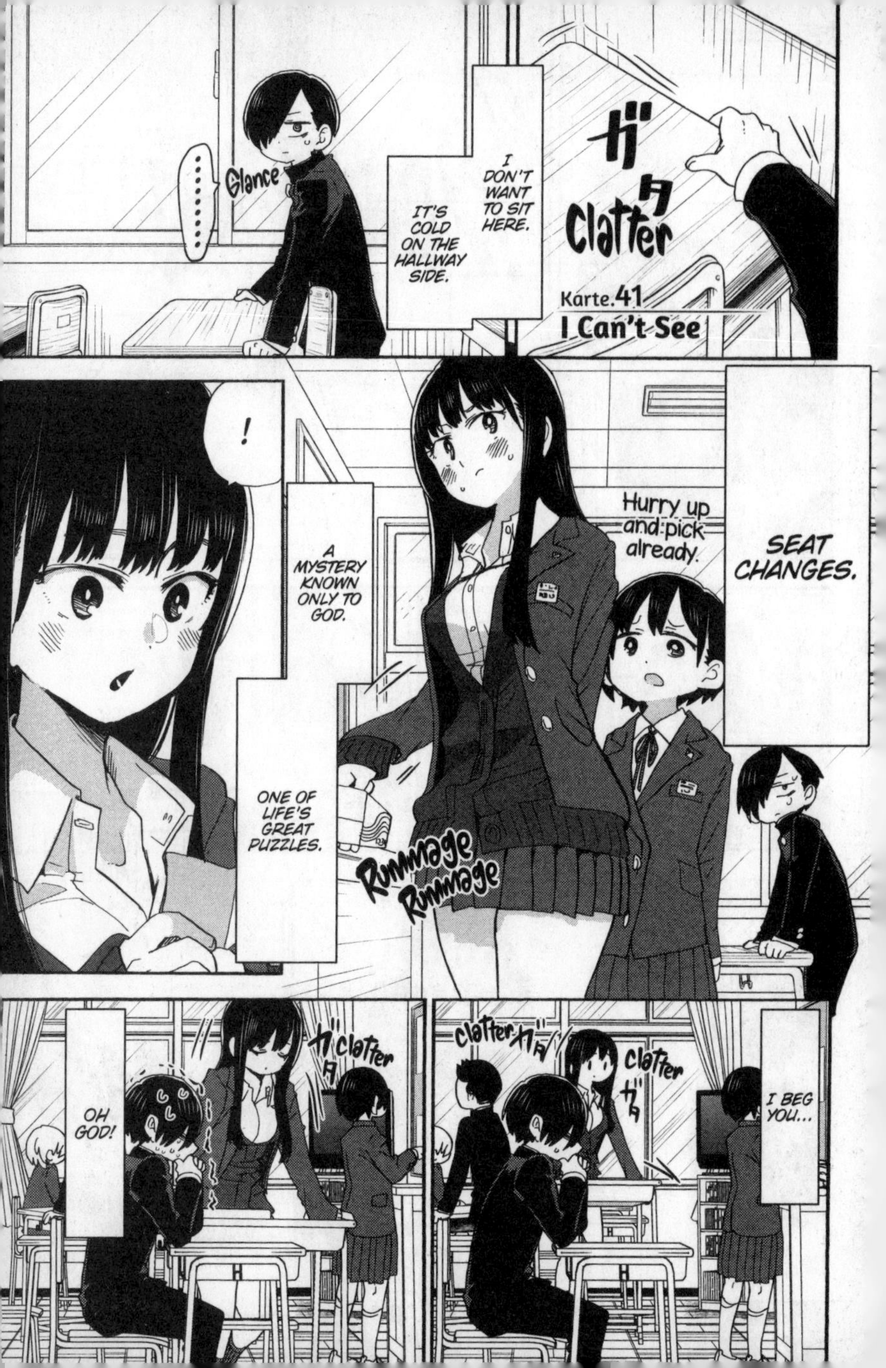
ガタ
Clatter
Karte.41
I Can't See
I DON'T WANT TO SIT HERE.
IT'S COLD ON THE HALLWAY SIDE.
Glance
……
SEAT CHANGES.
Hurry up and pick already.
A MYSTERY KNOWN ONLY TO GOD.
ONE OF LIFE'S GREAT PUZZLES.
Rummage Rummage
!
I BEG YOU...
Clatter ガタ
clatter ガタ
ガタ clatter
OH GOD!

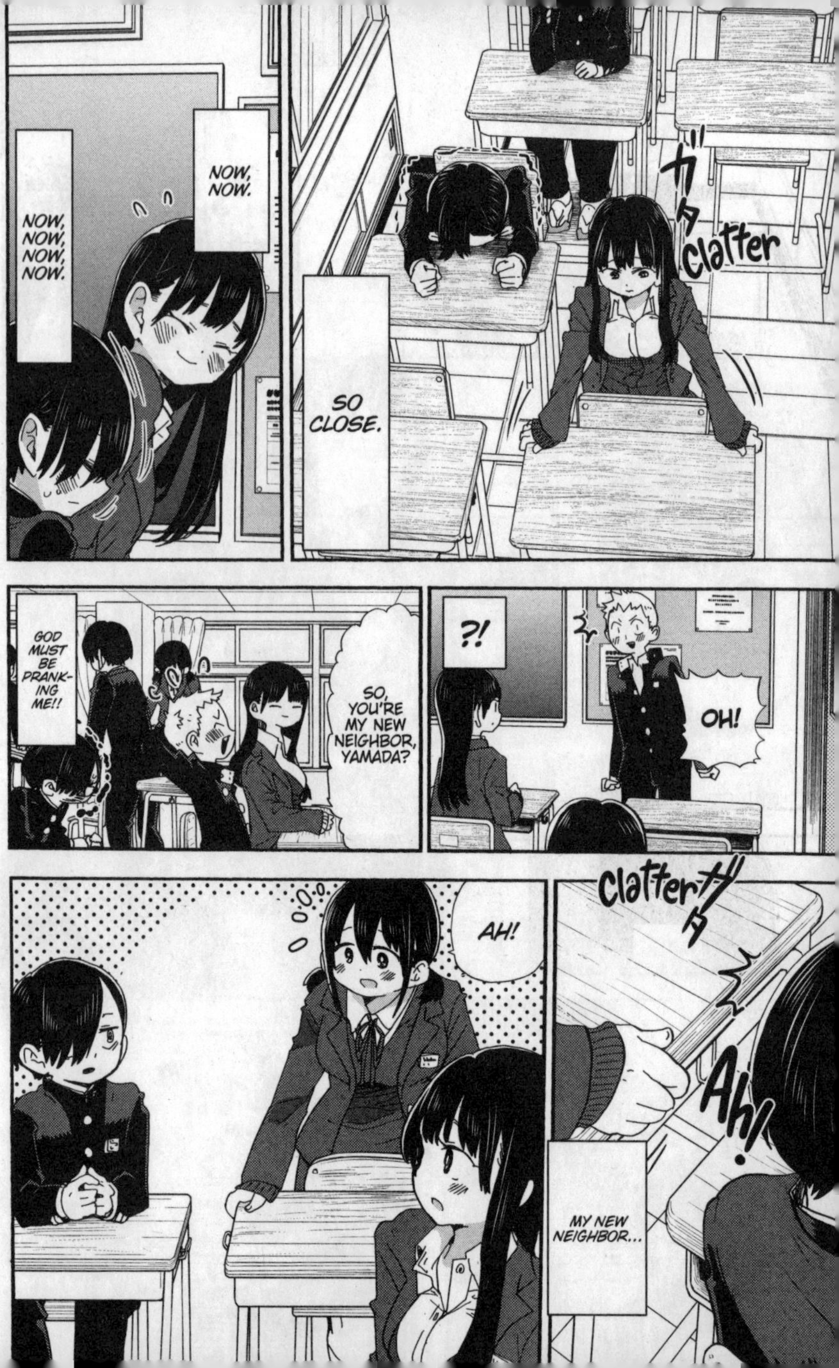
ガタ
Clatter
SO CLOSE.
NOW, NOW.
NOW, NOW, NOW, NOW.
?!
OH!
SO, YOU'RE MY NEW NEIGHBOR, YAMADA?
GOD MUST BE PRANKING ME!!
Clatter ガタ
Ah!
MY NEW NEIGHBOR...
AH!

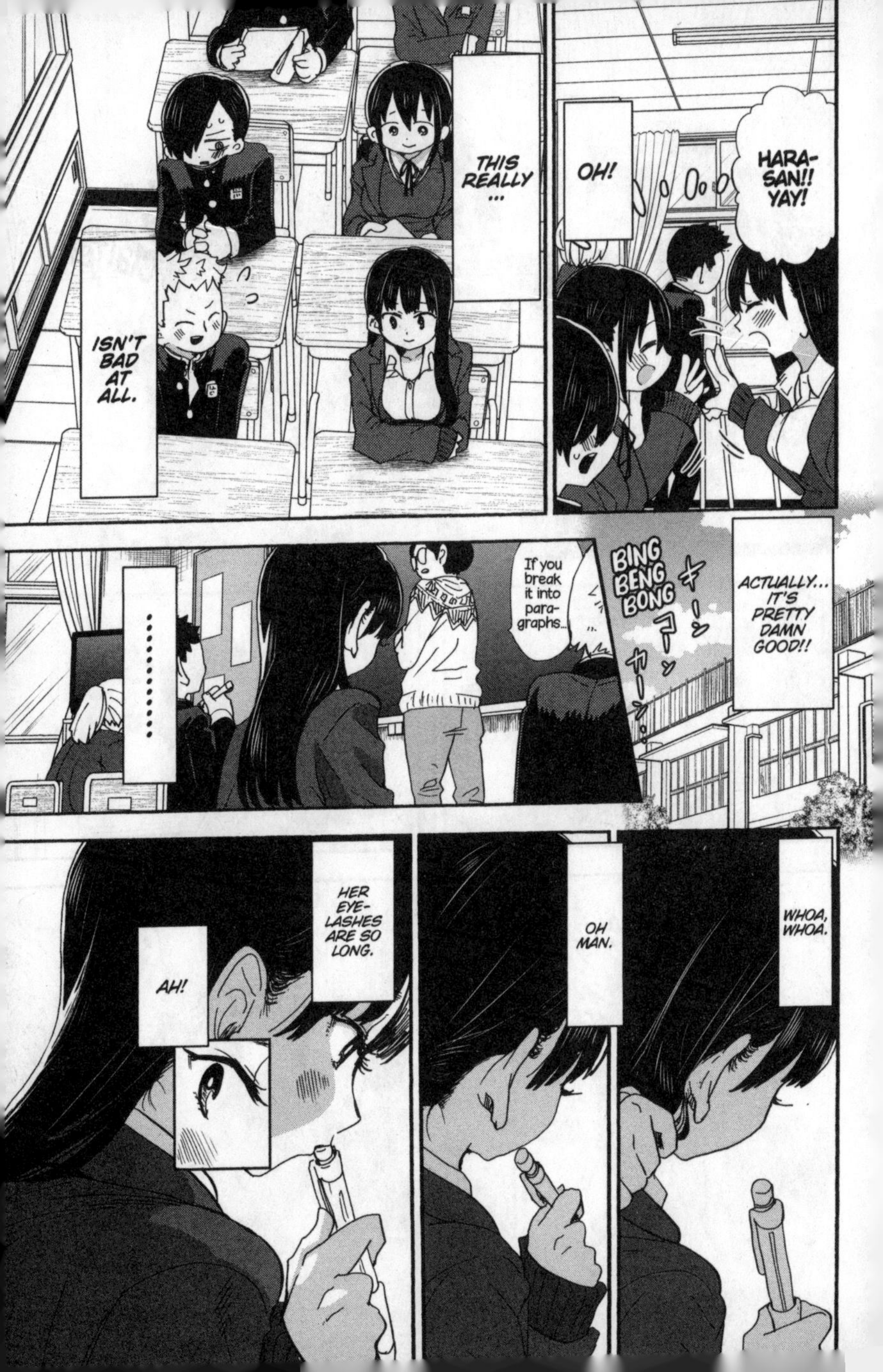

HARA-SAN!! YAY!
OH!
THIS REALLY ...
ISN'T BAD AT ALL.
ACTUALLY... IT'S PRETTY DAMN GOOD!!
BING BENG BONG
If you break it into paragraphs...
....
WHOA, WHOA.
OH MAN.
HER EYE-LASHES ARE SO LONG.
AH!

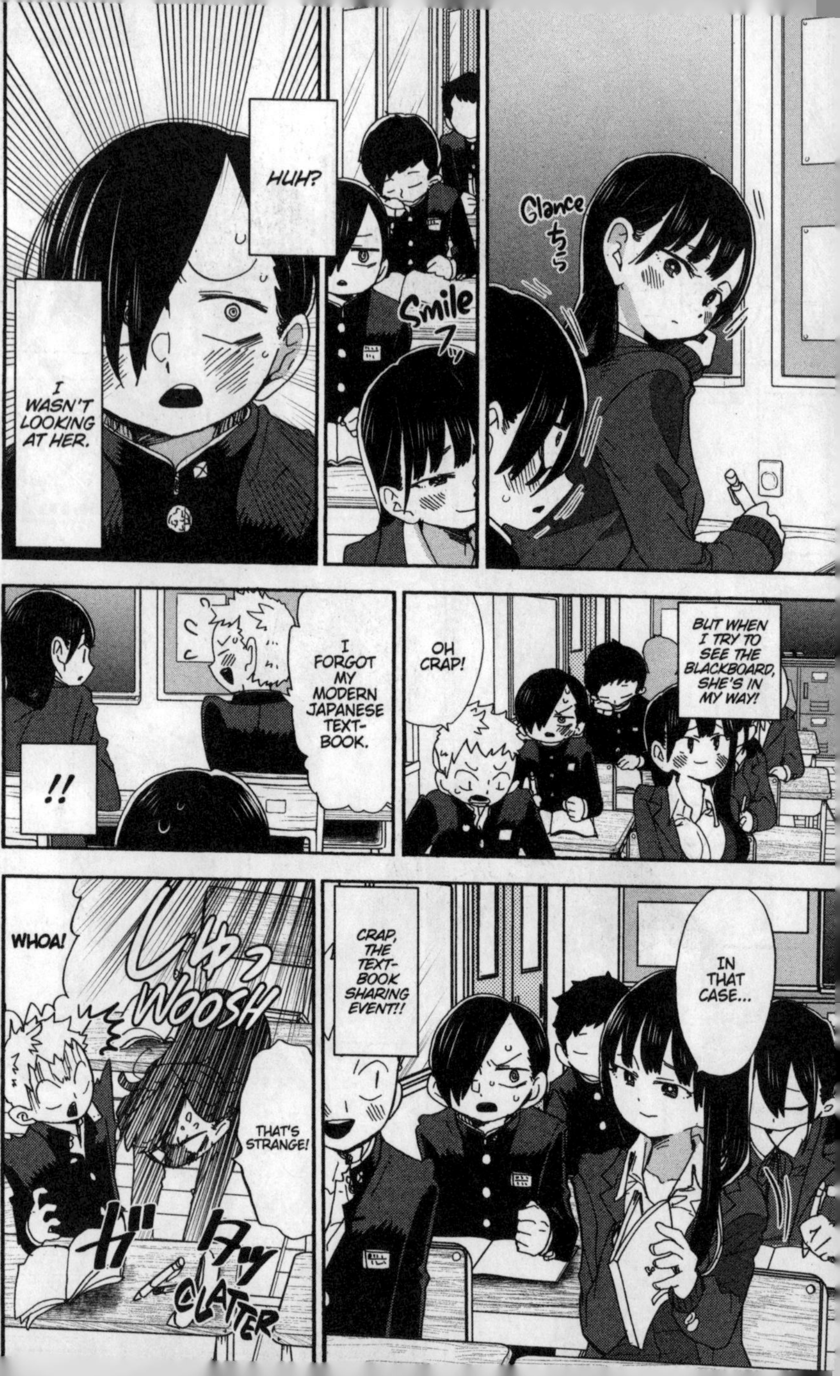
Glance
ちら
Smile
ニッ
HUH?
I WASN'T LOOKING AT HER.
BUT WHEN I TRY TO SEE THE BLACKBOARD, SHE'S IN MY WAY!
OH CRAP!
I FORGOT MY MODERN JAPANESE TEXT-BOOK.
!!
IN THAT CASE...
CRAP, THE TEXT-BOOK SHARING EVENT!!
しゅっ
WOOSH
WHOA!
THAT'S STRANGE!
ガタッ
CLATTER

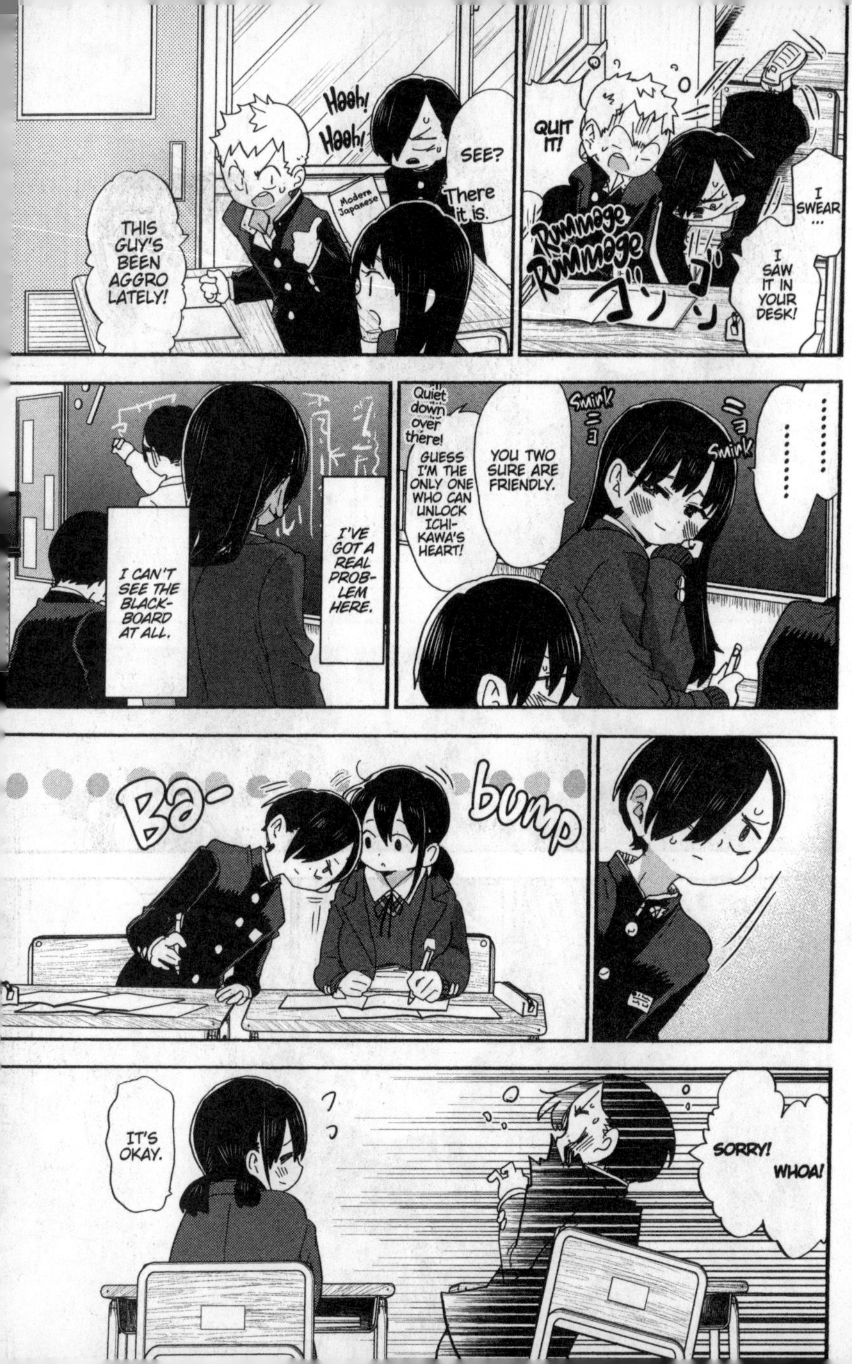
I SWEAR...
I SAW IT IN YOUR DESK!
QUIT IT!
Rummage
Rummage
SEE?
There it is.
Haah!
Haah!
Modern Japanese
THIS GUY'S BEEN AGGRO LATELY!
......
Smirk
Smirk
YOU TWO SURE ARE FRIENDLY.
Quiet down over there!
GUESS I'M THE ONLY ONE WHO CAN UNLOCK ICHI-KAWA'S HEART!
I'VE GOT A REAL PROB-LEM HERE.
I CAN'T SEE THE BLACK-BOARD AT ALL.
Ba-
bump
SORRY!
WHOA!
IT'S OKAY.

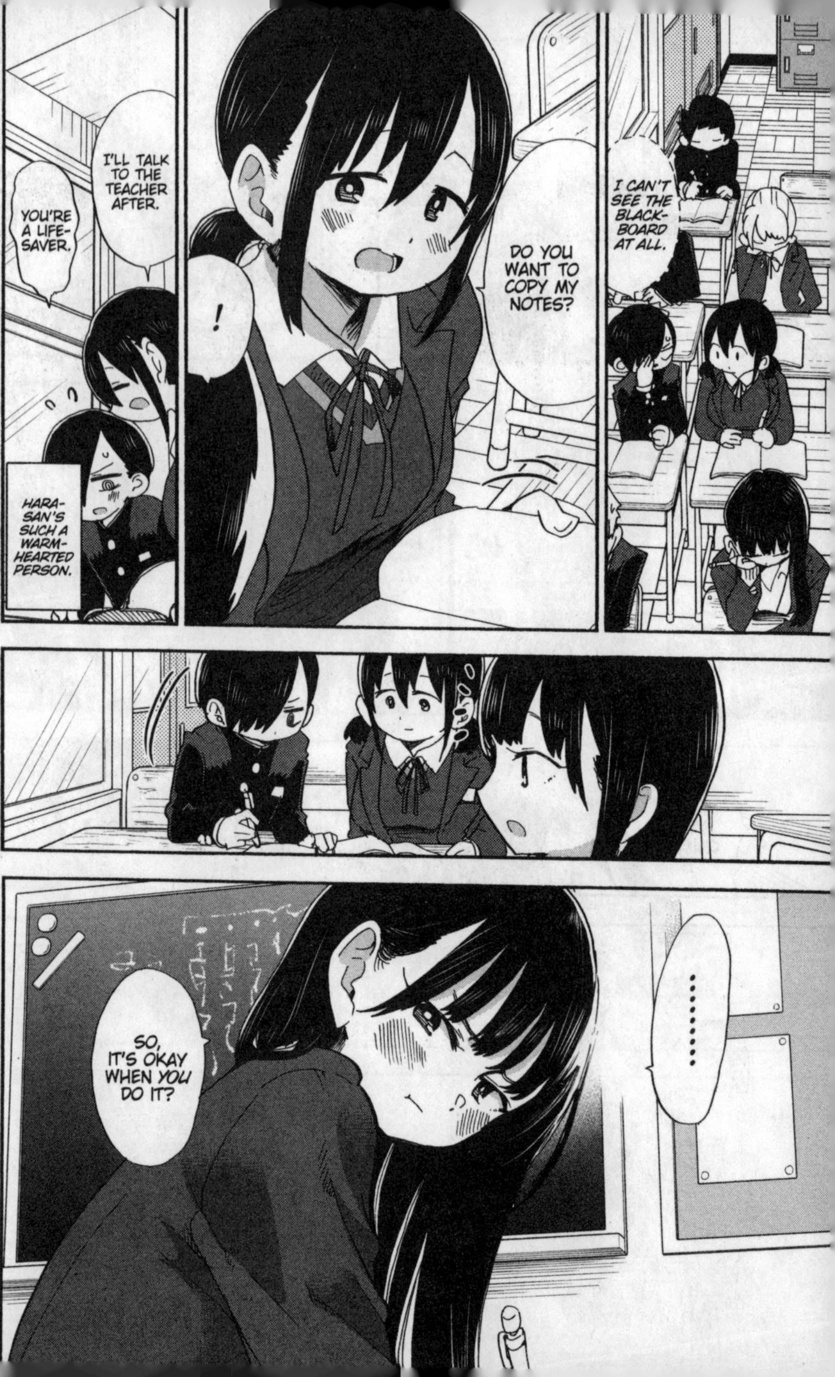
I CAN'T SEE THE BLACK-BOARD AT ALL.
DO YOU WANT TO COPY MY NOTES?
!
I'LL TALK TO THE TEACHER AFTER.
YOU'RE A LIFE-SAVER.
HARA-SAN'S SUCH A WARM-HEARTED PERSON.
....
SO, IT'S OKAY WHEN YOU DO IT?

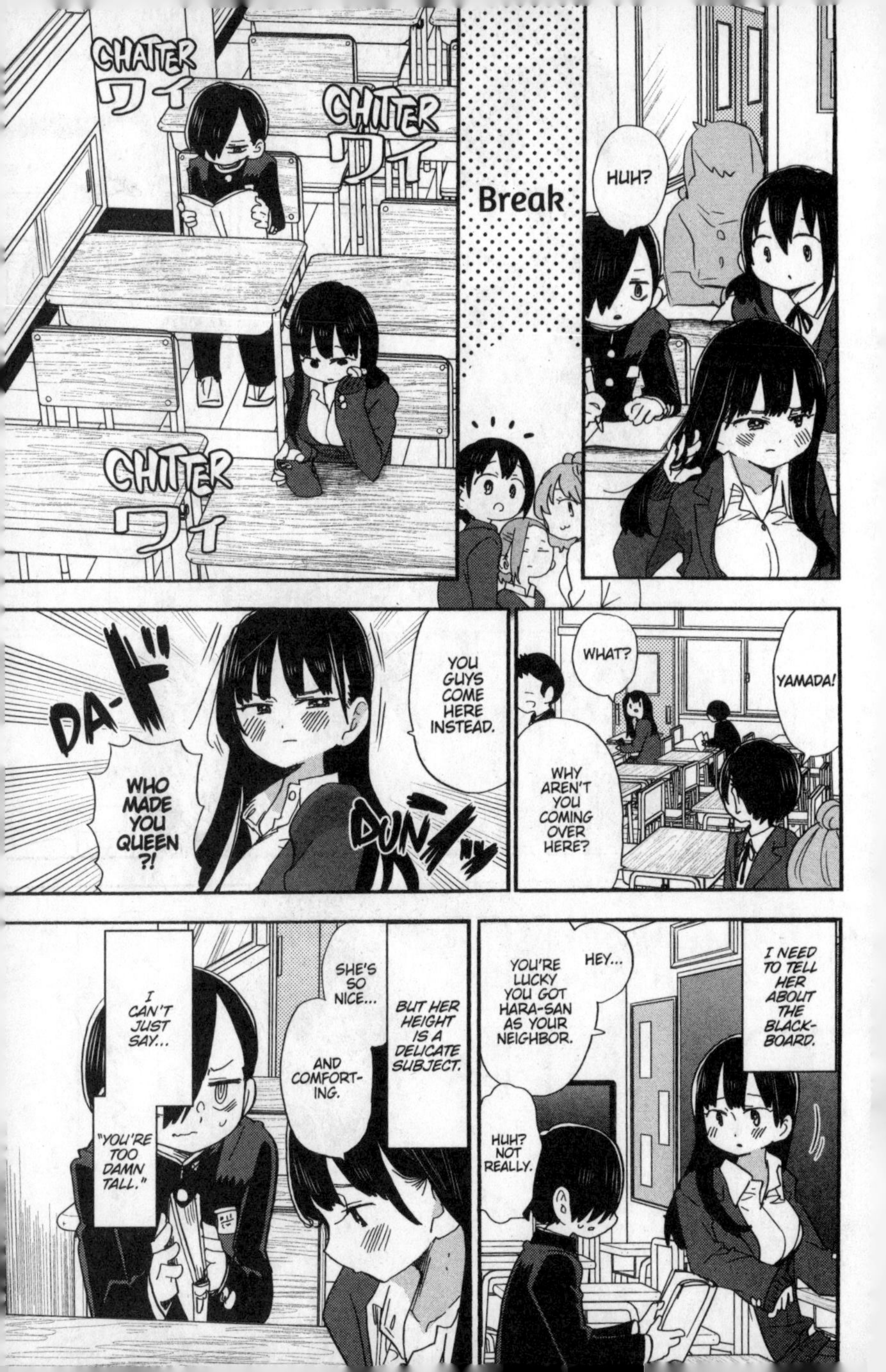
HUH?
Break
CHATER ワイ
CHITER ワイ
CHITER ワイ
YAMADA!
WHAT?
WHY AREN'T YOU COMING OVER HERE?
YOU GUYS COME HERE INSTEAD.
DA-ド
WHO MADE YOU QUEEN?!
DUN ッ
I NEED TO TELL HER ABOUT THE BLACK-BOARD.
HEY...
YOU'RE LUCKY YOU GOT HARA-SAN AS YOUR NEIGHBOR.
HUH? NOT REALLY.
BUT HER HEIGHT IS A DELICATE SUBJECT.
SHE'S SO NICE...
AND COMFORT-ING.
I CAN'T JUST SAY...
"YOU'RE TOO DAMN TALL."

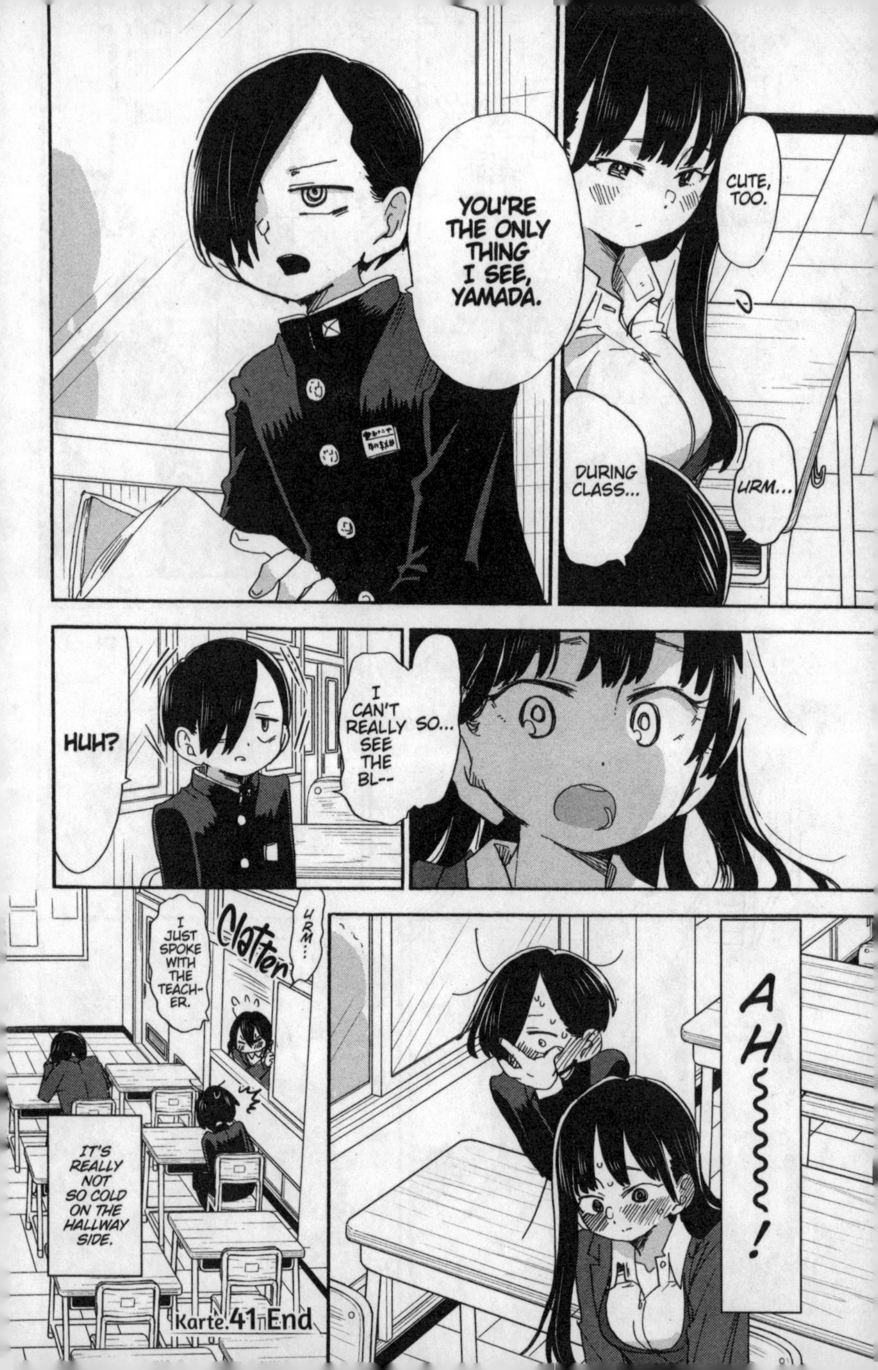
CUTE, TOO.
URM...
DURING CLASS...
YOU'RE THE ONLY THING I SEE, YAMADA.
SO...
I CAN'T REALLY SEE THE BL--
HUH?
AH~~~!
URM...
Clatter
I JUST SPOKE WITH THE TEACHER.
IT'S REALLY NOT SO COLD ON THE HALLWAY SIDE.
Karte.41 End

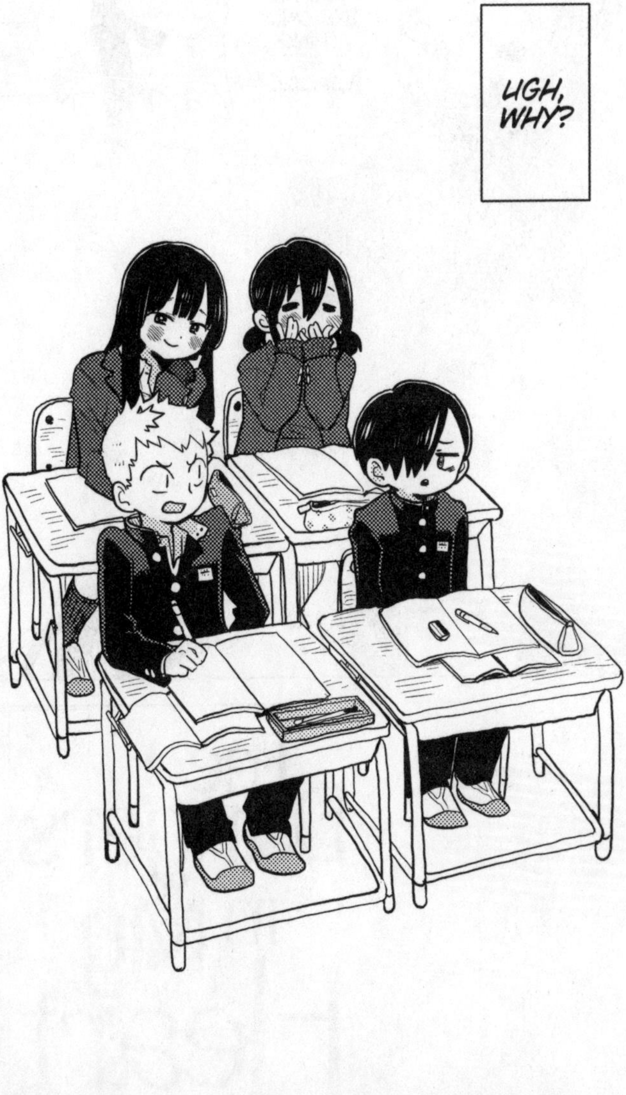
UGH, WHY?

The
Dangers
in My
Heart

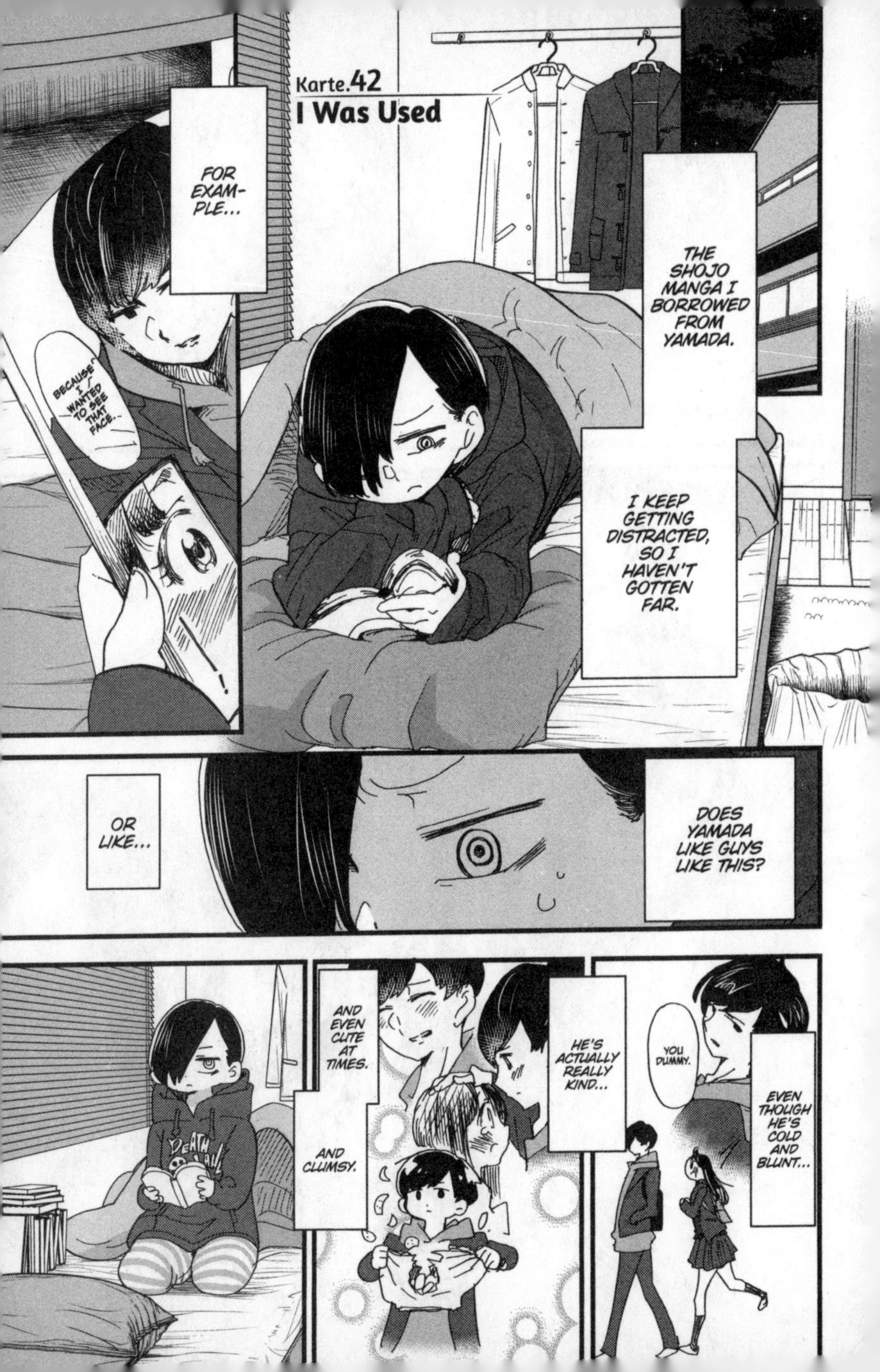
Karte. 42
I Was Used
THE SHOJO MANGA I BORROWED FROM YAMADA.
I KEEP GETTING DISTRACTED, SO I HAVEN'T GOTTEN FAR.
FOR EXAMPLE...
BECAUSE I WANTED TO SEE THAT FACE...
DOES YAMADA LIKE GUYS LIKE THIS?
OR LIKE...
EVEN THOUGH HE'S COLD AND BLUNT...
YOU DUMMY.
HE'S ACTUALLY REALLY KIND...
AND EVEN CUTE AT TIMES.
AND CLUMSY.
DEATH

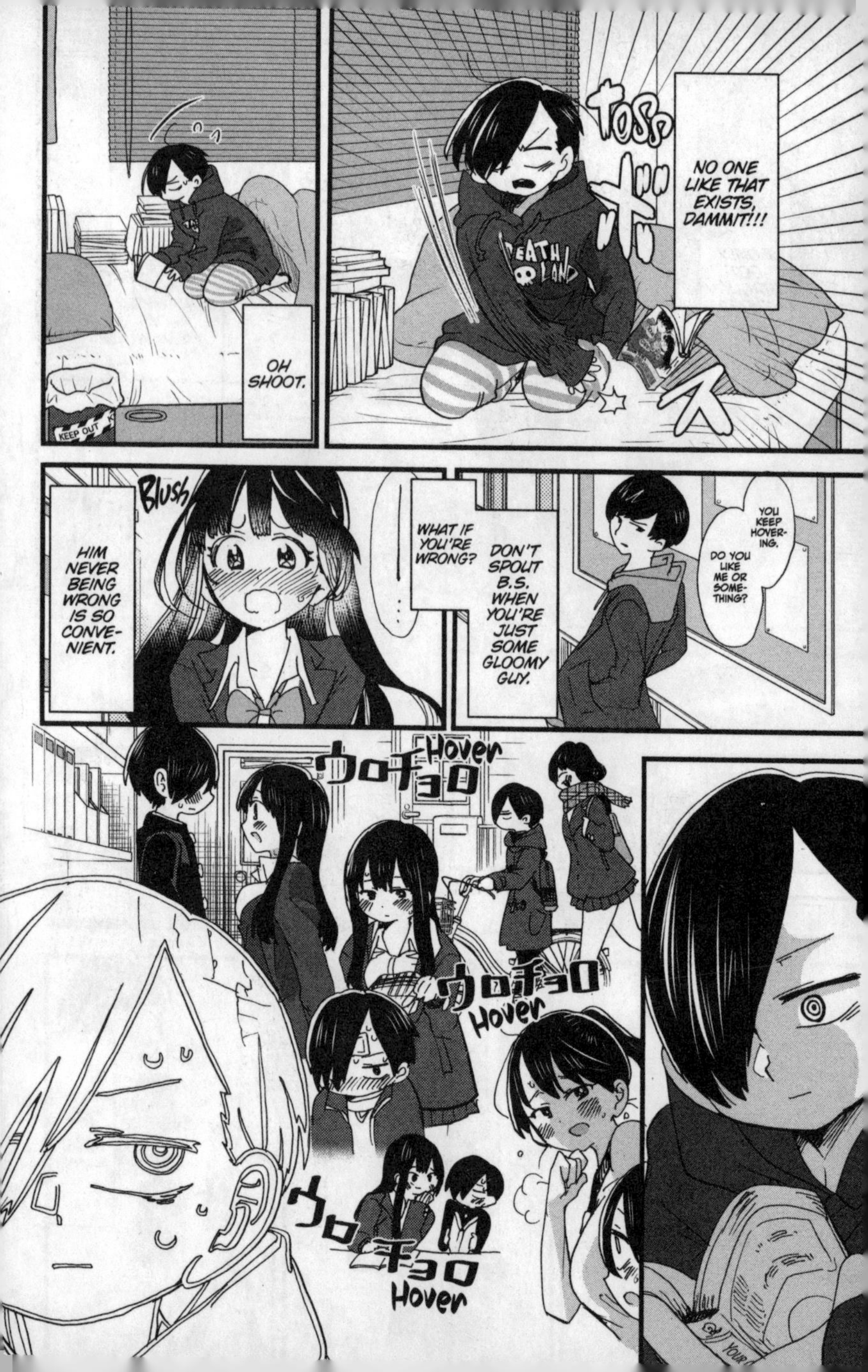
TOSS
NO ONE LIKE THAT EXISTS, DAMMIT!!!
OH SHOOT.
YOU KEEP HOVERING.
DO YOU LIKE ME OR SOMETHING?
DON'T SPOUT B.S. WHEN YOU'RE JUST SOME GLOOMY GUY.
WHAT IF YOU'RE WRONG?
Blush
HIM NEVER BEING WRONG IS SO CONVENIENT.
ウロチョロ
Hover
ウロチョロ
Hover
ウロチョロ
Hover

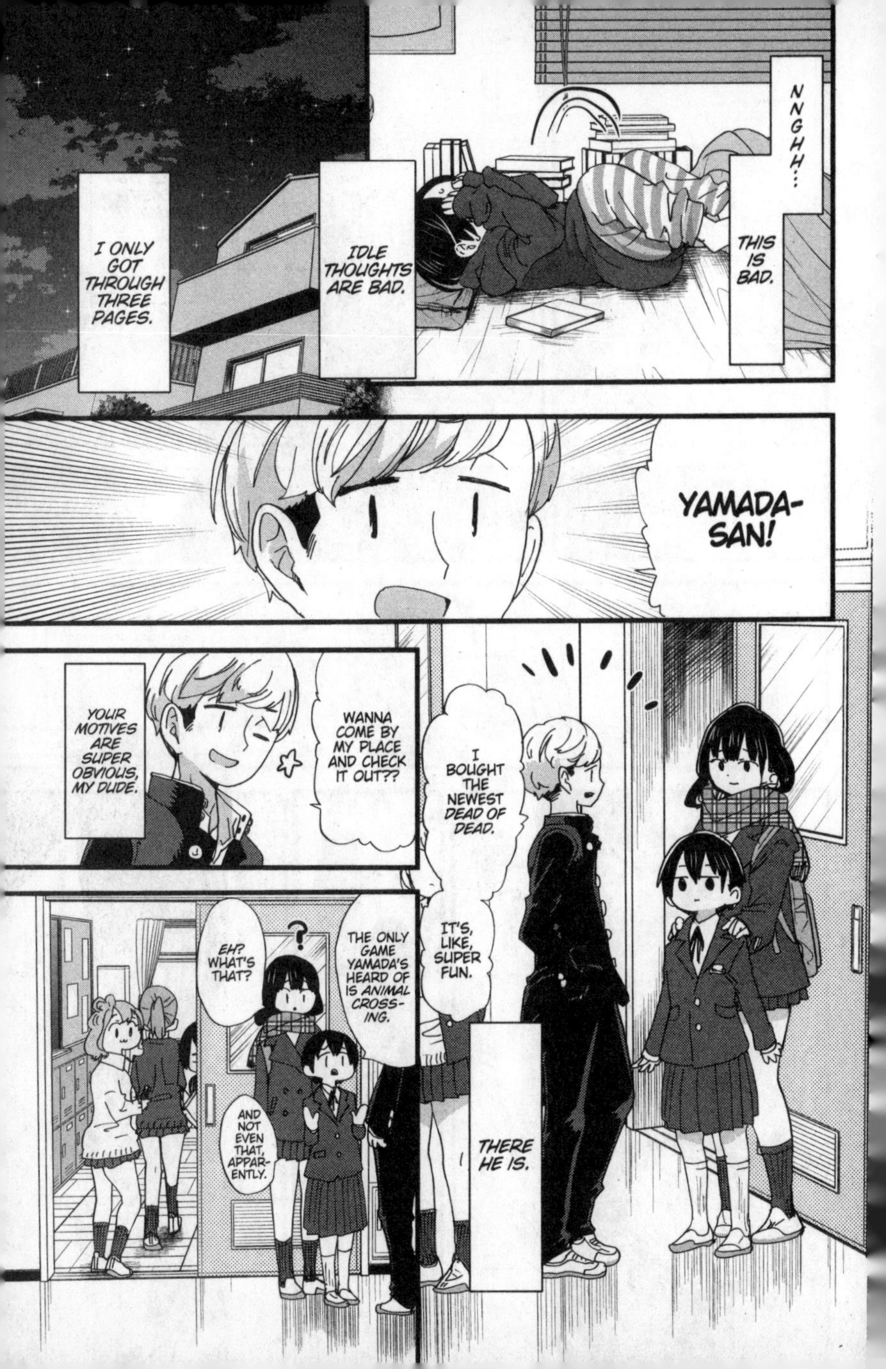
NNGHH...
THIS IS BAD.
IDLE THOUGHTS ARE BAD.
I ONLY GOT THROUGH THREE PAGES.
YAMADA-SAN!
I BOUGHT THE NEWEST DEAD OF DEAD.
IT'S, LIKE, SUPER FUN.
THERE HE IS.
WANNA COME BY MY PLACE AND CHECK IT OUT??
YOUR MOTIVES ARE SUPER OBVIOUS, MY DUDE.
THE ONLY GAME YAMADA'S HEARD OF IS ANIMAL CROSSING.
EH? WHAT'S THAT?
AND NOT EVEN THAT, APPARENTLY.

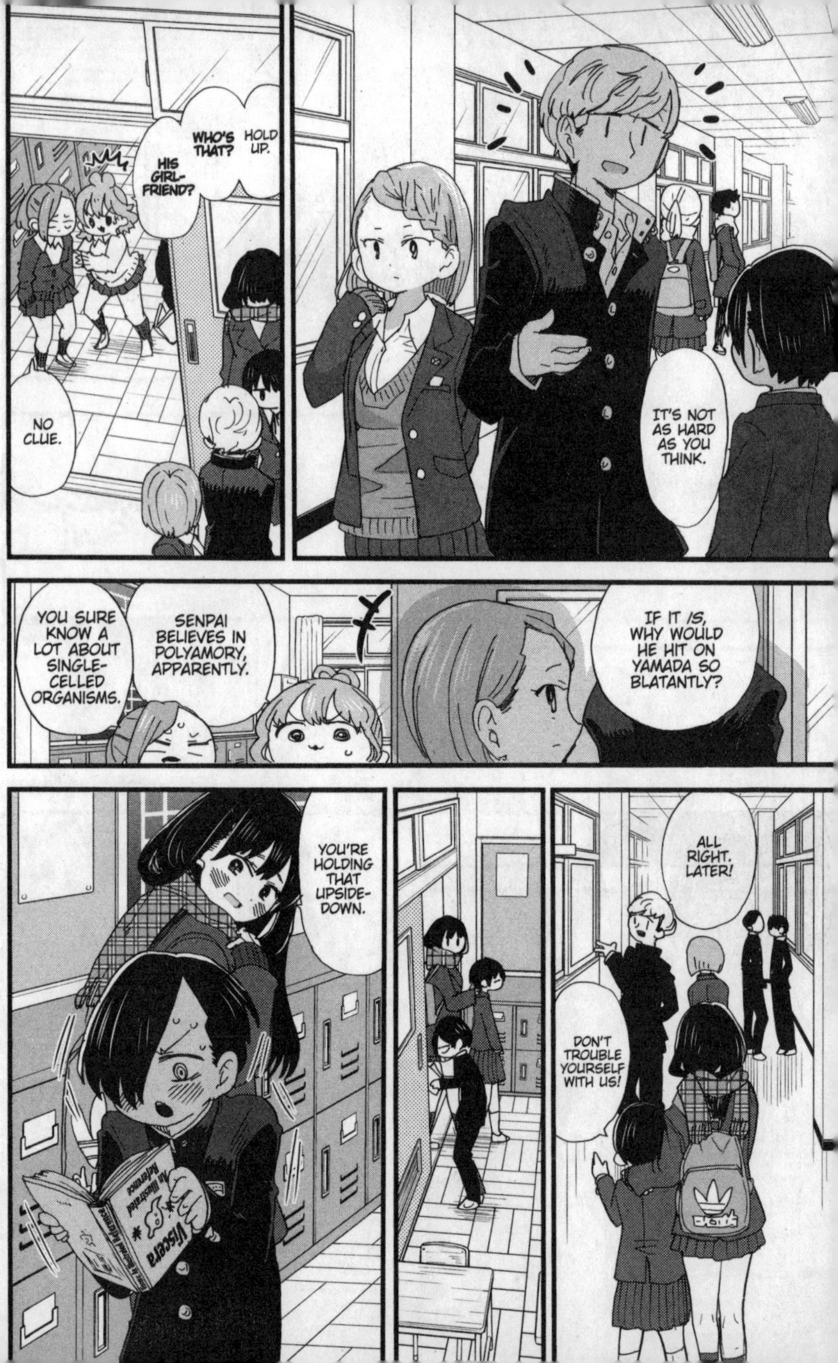
IT'S NOT AS HARD AS YOU THINK.
HOLD UP.
WHO'S THAT?
HIS GIRL-FRIEND?
NO CLUE.
IF IT *IS*, WHY WOULD HE HIT ON YAMADA SO BLATANTLY?
SENPAI BELIEVES IN POLYAMORY, APPARENTLY.
YOU SURE KNOW A LOT ABOUT SINGLE-CELLED ORGANISMS.
ALL RIGHT. LATER!
DON'T TROUBLE YOURSELF WITH US!
YOU'RE HOLDING THAT UPSIDE-DOWN.
Viscera
An Illustrated Reference

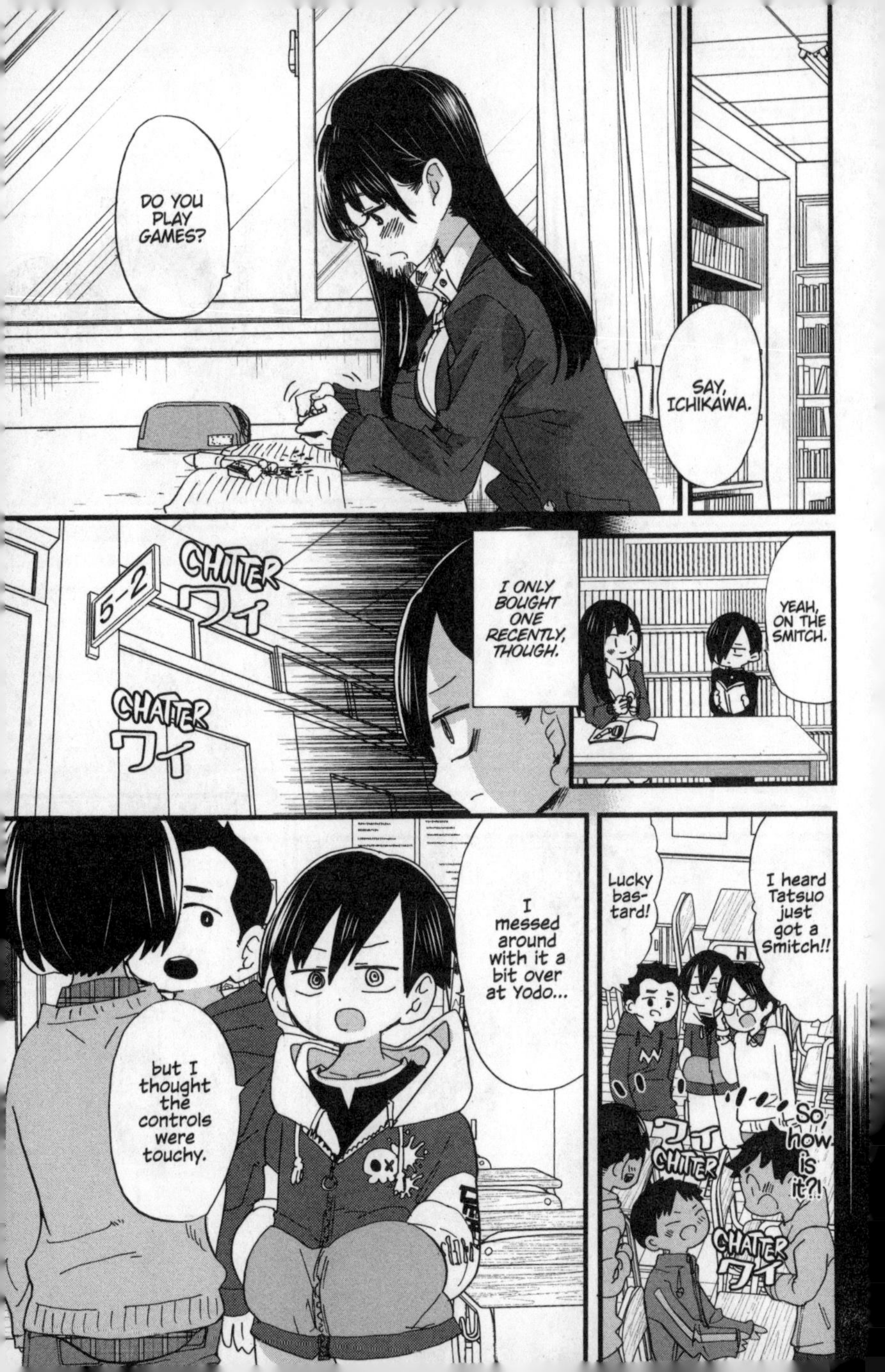
SAY, ICHIKAWA.
DO YOU PLAY GAMES?
YEAH, ON THE SMITCH.
I ONLY BOUGHT ONE RECENTLY, THOUGH.
5-2
CHITTER
ワイ
CHATTER
ワイ
I heard Tatsuo just got a Smitch!!
Lucky bas-tard!
So, how is it?!
ワイ
CHITTER
CHATTER
ワイ
I messed around with it a bit over at Yodo...
but I thought the controls were touchy.

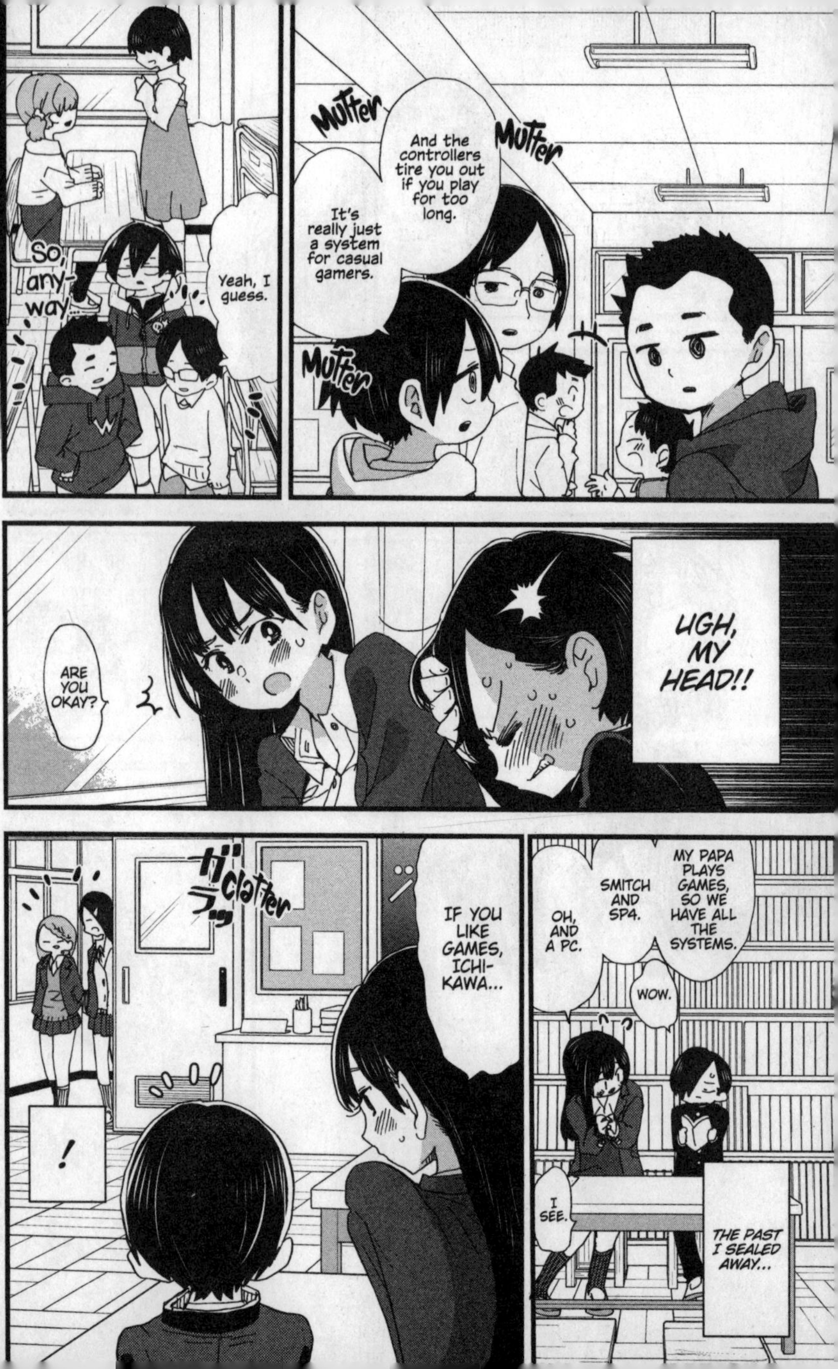
Mutter
And the controllers tire you out if you play for too long.
Mutter
It's really just a system for casual gamers.
Mutter
Yeah, I guess.
So, any-way
UGH, MY HEAD!!
ARE YOU OKAY?
MY PAPA PLAYS GAMES, SO WE HAVE ALL THE SYSTEMS.
SMITCH AND SP4.
OH, AND A PC.
WOW.
THE PAST I SEALED AWAY...
I SEE.
IF YOU LIKE GAMES, ICHI-KAWA...
clatter
!

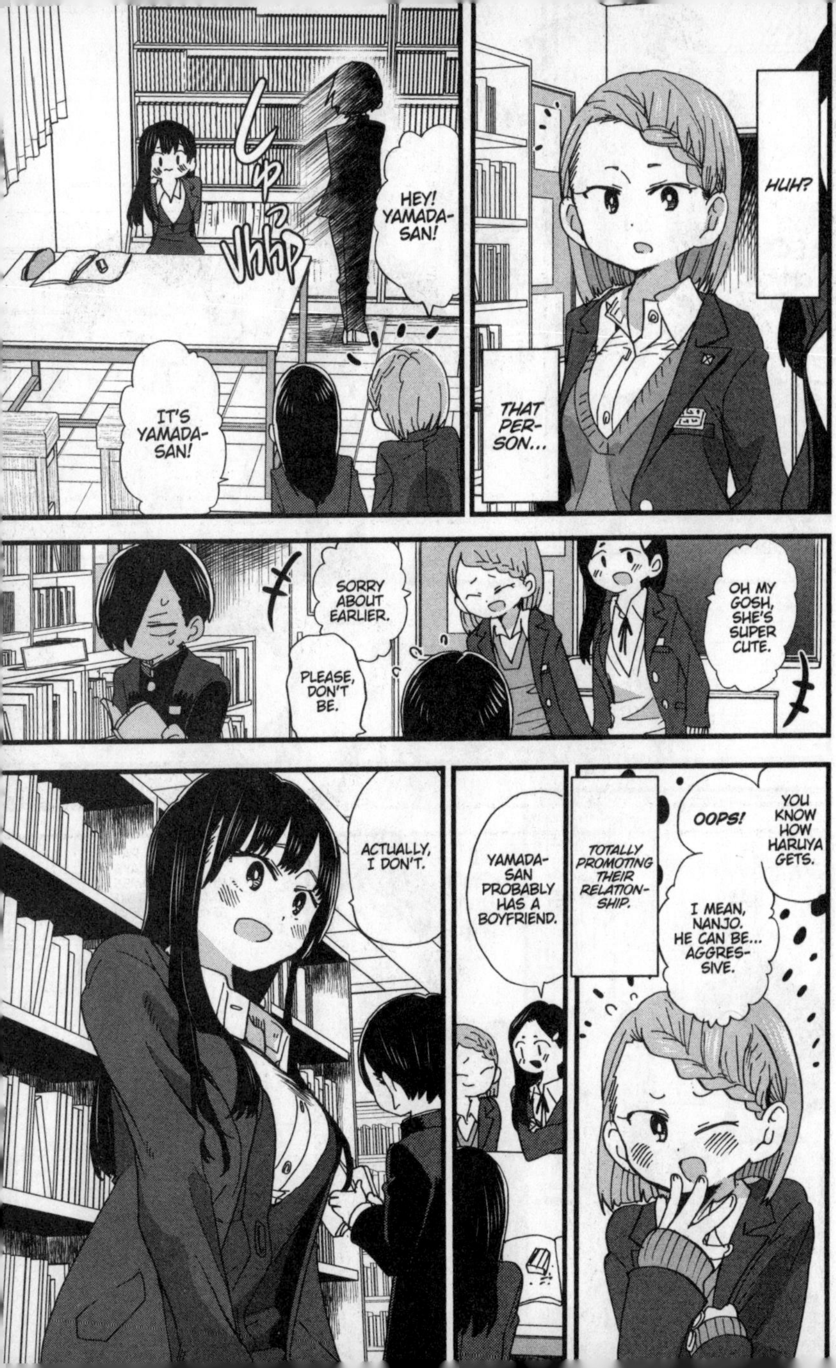
HUH?
THAT PER-SON...
HEY! YAMADA-SAN!
しゅっ
vhhp
IT'S YAMADA-SAN!
OH MY GOSH, SHE'S SUPER CUTE.
SORRY ABOUT EARLIER.
PLEASE, DON'T BE.
YOU KNOW HOW HARUYA GETS.
OOPS!
I MEAN, NANJO. HE CAN BE... AGGRES-SIVE.
TOTALLY PROMOTING THEIR RELATION-SHIP.
YAMADA-SAN PROBABLY HAS A BOYFRIEND.
ACTUALLY, I DON'T.

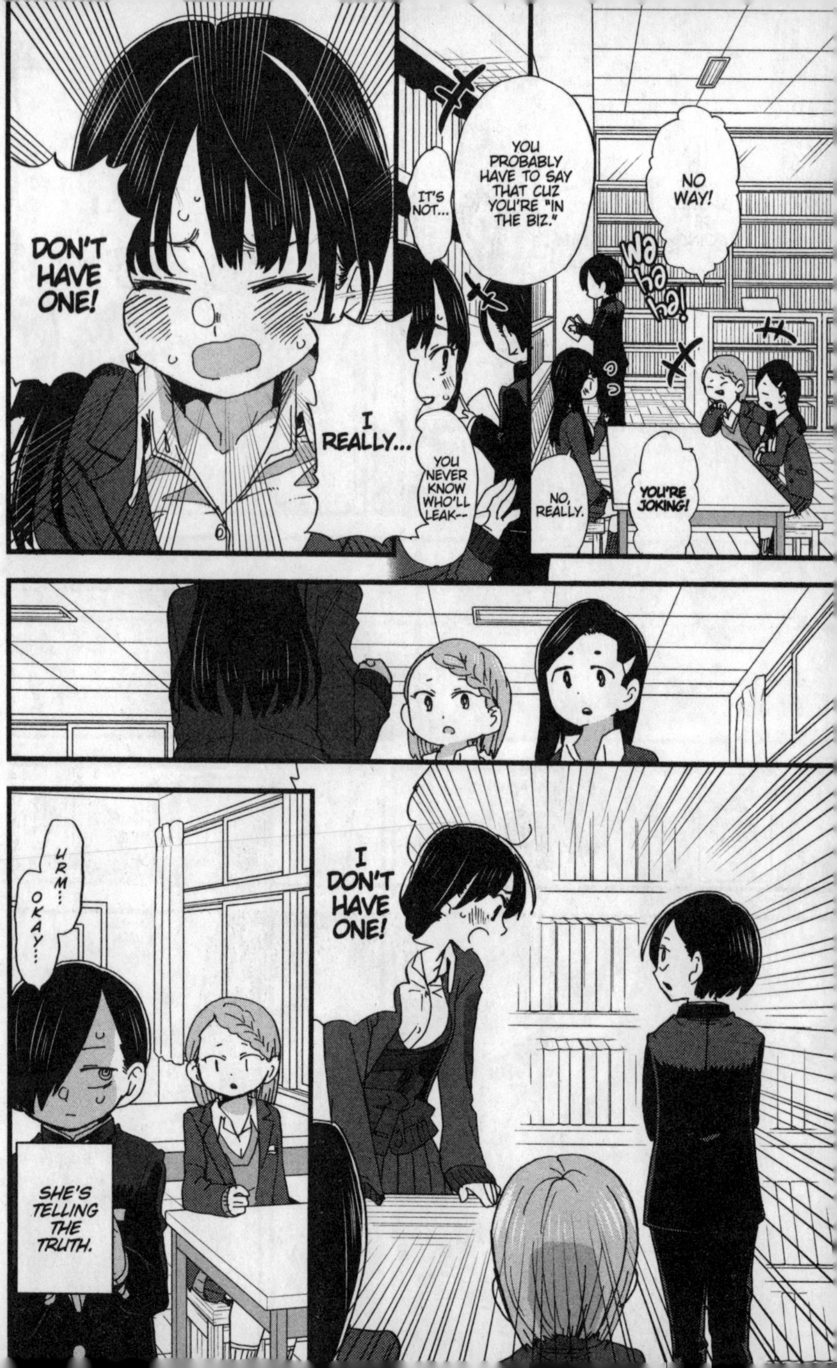
NO WAY!
Wa ha ha!
YOU'RE JOKING!
NO, REALLY.
YOU PROBABLY HAVE TO SAY THAT CUZ YOU'RE "IN THE BIZ."
IT'S NOT...
YOU NEVER KNOW WHO'LL LEAK--
I REALLY...
DON'T HAVE ONE!
I DON'T HAVE ONE!
URM... OKAY...
SHE'S TELLING THE TRUTH.

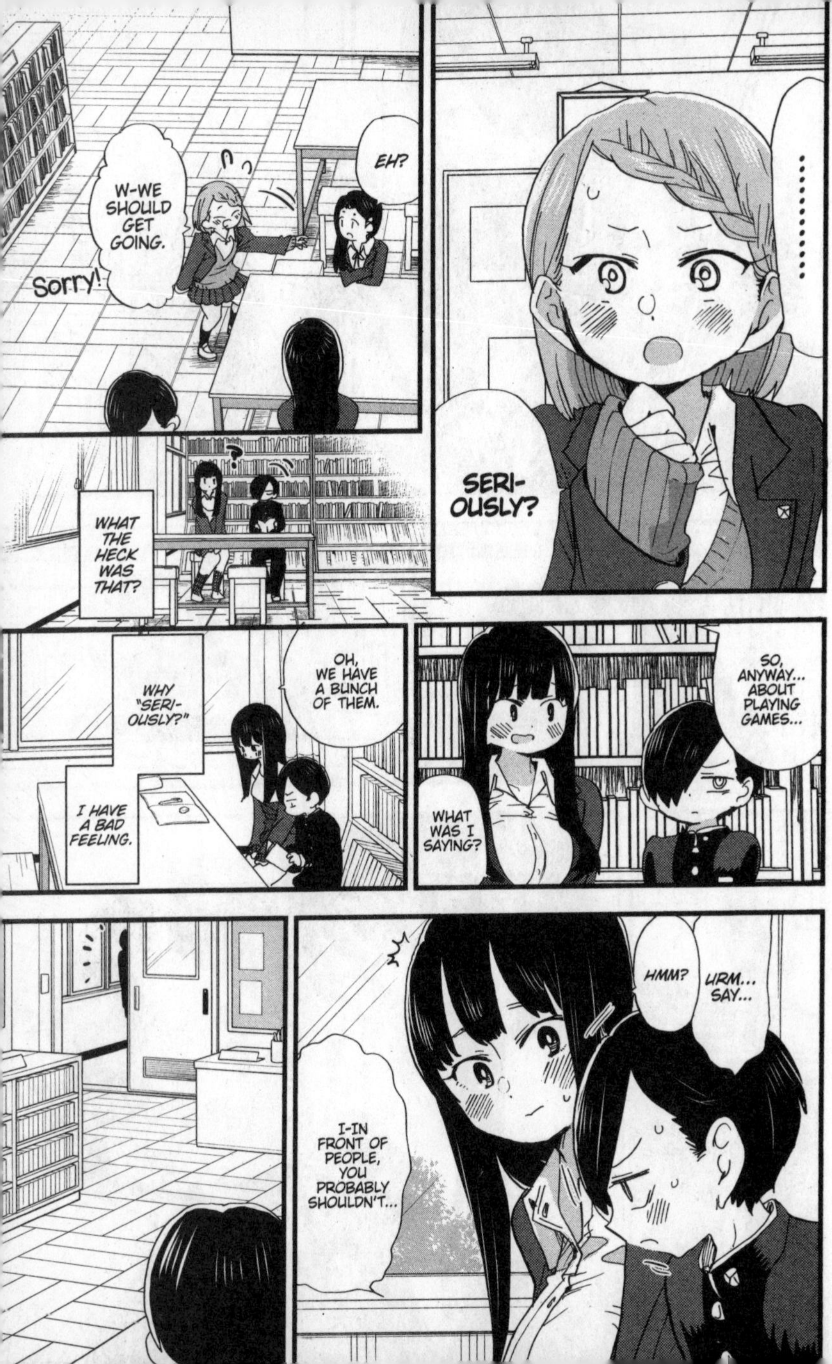
......
SERI-OUSLY?
EH?
W-WE SHOULD GET GOING.
Sorry!
WHAT THE HECK WAS THAT?
SO, ANYWAY... ABOUT PLAYING GAMES...
WHAT WAS I SAYING?
OH, WE HAVE A BUNCH OF THEM.
WHY "SERI-OUSLY?"
I HAVE A BAD FEELING.
URM... SAY...
HMM?
I-IN FRONT OF PEOPLE, YOU PROBABLY SHOULDN'T...

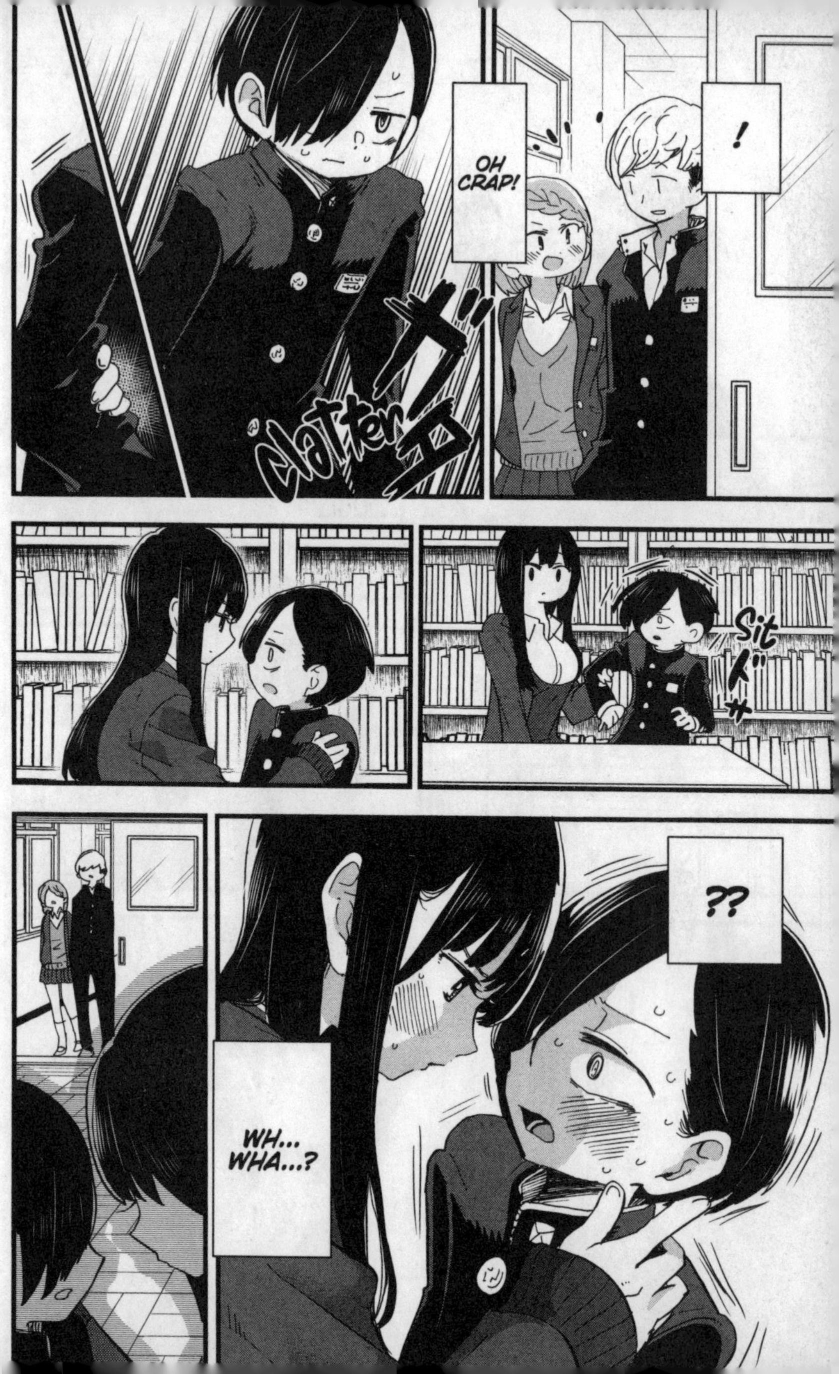
!
OH CRAP!
clatter
Sit
??
WH... WHA...?

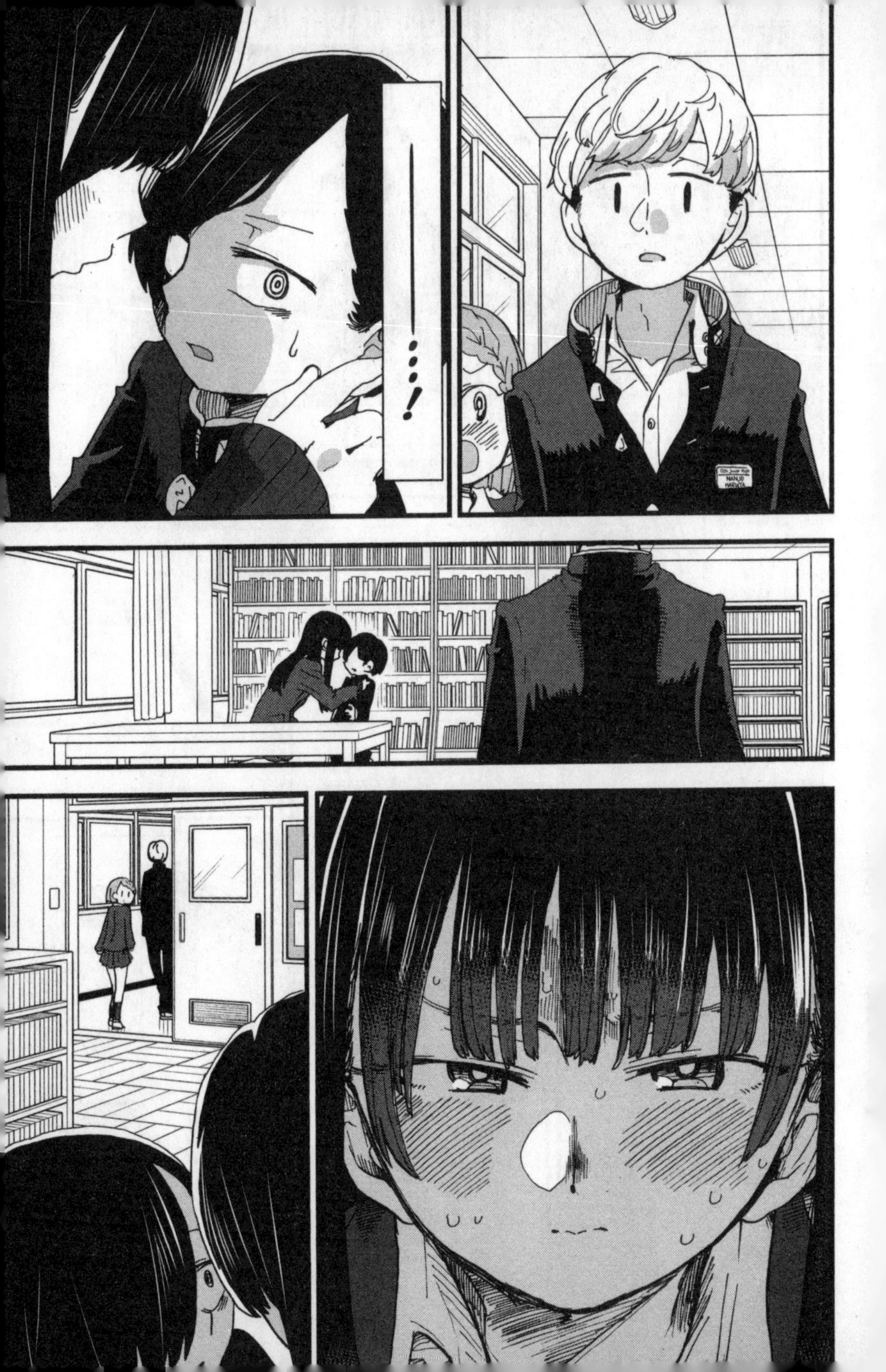
……!

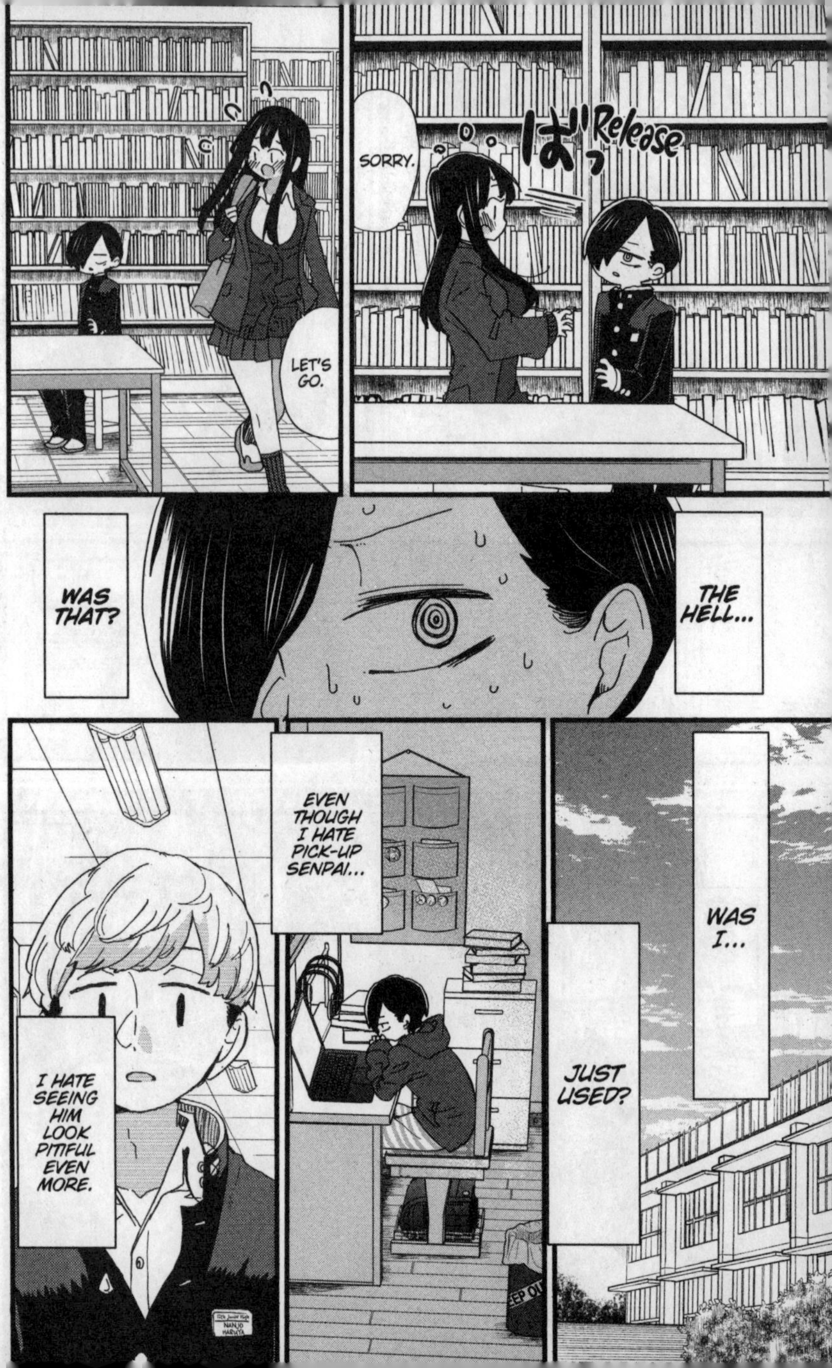
ぱっ
Release
SORRY.
LET'S GO.
THE HELL...
WAS THAT?
WAS I...
JUST USED?
EVEN THOUGH I HATE PICK-UP SENPAI...
I HATE SEEING HIM LOOK PITIFUL EVEN MORE.

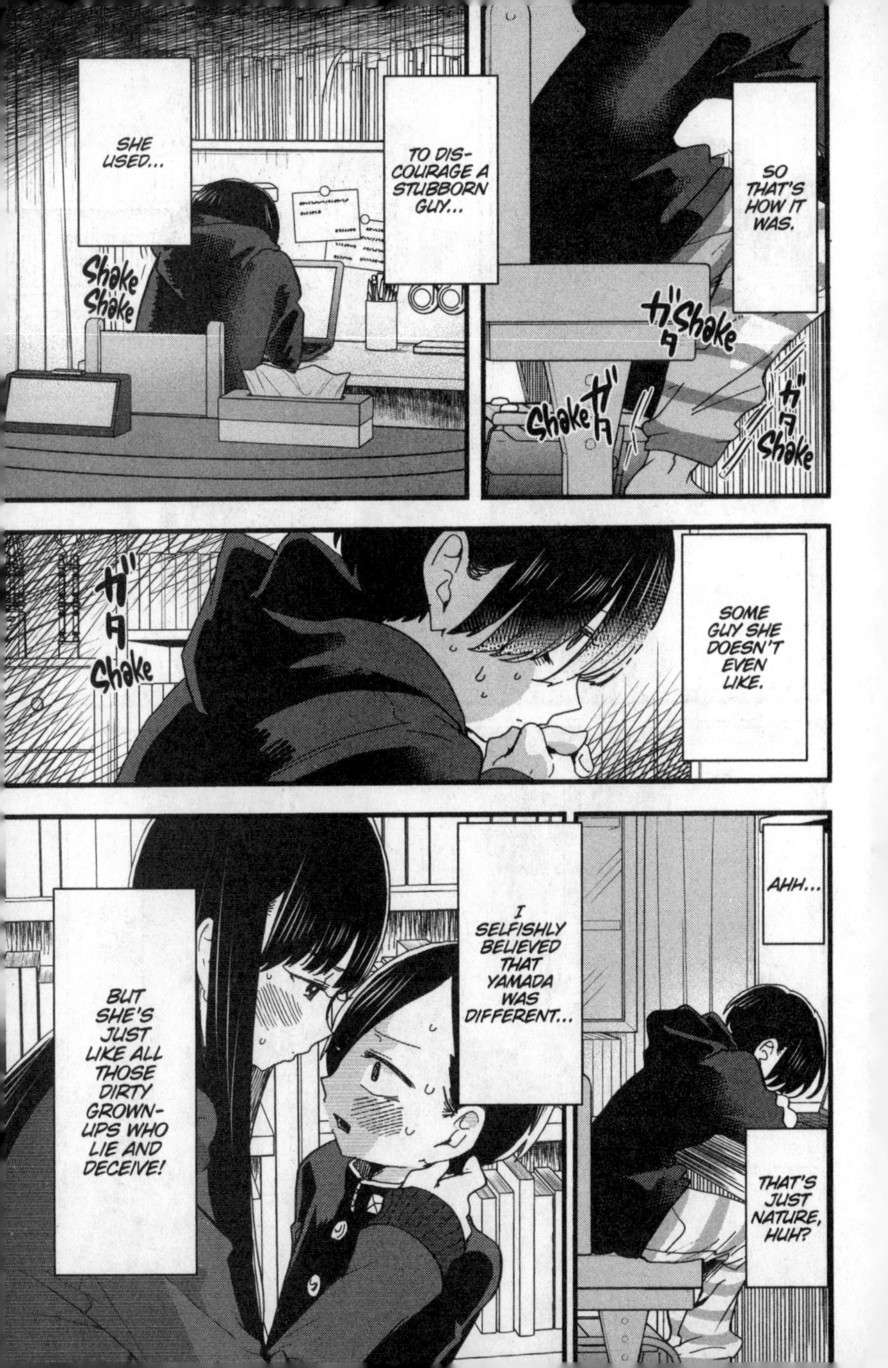
SO THAT'S HOW IT WAS.
ガタ Shake
ガタ Shake
Shake ガタ
TO DIS-COURAGE A STUBBORN GUY...
SHE USED...
Shake Shake
SOME GUY SHE DOESN'T EVEN LIKE.
ガタ Shake
AHH...
THAT'S JUST NATURE, HUH?
I SELFISHLY BELIEVED THAT YAMADA WAS DIFFERENT...
BUT SHE'S JUST LIKE ALL THOSE DIRTY GROWN-UPS WHO LIE AND DECEIVE!

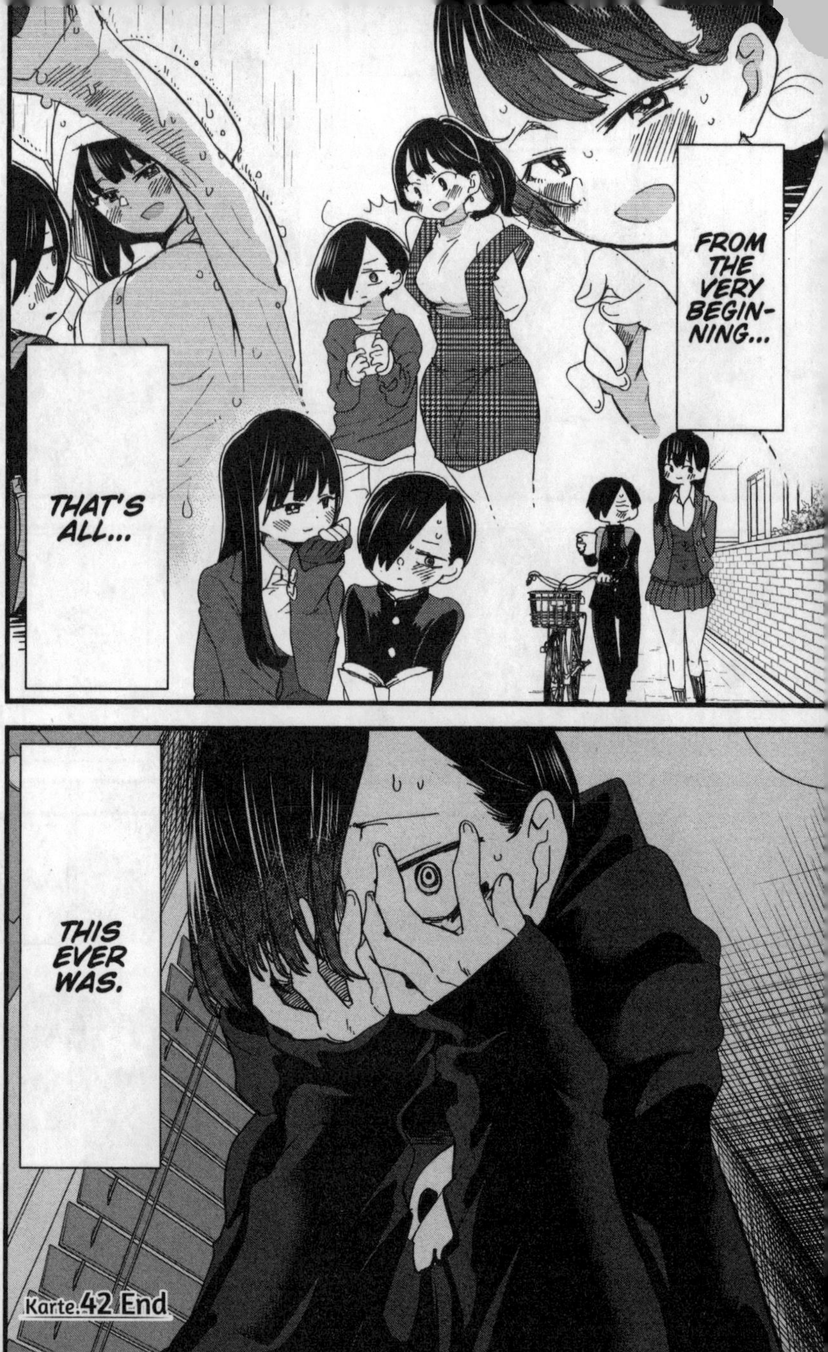
FROM THE VERY BEGIN-NING...
THAT'S ALL...
THIS EVER WAS.
Karte.42 End

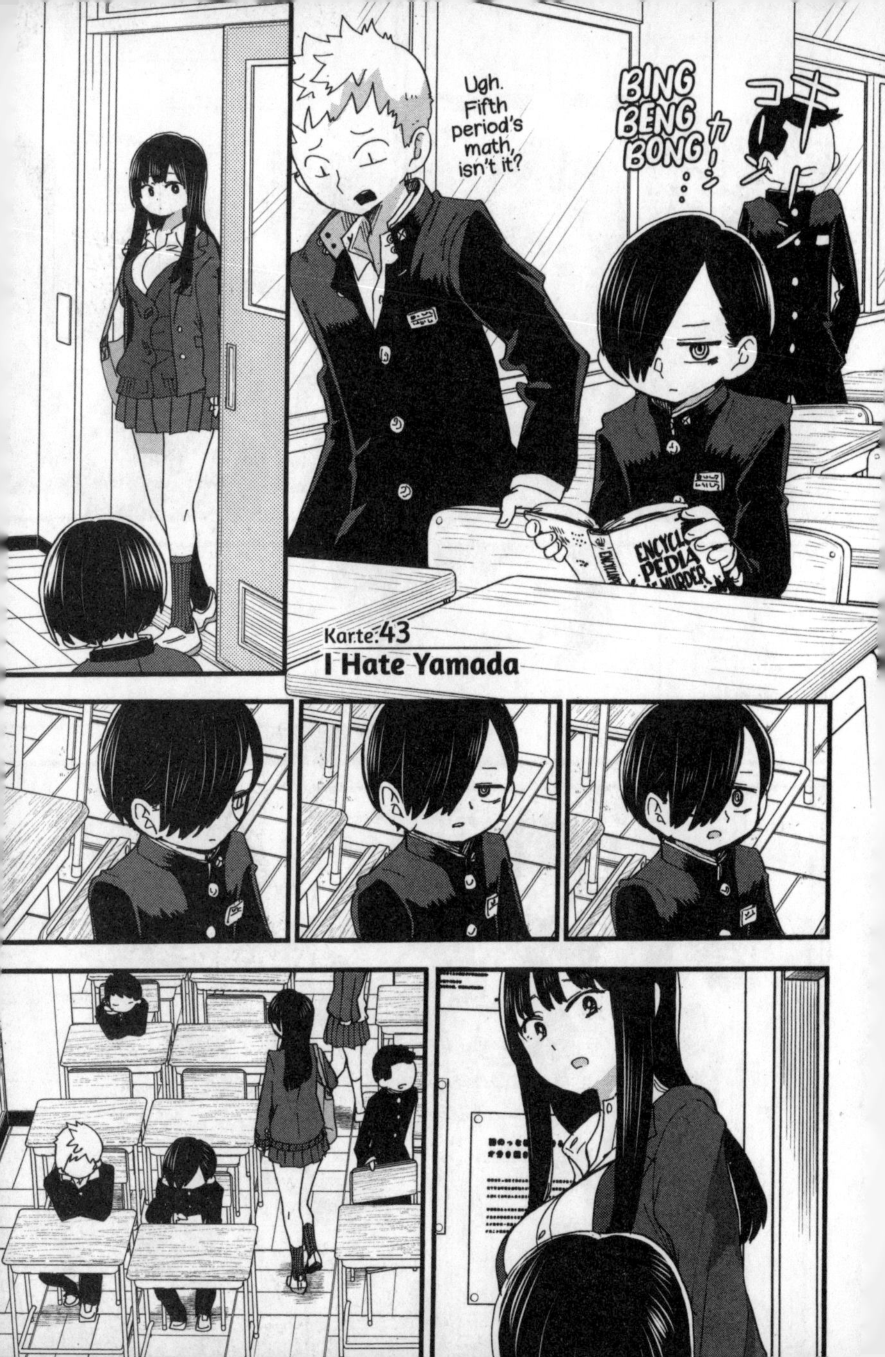
BING BENG BONG
Ugh. Fifth period's math, isn't it?
Kar.te.43
I Hate Yamada

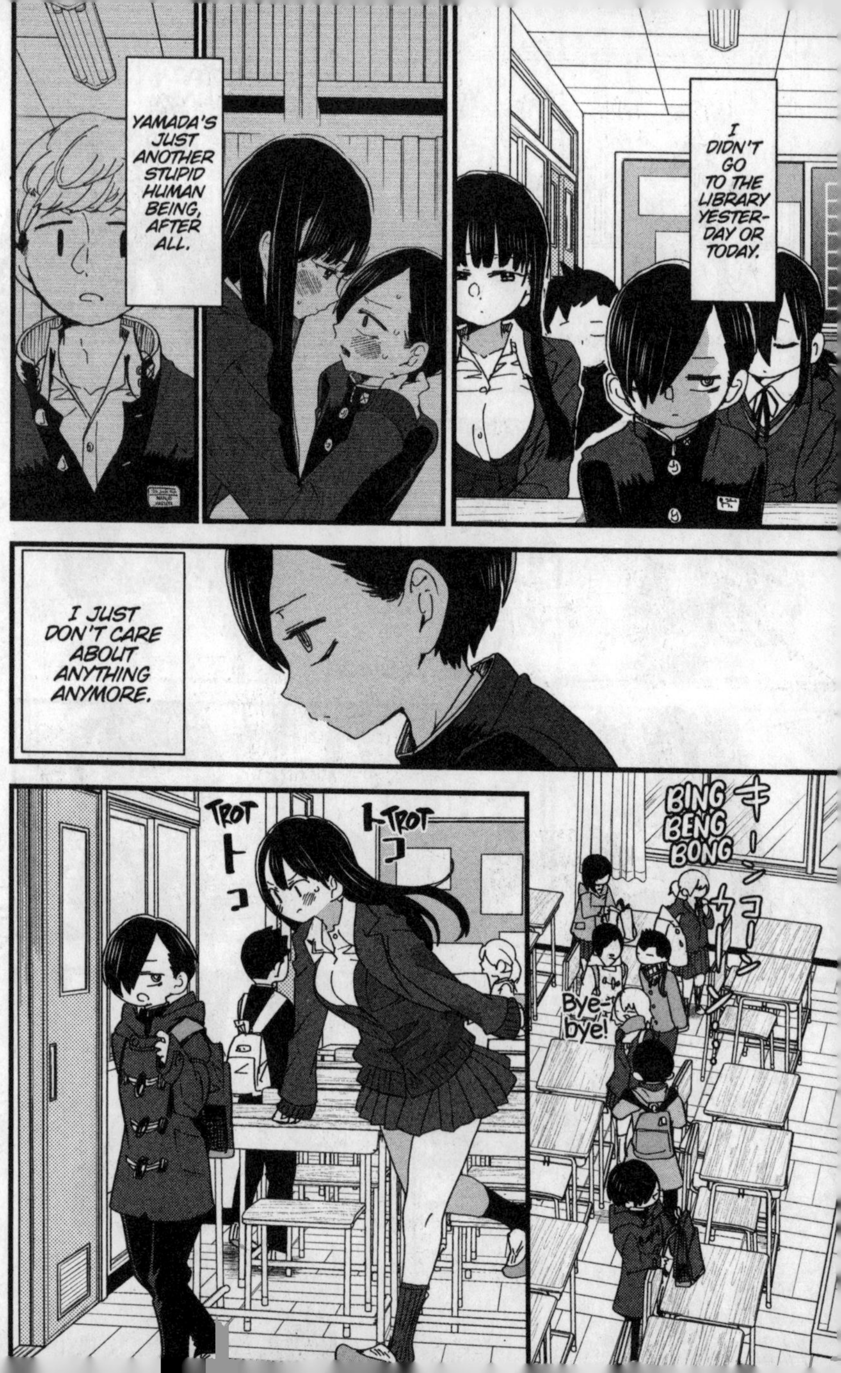
I DIDN'T GO TO THE LIBRARY YESTER-DAY OR TODAY.
YAMADA'S JUST ANOTHER STUPID HUMAN BEING, AFTER ALL.
I JUST DON'T CARE ABOUT ANYTHING ANYMORE.
BING BENG BONG
キーンコーン
Bye-bye!
TROT
トコ
TROT
トコ

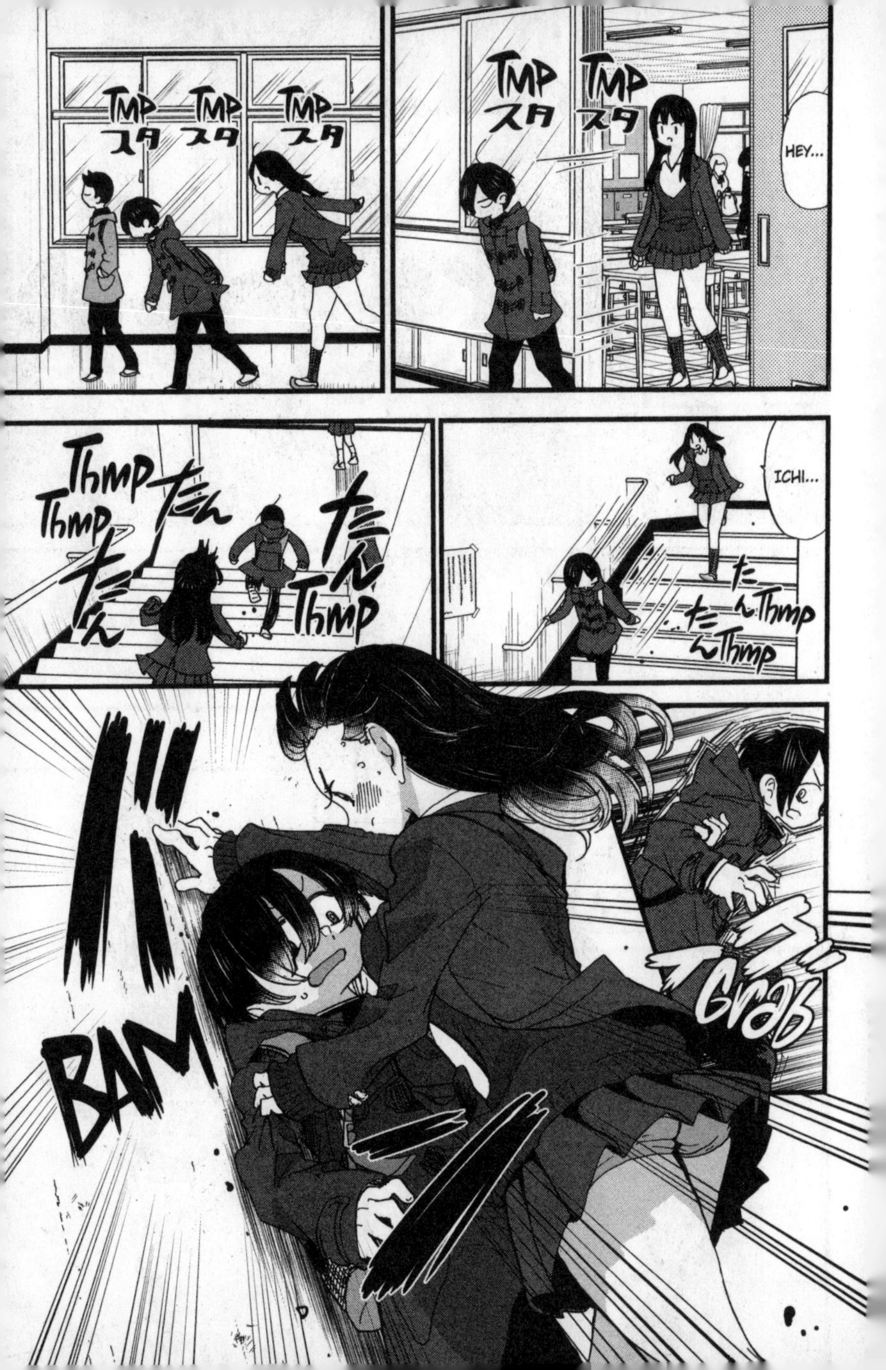
HEY...
TMP スタ
TMP スタ
TMP スタ
TMP スタ
TMP スタ
ICHI...
たん Thmp
たん Thmp
たん Thmp
Thmp たん
Thmp たん
Grab
BAM

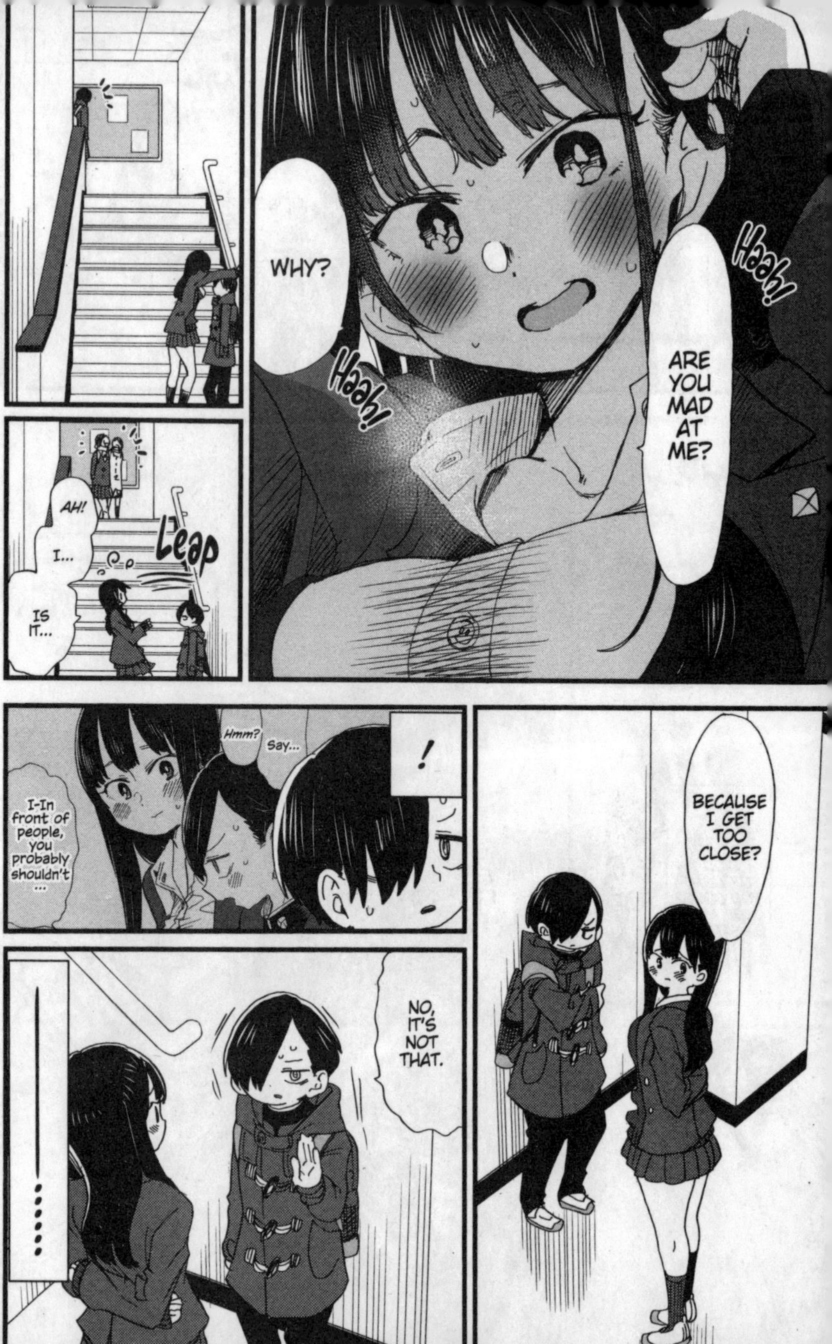
Haah!
ARE YOU MAD AT ME?
WHY?
Haah!
AH!
I...
Leap
IS IT...
BECAUSE I GET TOO CLOSE?
!
Say...
Hmm?
I-In front of people, you probably shouldn't ...
NO, IT'S NOT THAT.
......

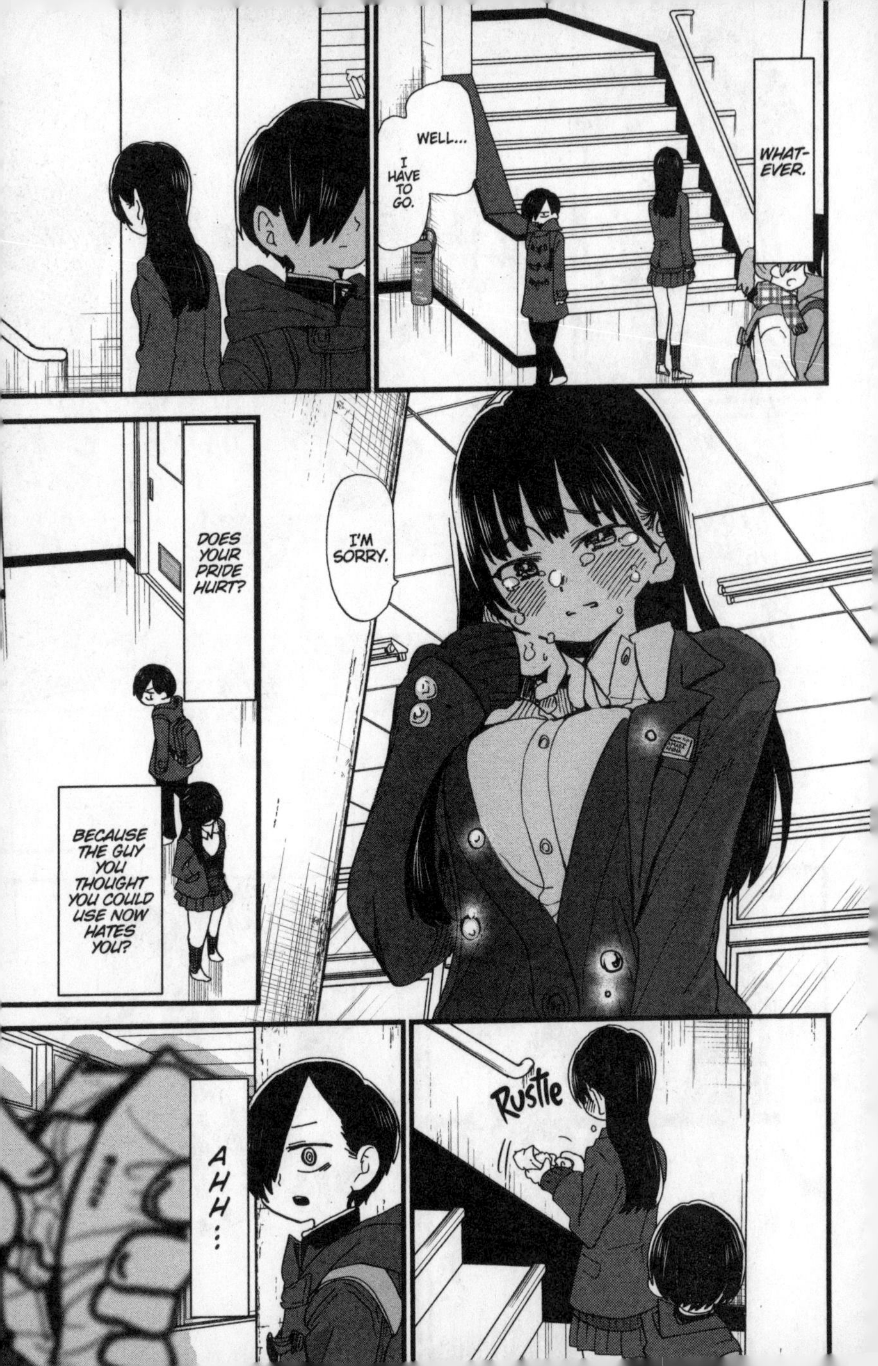
WHAT-EVER.
WELL... I HAVE TO GO.
I'M SORRY.
DOES YOUR PRIDE HURT?
BECAUSE THE GUY YOU THOUGHT YOU COULD USE NOW HATES YOU?
Rustle
AHH...

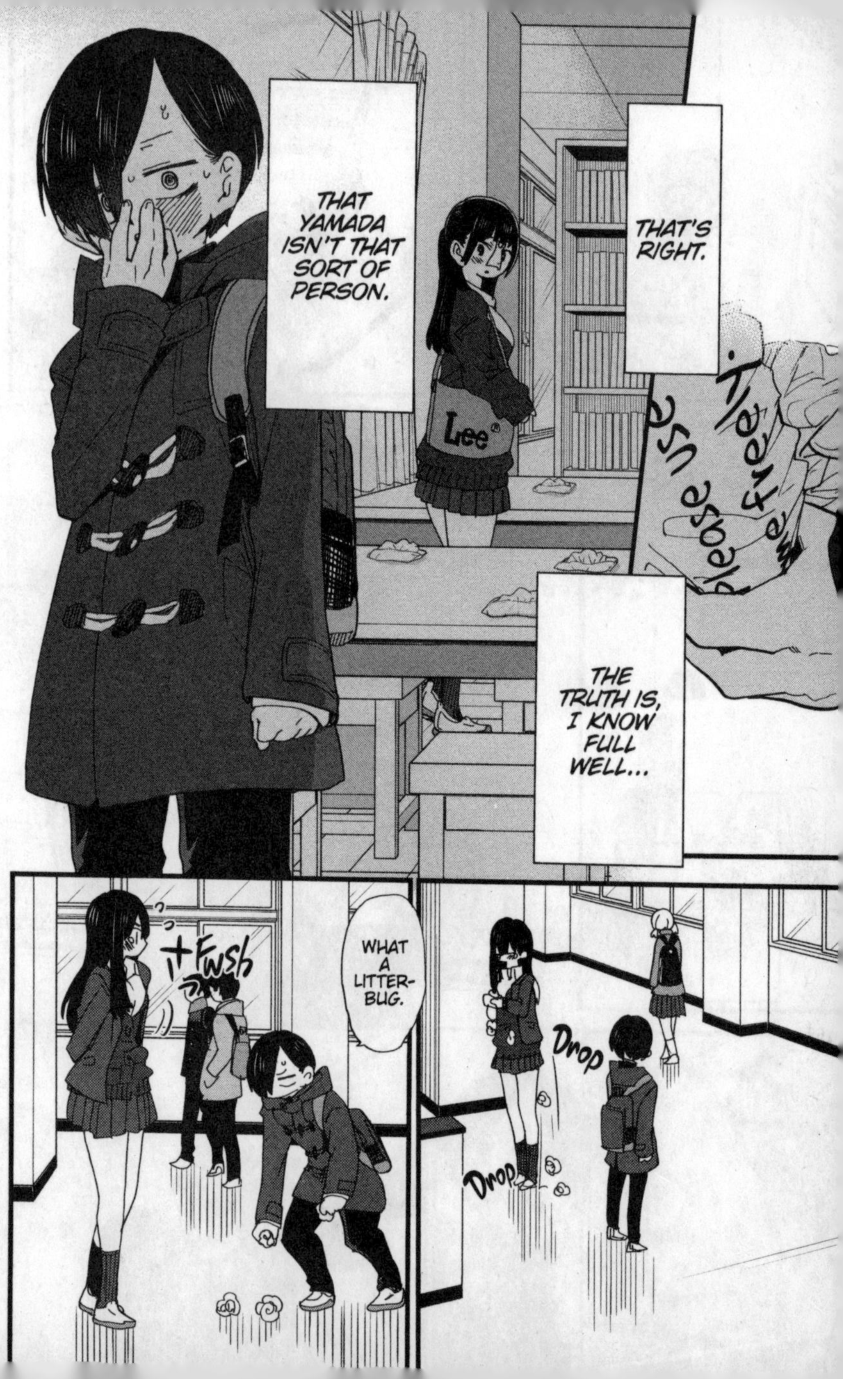
THAT'S RIGHT.
THAT YAMADA ISN'T THAT SORT OF PERSON.
THE TRUTH IS, I KNOW FULL WELL...
Drop
Drop
Fwsh
WHAT A LITTER-BUG.

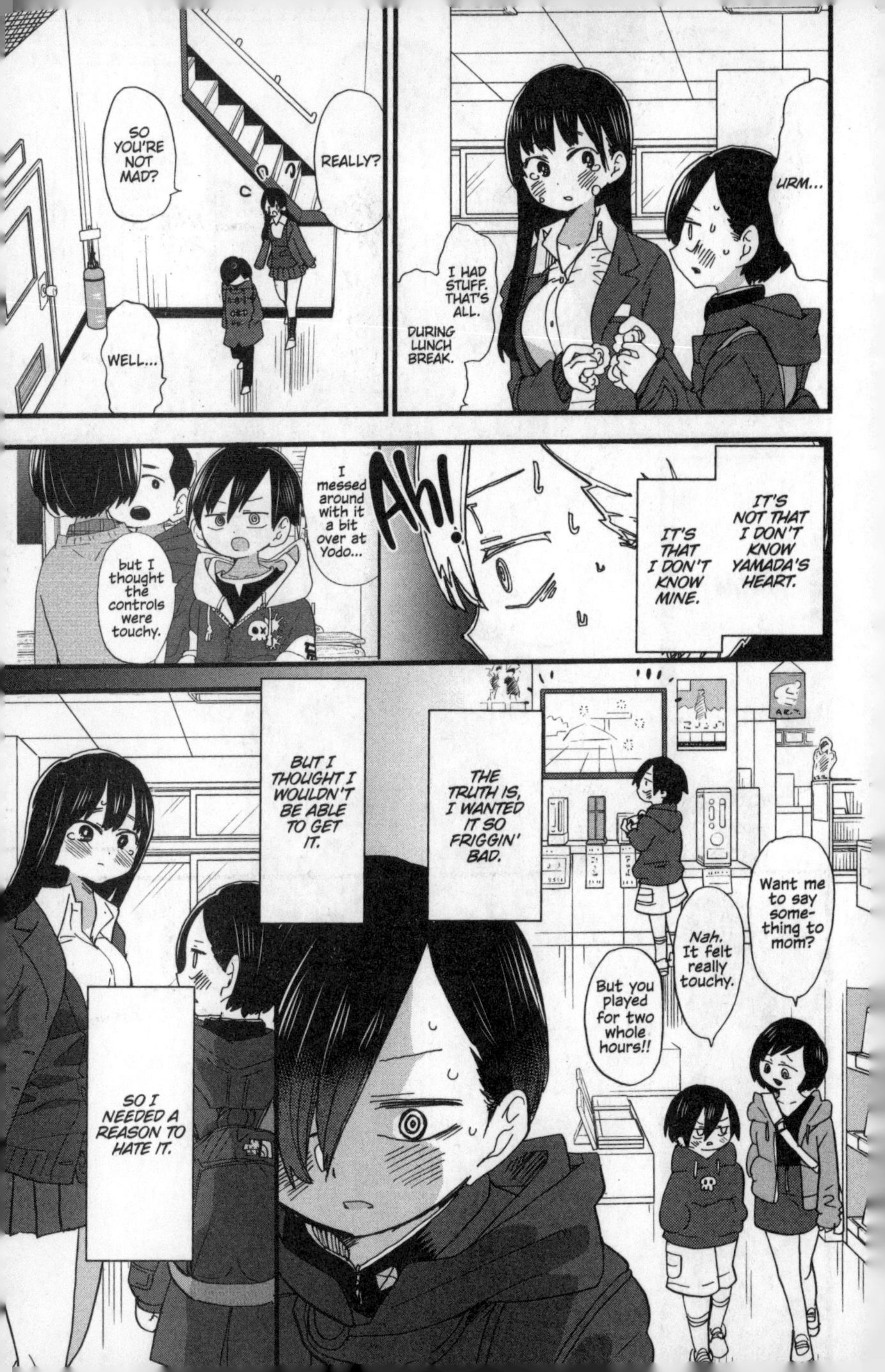
URM...
I HAD STUFF. THAT'S ALL.
DURING LUNCH BREAK.
REALLY?
SO YOU'RE NOT MAD?
WELL...
IT'S NOT THAT I DON'T KNOW YAMADA'S HEART.
IT'S THAT I DON'T KNOW MINE.
Ah!
I messed around with it a bit over at Yodo...
but I thought the controls were touchy.
THE TRUTH IS, I WANTED IT SO FRIGGIN' BAD.
BUT I THOUGHT I WOULDN'T BE ABLE TO GET IT.
Want me to say some-thing to mom?
Nah. It felt really touchy.
But you played for two whole hours!!
SO I NEEDED A REASON TO HATE IT.

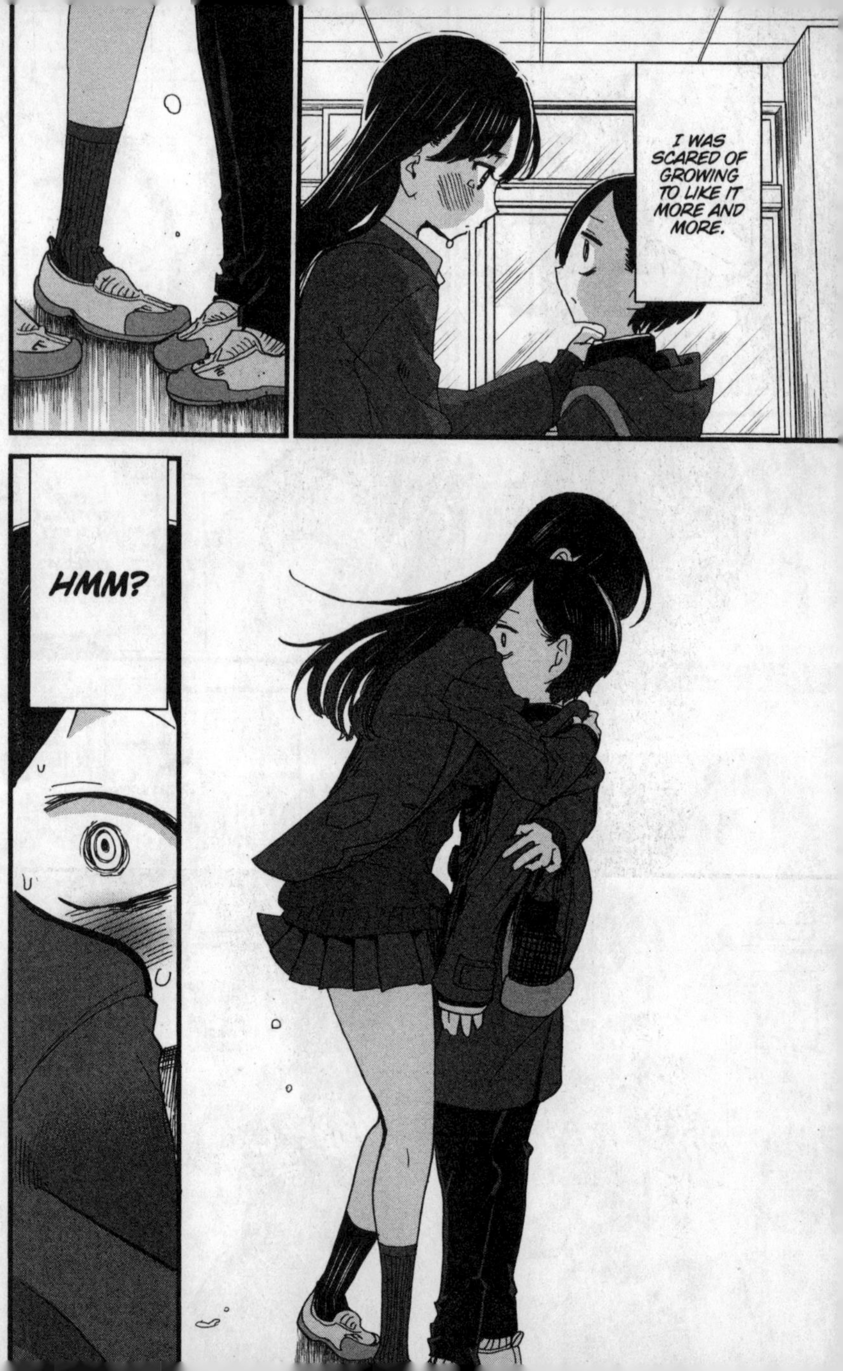
I WAS SCARED OF GROWING TO LIKE IT MORE AND MORE.
HMM?

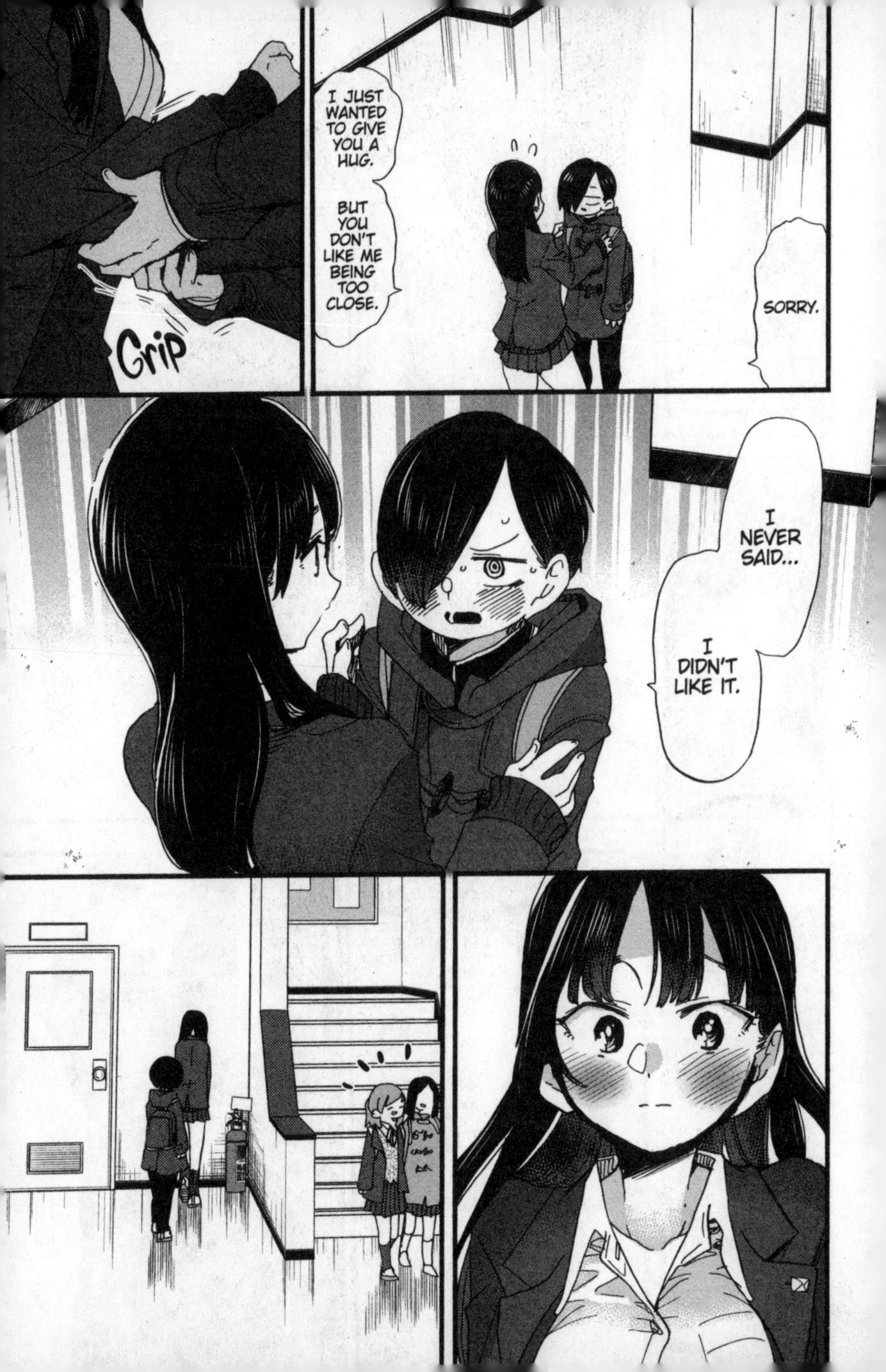
I JUST WANTED TO GIVE YOU A HUG.
BUT YOU DON'T LIKE ME BEING TOO CLOSE.
SORRY.
Grip
I NEVER SAID...
I DIDN'T LIKE IT.

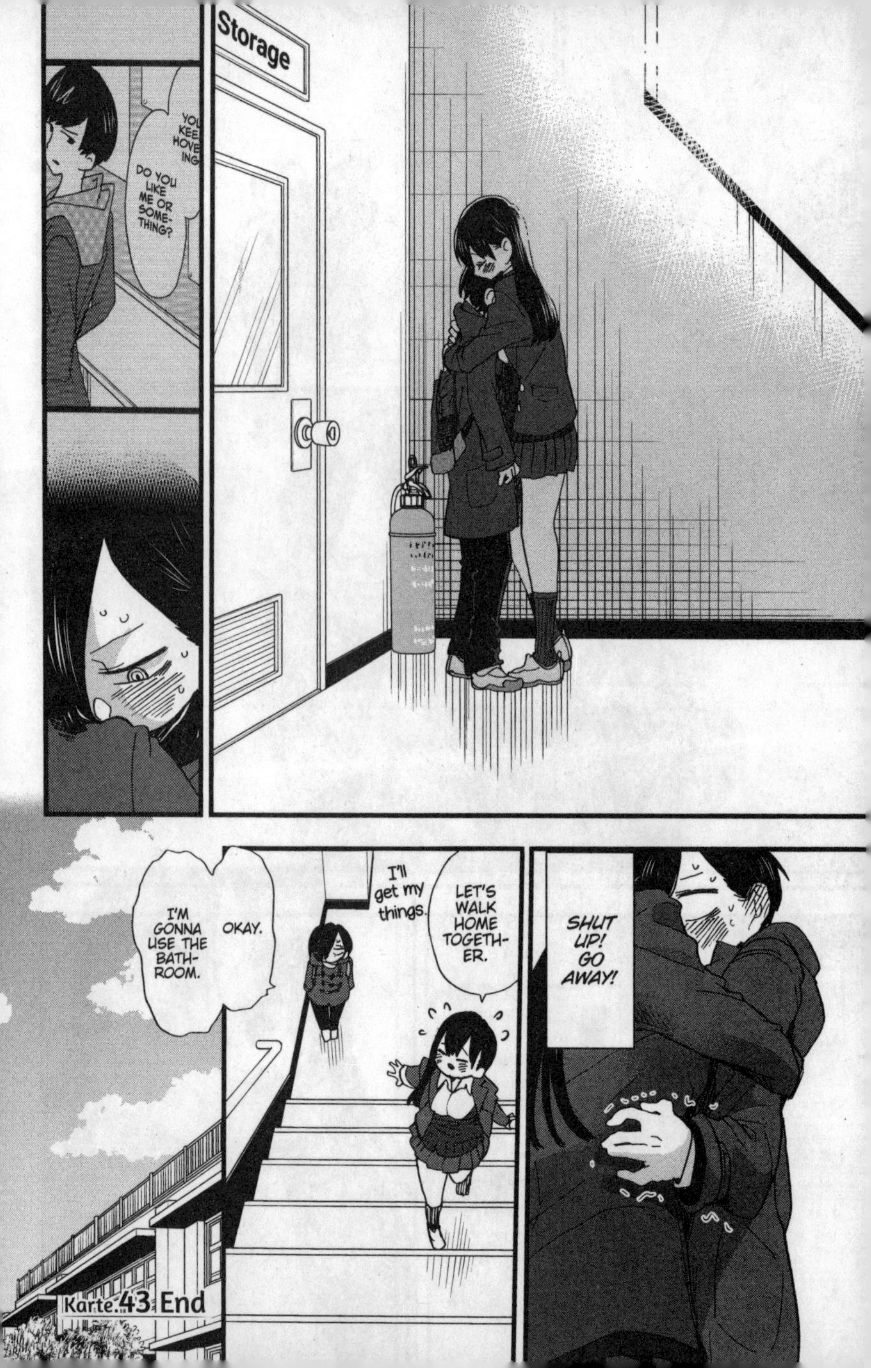
Storage
YOU KEE HOVE ING
DO YOU LIKE ME OR SOME-THING?
SHUT UP! GO AWAY!
LET'S WALK HOME TOGETH-ER.
I'll get my things.
OKAY.
I'M GONNA USE THE BATH-ROOM.
Karte.43 End

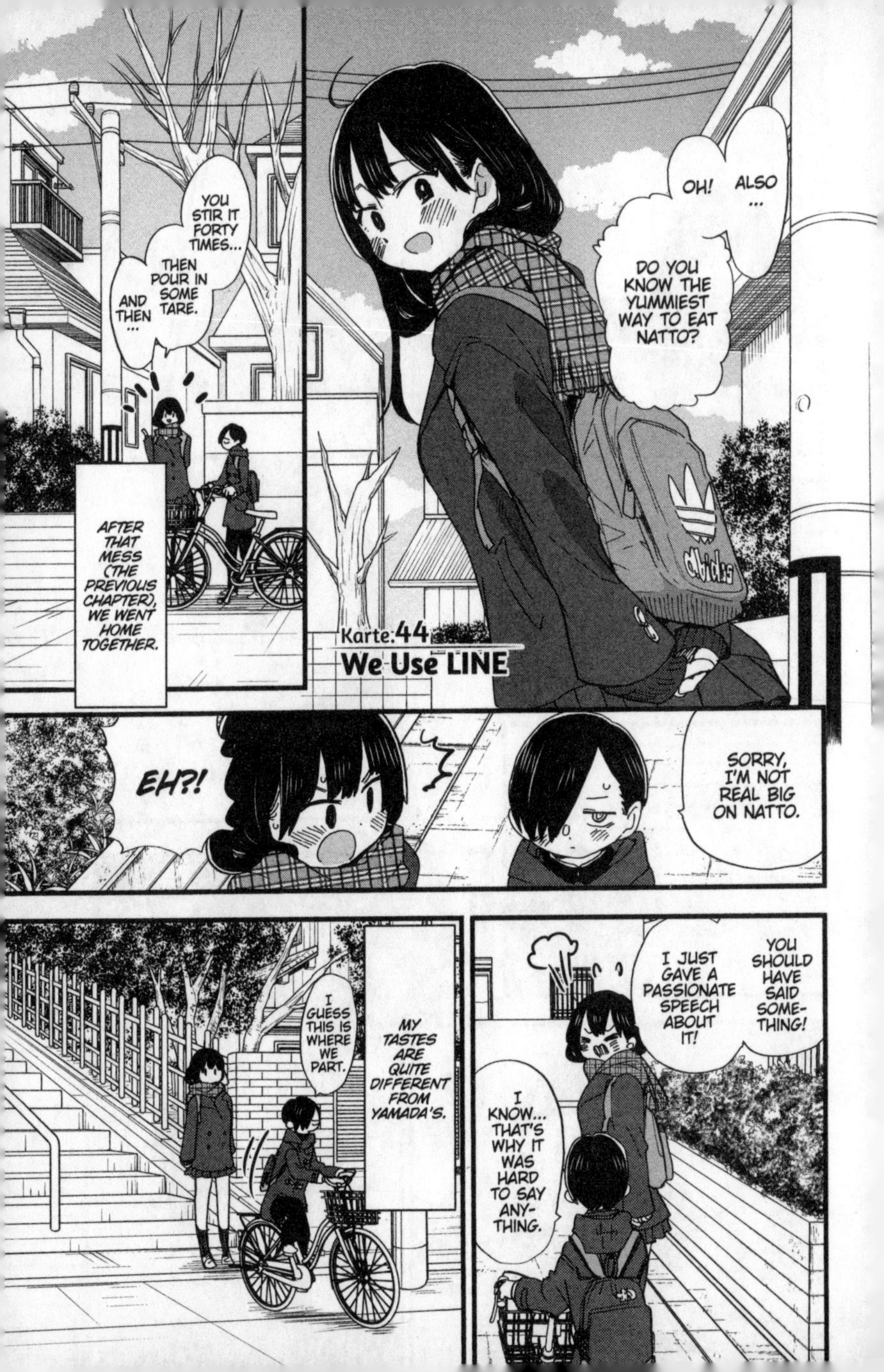
OH! ALSO ...
DO YOU KNOW THE YUMMIEST WAY TO EAT NATTO?
Karte: 44
We Use LINE
YOU STIR IT FORTY TIMES...
THEN POUR IN SOME TARE.
AND THEN ...
AFTER THAT MESS (THE PREVIOUS CHAPTER), WE WENT HOME TOGETHER.
SORRY, I'M NOT REAL BIG ON NATTO.
EH?!
YOU SHOULD HAVE SAID SOME-THING!
I JUST GAVE A PASSIONATE SPEECH ABOUT IT!
I KNOW... THAT'S WHY IT WAS HARD TO SAY ANY-THING.
MY TASTES ARE QUITE DIFFERENT FROM YAMADA'S.
I GUESS THIS IS WHERE WE PART.

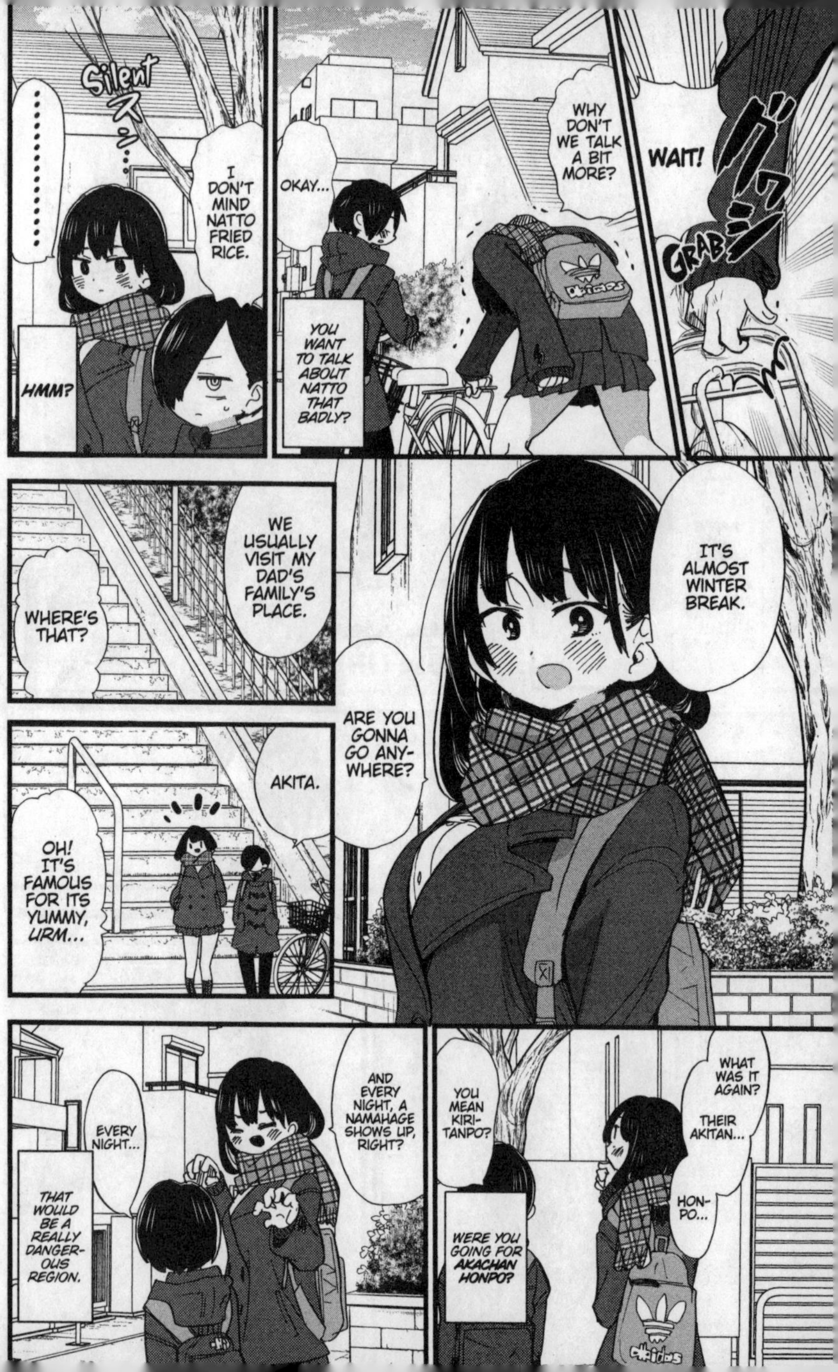

グワシ
WAIT!
GRAB
WHY DON'T WE TALK A BIT MORE?
OKAY...
YOU WANT TO TALK ABOUT NATTO THAT BADLY?
I DON'T MIND NATTO FRIED RICE.
Silent
スッ
......
HMM?
IT'S ALMOST WINTER BREAK.
ARE YOU GONNA GO ANY-WHERE?
WE USUALLY VISIT MY DAD'S FAMILY'S PLACE.
WHERE'S THAT?
AKITA.
OH! IT'S FAMOUS FOR ITS YUMMY, URM...
WHAT WAS IT AGAIN?
THEIR AKITAN...
HON-PO...
YOU MEAN KIRI-TANPO?
WERE YOU GOING FOR AKACHAN HONPO?
AND EVERY NIGHT, A NAMAHAGE SHOWS UP, RIGHT?
EVERY NIGHT...
THAT WOULD BE A REALLY DANGER-OUS REGION.

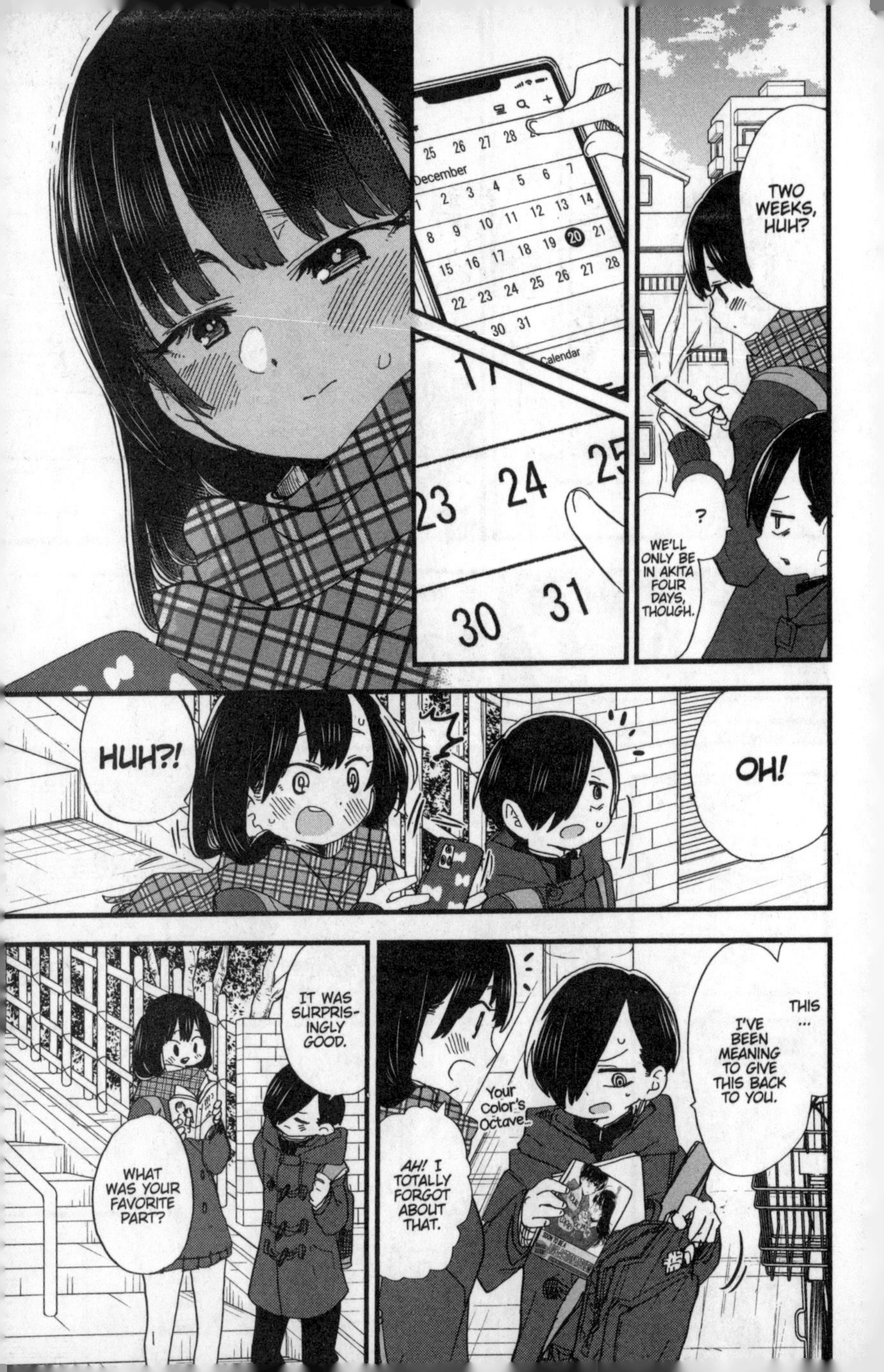
TWO WEEKS, HUH?
?
WE'LL ONLY BE IN AKITA FOUR DAYS, THOUGH.
December
Calendar
OH!
HUH?!
THIS ... I'VE BEEN MEANING TO GIVE THIS BACK TO YOU.
Your Color's Octave...
AH! I TOTALLY FORGOT ABOUT THAT.
IT WAS SURPRISINGLY GOOD.
WHAT WAS YOUR FAVORITE PART?

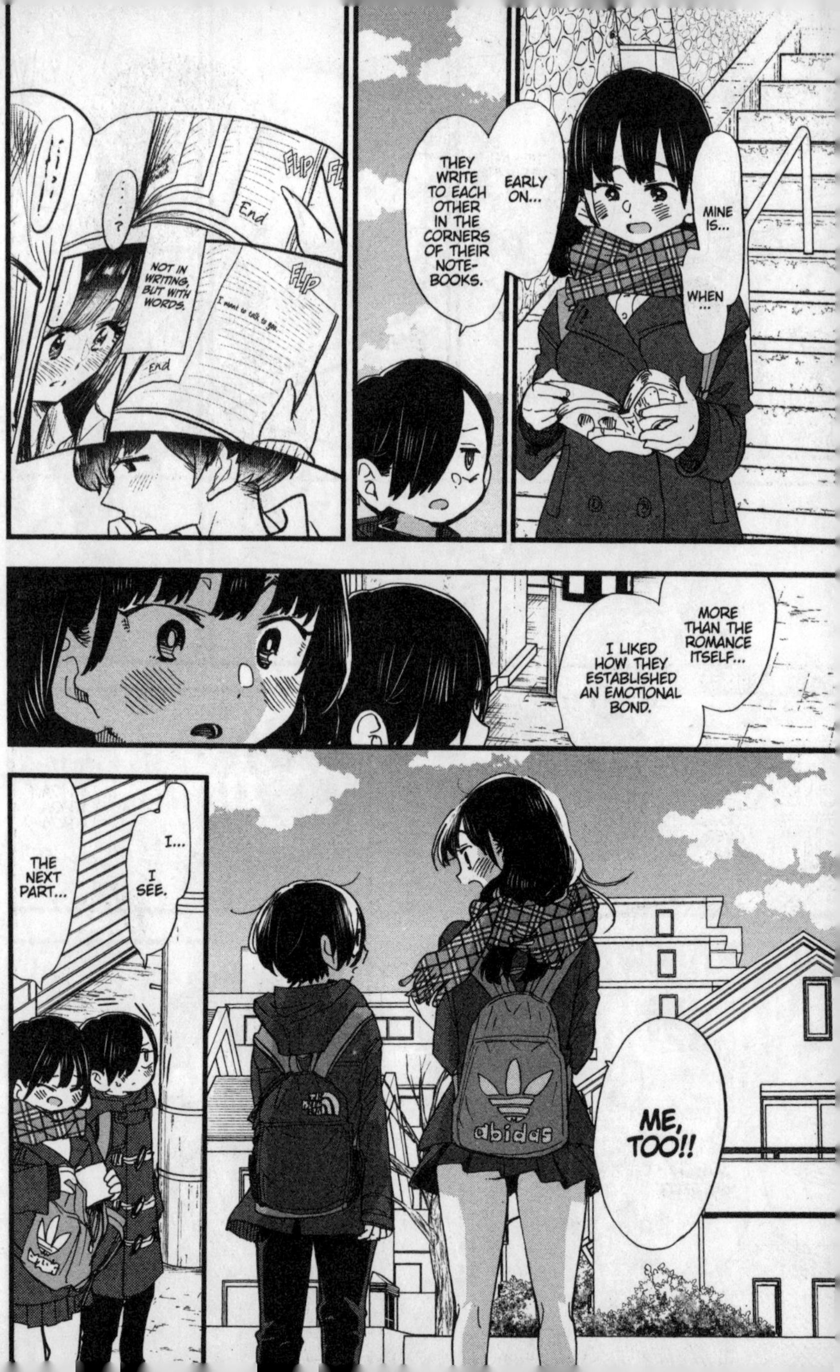
MINE IS... WHEN ...
EARLY ON...
THEY WRITE TO EACH OTHER IN THE CORNERS OF THEIR NOTE-BOOKS.
FLIP FLIP
FLIP
End
...?
...!
NOT IN WRITING, BUT WITH WORDS.
I want to talk to you.
End
MORE THAN THE ROMANCE ITSELF...
I LIKED HOW THEY ESTABLISHED AN EMOTIONAL BOND.
ME, TOO!!
abidas
I... I SEE.
THE NEXT PART...

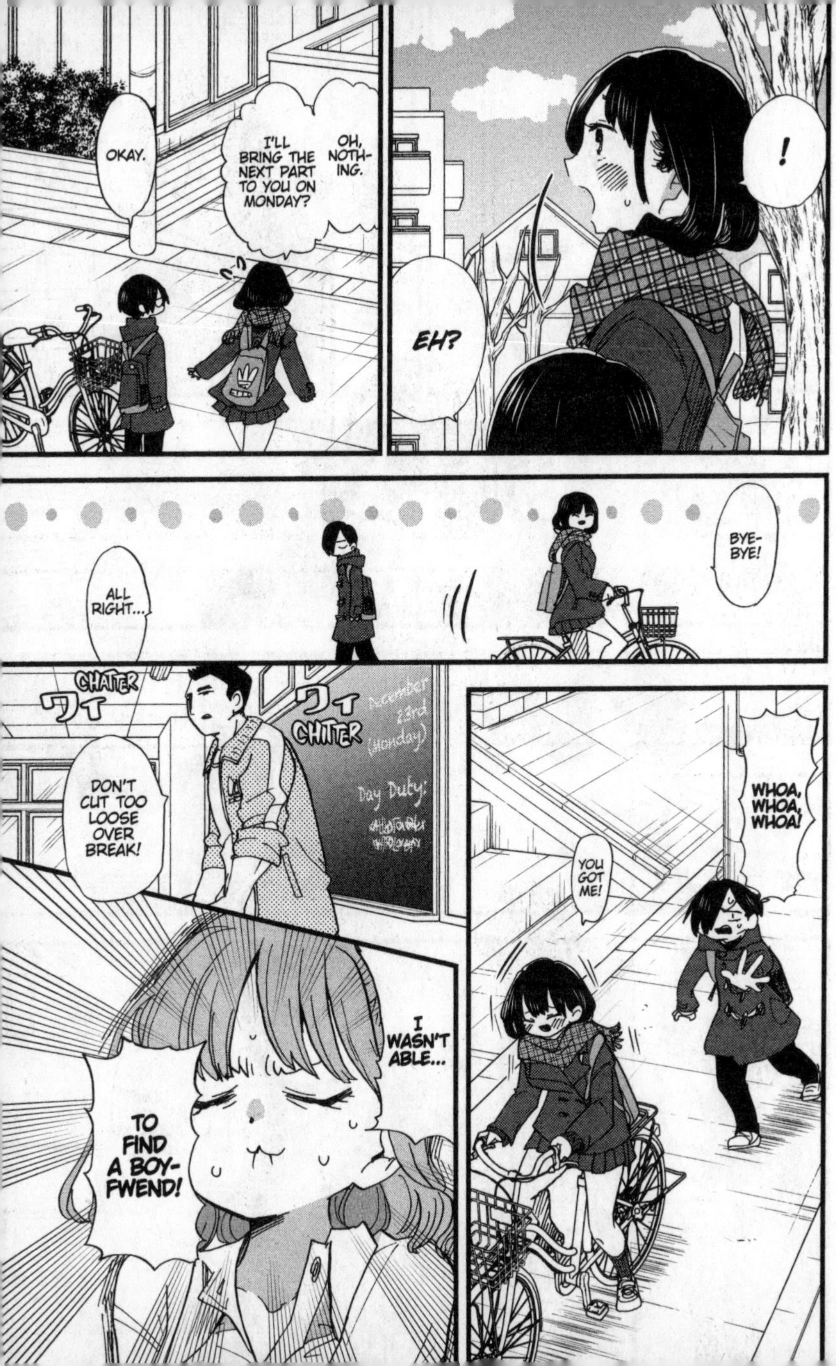
!
EH?
OH, NOTHING.
I'LL BRING THE NEXT PART TO YOU ON MONDAY?
OKAY.
BYE-BYE!
ALL RIGHT...
WHOA, WHOA, WHOA!
YOU GOT ME!
ワィ CHITER
December 23rd (Monday)
Day Duty:
ワイ CHATER
DON'T CUT TOO LOOSE OVER BREAK!
I WASN'T ABLE...
TO FIND A BOY-FWEND!

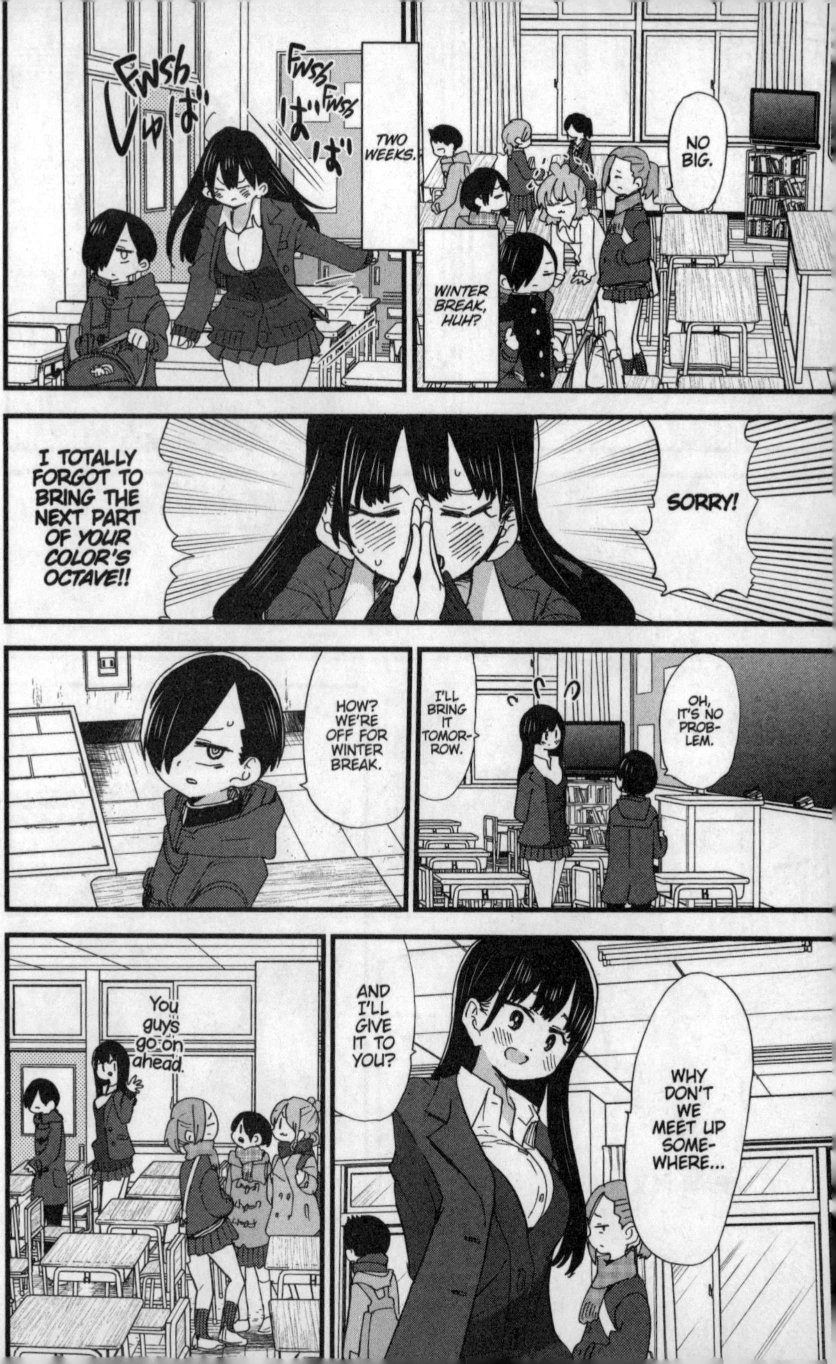
NO BIG.
WINTER BREAK, HUH?
TWO WEEKS.
Fwsh Fwsh ばば
Fwsh しゅば
SORRY!
I TOTALLY FORGOT TO BRING THE NEXT PART OF YOUR COLOR'S OCTAVE!!
OH, IT'S NO PROB-LEM.
I'LL BRING IT TOMOR-ROW.
HOW? WE'RE OFF FOR WINTER BREAK.
WHY DON'T WE MEET UP SOME-WHERE...
AND I'LL GIVE IT TO YOU?
You guys go on ahead.

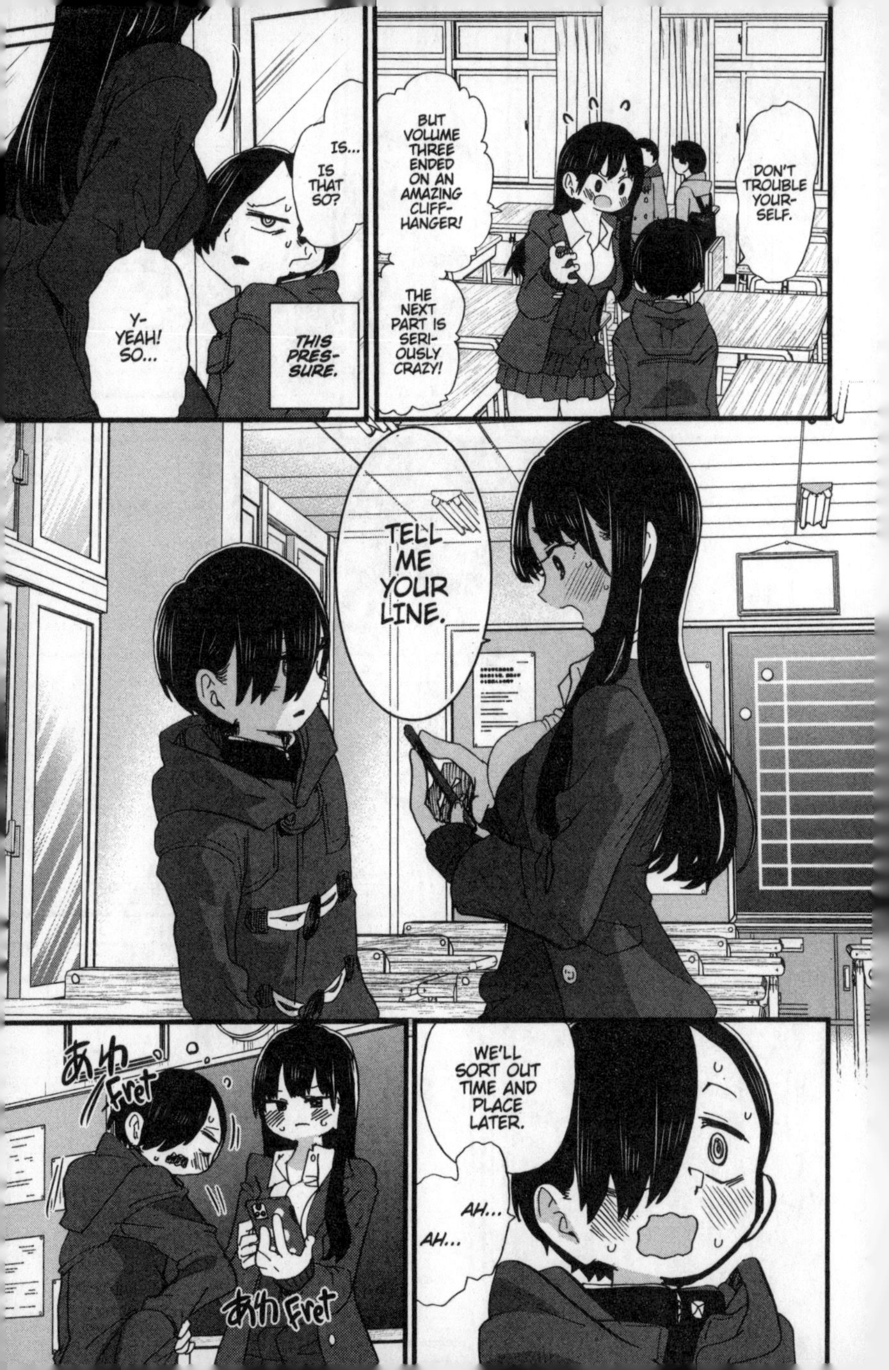

DON'T TROUBLE YOURSELF.
BUT VOLUME THREE ENDED ON AN AMAZING CLIFF-HANGER!
THE NEXT PART IS SERIOUSLY CRAZY!
IS... IS THAT SO?
THIS PRESSURE.
Y-YEAH! SO...
TELL ME YOUR LINE.
WE'LL SORT OUT TIME AND PLACE LATER.
AH... AH...
あわ Fret
あわ Fret

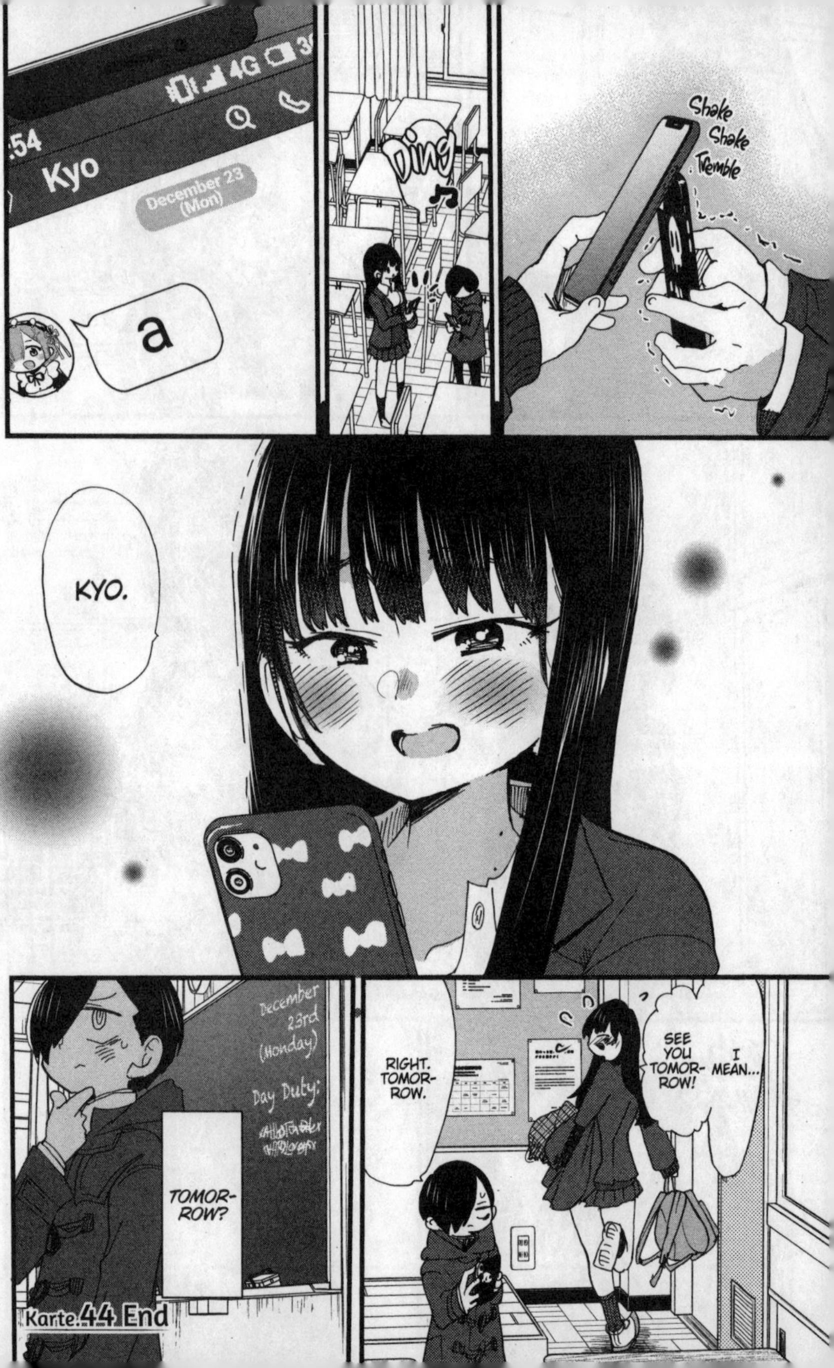
Shake
Shake
Tremble
Ding ♪
:54
4G
Kyo
December 23 (Mon)
a
KYO.
SEE YOU TOMORROW!
I MEAN...
RIGHT. TOMORROW.
December 23rd (Monday)
Day Duty:
TOMORROW?
Karte.44 End

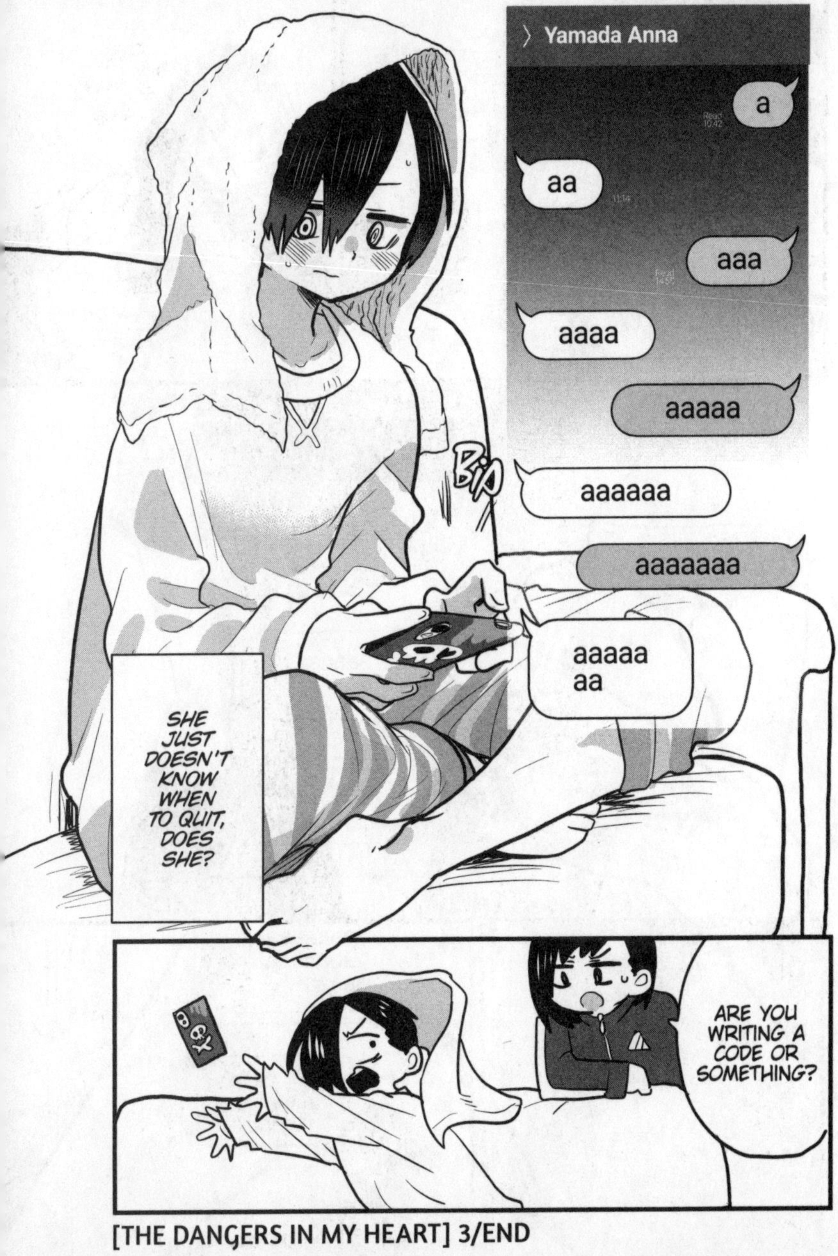
Yamada Anna
a
aa
aaa
aaaa
aaaaa
aaaaaa
aaaaaaa
aaaaa aa
SHE JUST DOESN'T KNOW WHEN TO QUIT, DOES SHE?
ARE YOU WRITING A CODE OR SOMETHING?

[THE DANGERS IN MY HEART] 3/END

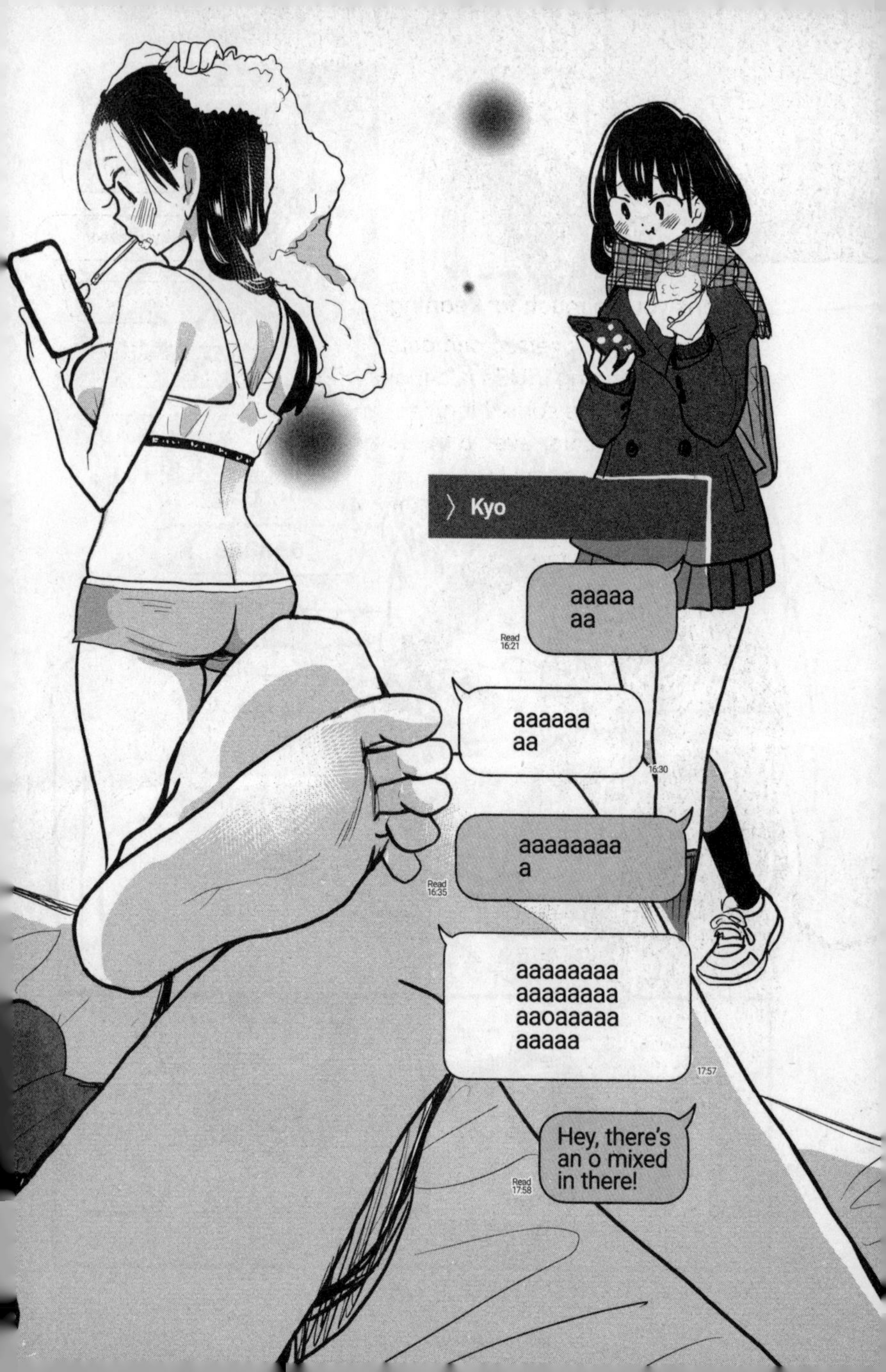
Kyo
aaaaaaa
Read 16:21
aaaaaaa
16:30
aaaaaaaaa
Read 16:35
aaaaaaaaaaaaaaaaaaoaaaaaaaaaa
17:57
Hey, there's an o mixed in there!
Read 17:58

Post script

Thank you so much for reading.
For a super introverted character,
even exchanging LINEs is a major affair.
But love really is something.
To be able to color even a trivial event
such as this so garishly...
I hope to see you again in Volume 4.
2020.4 Norio Sakurai

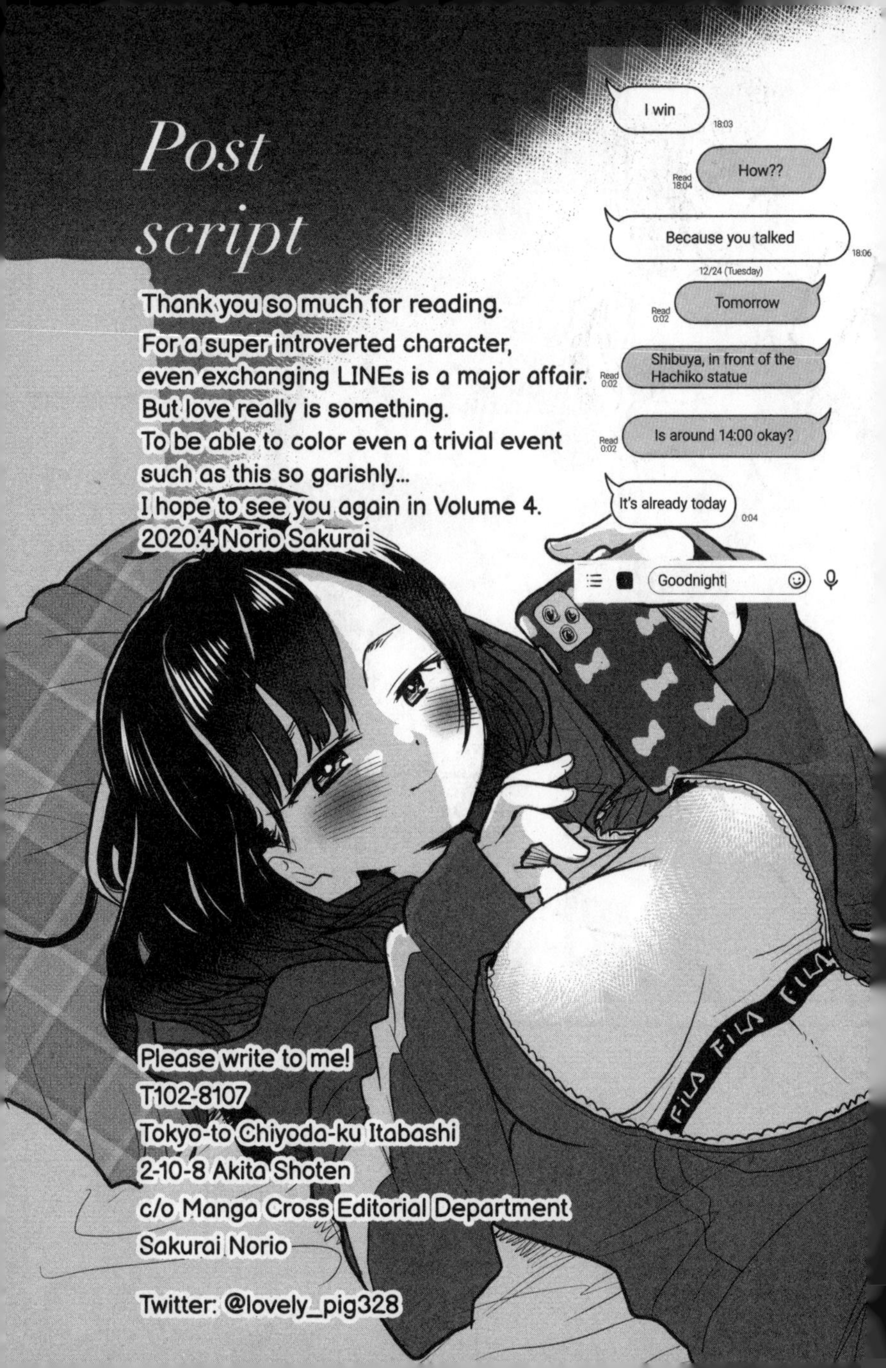

I win
18:03
Read 18:04
How??
Because you talked
18:06
12/24 (Tuesday)
Read 0:02
Tomorrow
Read 0:02
Shibuya, in front of the Hachiko statue
Read 0:02
Is around 14:00 okay?
It's already today
0:04
Goodnight
FILA

Please write to me!
T102-8107
Tokyo-to Chiyoda-ku Itabashi
2-10-8 Akita Shoten
c/o Manga Cross Editorial Department
Sakurai Norio

Twitter: @lovely_pig328

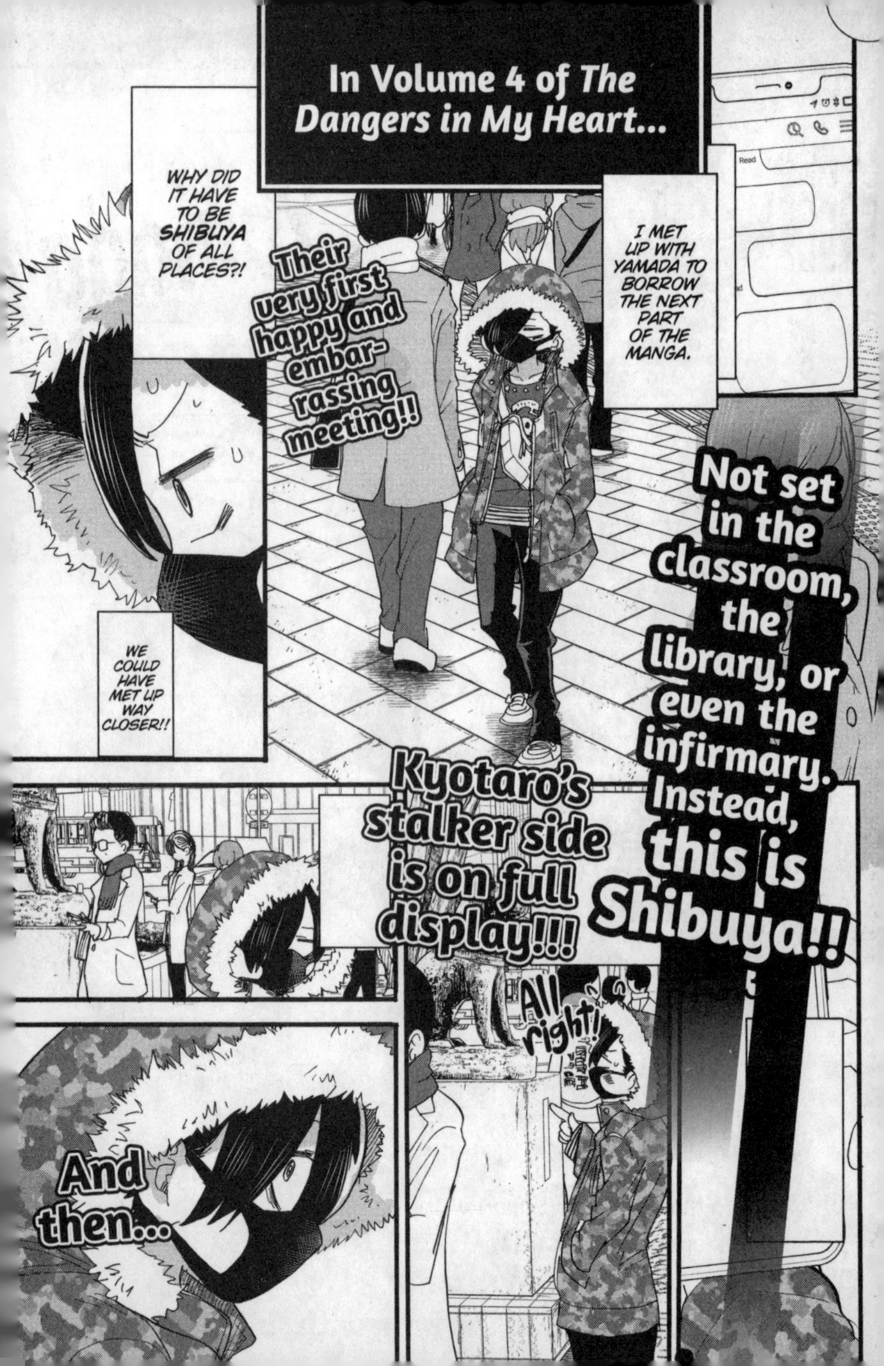
In Volume 4 of *The Dangers in My Heart*...
I MET UP WITH YAMADA TO BORROW THE NEXT PART OF THE MANGA.
Their very first happy and embar-rassing meeting!!
WHY DID IT HAVE TO BE SHIBUYA OF ALL PLACES?!
WE COULD HAVE MET UP WAY CLOSER!!
Not set in the classroom, the library, or even the infirmary. Instead, this is Shibuya!!
Kyotaro's stalker side is on full display!!!
All right!
And then...

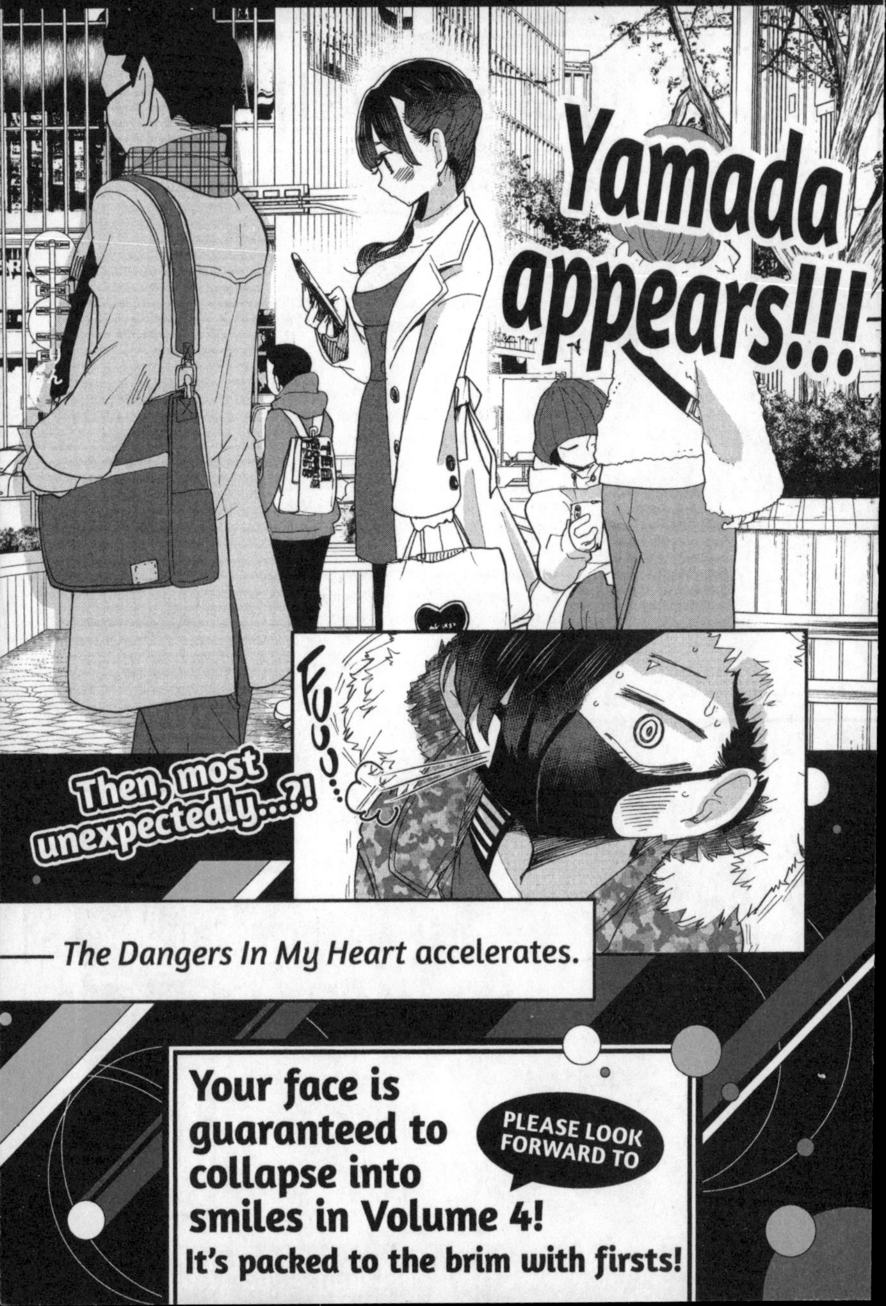
Yamada appears!!!
Then, most unexpectedly...?!
FUUU...
—— The Dangers In My Heart accelerates.
Your face is guaranteed to collapse into smiles in Volume 4!
PLEASE LOOK FORWARD TO
It's packed to the brim with firsts!

SEVEN SEAS ENTERTAINMENT PRESENTS

The Dangers in My Heart

story and art by **NORIO SAKURAI**　　　**VOLUME 3**

TRANSLATION
Nan Rymer

ADAPTATION
Jamal Joseph Jr.

LETTERING
Arbash Mughal

COVER DESIGN
Hanase Qi

EDITOR
Peter Adrian Behravesh

PREPRESS TECHNICIAN
Rhiannon Rasmussen-Silverstein

PRODUCTION ASSOCIATE
Christa Miesner

PRODUCTION MANAGER
Lissa Pattillo

MANAGING EDITOR
Julie Davis

ASSOCIATE PUBLISHER
Adam Arnold

PUBLISHER
Jason DeAngelis

THE DANGERS IN MY HEART. VOLUME 3
© Norio Sakurai 2020
Originally published in Japan in 2020 by Akita Publishing Co., Ltd.
English translation rights arranged with Akita Publishing Co., Ltd.
through TOHAN CORPORATION, Tokyo.

Seven Seas press and purchase enquiries can be sent to Marketing Manager Lianne Sentar at press@gomanga.com. Information regarding the distribution and purchase of digital editions is available from Digital Manager CK Russell at digital@gomanga.com.

Seven Seas and the Seven Seas logo are trademarks of Seven Seas Entertainment. All rights reserved.

ISBN: 978-1-64827-462-6
Printed in Canada
First Printing: November 2021
10 9 8 7 6 5 4 3 2 1

////// READING DIRECTIONS //////

This book reads from *right to left*, Japanese style. If this is your first time reading manga, you start reading from the top right panel on each page and take it from there. If you get lost, just follow the numbered diagram here. It may seem backwards at first, but you'll get the hang of it! Have fun!!

Follow us online: www.SevenSeasEntertainment.com